THE NEW POODLE

Ch. Tedwin's Top Billing, Miniature, one of the top winning Poodles of all time with 56 all-breed Bests in Show and 11 Specialty Bests in Show including the Poodle Club of America shows, 1963 and 1965. Bred by Ted Young, Jr., campaigned under ownership of E.E. Ferguson and last owned by Frank T. Sabella, Jr.

The NEW
POODLE

by

MACKEY J. IRICK, Jr.

ILLUSTRATED

SIXTH EDITION
First Printing — 1986

HOWELL BOOK HOUSE Inc.
230 Park Avenue, New York, N.Y. 10169

History of **THE NEW POODLE:**

First published (as *The Complete Poodle* by Lydia K. Hopkins), 1951
Second edition, 1952
Third edition, 1953
Fourth edition (as *The New Complete Poodle*), 1964
Fifth edition (revised by Mackey J. Irick, Jr.), 1969, 1975
Sixth edition (as *The New Poodle* by Mackey J. Irick, Jr.), 1986

Library of Congress Cataloging-in-Publication Data

Irick, Mackey J.
     The new poodle.

     Rev. ed. of: New complete poodle / by Lydia
Hopkins. 5th ed. 1969.
     Includes index.
     1. Poodles.   I. Hopkins, Lydia, 1887-1965.   New
complete poodle.   II. Title.
SF429.P85175   1986   636.7'2   86-3124
ISBN 0-87605-256-1

Contents

Ch. Valhalla's Jacquelyn winning Best of Breed at the 1985 Poodle Club of America Specialty. Shown with Doris Cozart; Francis Fretwell; Frank Sabella, Inter-Variety Judge; Anne Rogers Clark; Dennis McCoy, Handler; Sterg O'Dell, Club President; Janet Kiczek and Rebecca Mason. Owned by Wallace Yost and Catherine Kish.

Foreword

by W. H. Sterg O'Dell

Mr. O'Dell, a long time breeder and judge of Poodles, has been a member of the Board of Directors of the Poodle Club of America intermittently since 1963, and President 1974-1978 and 1984-1986. He holds a Harvard Ph.D. in English Renaissance Philosophy and Literature and is a retired university professor and administrator.

IN 1949 only 2,165 Poodles of all three varieties were registered with the American Kennel Club. By 1959 the annual registration had risen to 58,661, and for many years the Poodle was the most popular breed in America.

The Poodle Review magazine, founded by Mackey Irick in 1955, became a central educational contributor to the development of Poodles. Edited with objectivity and scholarly taste, the periodical became a source book for information on breeding, care, and showing of Poodles. The gallery of handsome Poodles pictured on its pages became models to be emulated, and the annual Stud Issue became the handbook for selecting studs. For over thirty years Mr. Irick has, as editor and publisher of *The Poodle Review*, known all of the top breeders, their Poodles, and their problems. He has generously shared his experience, wisdom and sympathy.

Involved with dogs from his boyhood, he started High Heritage Kennels in 1953, and bred over 33 Toy Poodle champions, including Best in Show winners, Group winners, and Top Producers. High Heritage Toys have become champions in the United States, Canada, Germany and Japan.

Mr. Irick has been an active member of the Poodle Club of America for many years. He served on the Breed Standard Committee when the Standard was revised in 1978, and was on the Committee for the proposed revisions in 1985. He is Chairman of the P.C.A. Illustrated Breed Standard Committee, Chairman of the P.C.A. Archives Committee, and served on the Committee for *Poodles In America*, Volumes III through VI. For his service to Poodles, the Poodle Club of America awarded him a Gold Medallion.

In 1969 Mr. Irick completely revised *The Complete Poodle*, written by the late Lydia Hopkins in 1951. The present book is not a revision; it is a new book by Mr. Irick. I cannot imagine anyone better equipped to write the definitive book on Poodles—*The NEW Poodle*.

Ch. Lou-Gin's Kiss Me Kate once held the title of the Top Winning Dog All Breeds, All Time with 140 All Breed Bests in Show and 19 Specialty Bests in Show. She is shown here going Best in Show at the 1979 Chicago International Dog Show under Henry Stoecker. Kiss Me Kate was bred by Lou Dunson, handled by Robert Walberg and owned by Mr. and Mrs. Jack Phelan and Terri Meyers.

Introduction

W HEN I first read *The Complete Poodle* by Lydia Hopkins in the early 1950's, I thought it the best breed book ever published. As my interest in Poodles grew, I continued to study the book, and—at a time when little information on the Poodle was available—found it invaluable.

I started a correspondence with Miss Hopkins, and found her extremely knowledgeable and helpful. When I asked her opinion on starting a Poodle magazine, she was most enthusiastic. She contributed an article for the very first issue of *The Poodle Review* in 1955, and followed with many more through the years for as long as her health permitted. I never ceased to be impressed with her brilliance of mind and great knowledge of the breed.

After her death in 1965 I was invited to do a revision of the book in 1969. This was the fifth edition of *The Complete Poodle* and it was enormously popular and with only minor changes from time to time has gone through ten printings.

Now that 20 years have passed since Miss Hopkins died, the time has come for a new book, incorporating the knowledge of the past with the present state of the breed. The Poodle with its wonderful disposition, intelligence and smart appearance has been one of the most popular breeds in America for the past quarter century. Enormous breeding and showing activity in all three varieties has taken place, with many new sires, dams, families and lines emerging as some of the older lines either contributed to the present or sadly fell by the wayside.

It is hoped that this new book will simplify the enormous task of sorting out the various lines and families within each of the three varieties so that novice and experienced breeder alike may more readily get an easier grasp on what has gone before and may also study those lines and individuals which are currently making the greatest contributions to the future.

The charts in all three varieties indicate how the Top Producing sires trace back to the foundation stud dogs in tail male line. The line of descent is from sire to son, and each indentation indicates a new generation. Colors are noted in parentheses, followed by the number of champions produced by each dog up to the time of publication.

A real effort has been made to include on the charts as many as possible of the vast number of Poodles which have sired 10 or more champions in their respective tail male lines. Any dog which has sired five or more champions is considered to be a Top Producer. In some cases, particularly in silvers and apricots, the number of champions produced have not been as numerous and impressive as the totals quoted for the more popular blacks and whites. These rarer colors have their devotees and should be encouraged by all breeders. The total number of champions on the charts are constantly changing, with new champions finishing every week. The charts are to be considered as a nucleus for future work by persons sufficiently interested. Even as they now exist, anyone can with a minimum of time and effort connect their own Poodles to their proper sire lines and learn more of their families through studying the text and photos which accompany the charts.

English and foreign dogs and their records and production history have been included where known, as Poodles are a truly international breed. In England a dog must win three "Challenge Certificates," or CC's, in order to become a champion of record. These Certificates are offered at just a certain number of the largest shows, and a great many of the smaller shows do not have them. Also, the practice in England is to show champions in competition in the classes and a really outstanding dog may win any number of CC's for any number of years, thus holding back younger dogs battling for the title.

In the presentation of pedigrees of outstanding individuals and on the charts, the key to the abbreviation of colors is: black (blk), blue (blu), gray (gr), silver (si), brown (brn), cream (crm), apricot (apr), and white (wh).

It should also be noted that in order for a bitch to be recognized as a Top Producer she must have three or more champion children.

A book of this size and dimension is not the work of any one person. I have been fortunate in having the enthusiastic cooperation of a number of experts within the breed. I want especially to thank Anne Rogers Clark for her chapter on grooming for the show ring, Catharine Reiley for her chapter on Poodles in Obedience, and the Princesse de Broglie for her explanation of Poodles in France. Also Beverly Jean Nelson for her tireless devotion as breed statistician and Frank Fretwell for sharing his vast records. The handsome photos by Evelyn Shafer, William Gilbert, the late Rudolph Tauskey and others help to depict the changes in the breed visually from its earliest to latest stages in both type and presentation. My appreciation extends also to Winnie Gillen and Anita McMullen for graphic illustrations and artwork. And further thanks to

Agnes Hamilton for her many hours typing copy and charts, to Ab Sidewater at Howell Book House for his excellent ideas in presentation, and to Nelson Garringer for his invaluable aid and encouragement.

—Mackey J. Irick, Jr.

Ch. Rimskittle Ruffian, black Standard, on her way to First in the Non-Sporting Group at the 1980 Westminster Kennel Club, handled by Timothy Brazier. Owned by Margaret Durney and Edward Jenner at time of this win, Ruffian was bred and last owned by Mr. and Mrs. James Edward Clark.

"Laying Down the Law," (also called "Trial By Jury"), a popular painting by Sir Edwin Landseer RA, dated 1840, with the Poodle serving as judge, considered the perfect satire of humanity in animal form. The original painting is in the collection at Chatsworth House in England.

1

Meet the Poodle

by Lydia Hopkins

THE POODLE is a gentleman with all the reserve, dignity, and delicacy of feeling the word implies. Although he is of the Spaniel family, there is nothing fawning about him. He makes up his mind about you with deliberation, and, after due consideration, he places you in his world and very seldom changes his idea about your worth. If you and he are to be friends or better, he gives you his full, undivided devotion, and, from that time on, your moods and your commands are his sole concern in life. But this is on a friend to friend basis of perfect equality; he expects from you the same loving understanding that he gives you. If you fail him, he will still love you but his admiration will slip a little and he will let you know it in no uncertain terms. His full devotion is usually for one person only, after which he includes the immediate family in various gradations of affectionate regard.

Poodles are polite to friends they know, but as a rule without enthusiasm. As a breed this distrust of strangers is quite marked, and makes of them guardians and watch dogs of the highest ability, both for the owner's possessions and for his person. There is a famous story of Moustache, the Poodle that went to war with his master who was killed in battle. The faithful dog refused to let the enemy soldiers touch his master's body and was killed defending it. When the French again took the field of battle, Moustache was buried with highest military honors with a grave marked "*Ce git le brave Moustache.*"

We flatter ourselves when we say that Poodles are the most intelligent of all breeds. It is very true that those who watch them work out difficult problems by themselves believe that their reasoning faculties are sometimes uncanny, but I have owned other breeds that could think, too. The real difference in Poodle intelligence is, I believe, this: whereas other dogs think in a doggy way, Poodles' brains react in a much more human fashion and one that we humans can better understand. Perhaps their three hundred or more years of earnest effort to understand us has given them this quality of mind.

For all their independence, Poodles as a breed are pathetically dependent upon human companionship and understanding. Without it they become distrustful, morose and dull. They must be sure of their masters before they can be sure of themselves. All dogs need affectionate understanding, but some other breeds can be happy in their own doggy sphere of life without much human companionship; Poodles cannot be even reasonably happy or smart without it.

It is their extreme sensitiveness that makes them such delightful companions, quick to respond to even unspoken thoughts; but this same quality makes them all the more sensitive to unkindness and severity. They seldom need correction other than the spoken word. A merited scolding—and it must be merited and perfectly just—will reduce them to the depths of woe, and it is only when the voice changes from grave disapproval to the all-clear signal of a brighter, approving tone that they regain their normal gaiety.

Their curiosity, like that of most intelligent creatures, is great, and they will share with you the pleasure of unwrapping a package—if done up with ribbons, so much the more intriguing. They always want to see just what is afoot, what's behind the closed door, or beyond the turn of the road. Although they will sometimes chase other little animals, domestic or wild, they seem to do it from a sense of fun rather than a desire to kill. Most of them enjoy playing with balls and other toys and have a lively sense of possession about such things.

Poodles, perhaps because of the attention their toilets always have received, show great pride in their appearance. When groomed and clipped and "in their best bib and tucker," they enjoy it keenly and the praise people give them. They are very fastidious and do not like to be dirty, tangled or unkempt. Unlike other types of dogs, they avoid mud puddles and dirty places and will not plow through muck of any sort.

As to food, Poodles are gourmets. Although they are never greedy, they will eat sensible kennel fare; but they can tell the difference between stew meat and prime rib roast, between top round and filet mignon; and they very much appreciate tidbits of the more sophisticated sort, such as cheese, pretzels, smoked fish, and so on.

As a breed, Poodles are rather old-maidish and set in their ways. They like regular hours, their particular chair always in the same spot, their own dish to eat out of and their own belongings just so. With this in mind, it is wise to make their routine what you want it to be from the very beginning, for this trait does not make them adaptable and they do not take readily to changes.

No other dog has so great a sense of humor. It is a mistake, however, to think of the Poodle as a circus clown merely because of the early childish association we have for him in this role, for his humor is very often quite subtle.

He unbends from the burden of his dignity to amuse you and himself in a bit of waggish fun, deliberately putting on an act, with an eye out for your reaction. This he doesn't take seriously nor does he expect you to, either. He simply feels he can relax among friends without permanent loss of dignity.

The teachability of Poodles is proverbial, and the only limit to what they can learn is that of your patience in teaching them. This applies to tricks, obedience work, hunting, or any other activity you may choose for them. They do not learn quickly as a rule and are sometimes rather stubborn; but with firmness, infinite repetition, kindness and patience, they can be taught almost anything a dog is capable of learning. Once a trick is mastered, they never forget it and even after years will remember what you wish of them, and respond with a finished performance to the same old command in the same voice.

The scores established by Poodles in Obedience trials, Standards, Miniatures, and even Toys, are indicative of the intelligence and trainability of the breed.

As a friend of children the Poodle is unique, and many who are older look back to a Poodle of their earlier days with deep and sentimental attachment, and to shared pranks and confidences exchanged with a patient and sympathetic companion. Poodles seem to understand children, are infinitely gentle with them, and will play for hours without becoming impatient. Poodles have for children a tenderness and protective instinct which is extremely deep. In addition, their resourcefulness in inventing childish entertainment is unlimited.

Many noted people have been Poodle enthusiasts—Gertrude Stein, Helen Hayes, Booth Tarkington, Greer Garson, Ben Hecht, Winston Churchill, the Nobel prizewinner John Steinbeck, whose "Travels with Charlie (a Standard Poodle) in Search of America" won the Dog Writers' Association award in 1962, and many others including Alexander Woollcott, who says in his book, *Long, Long Ago*, "I belong—and for many years have belonged—to the brotherhood of the Poodle. This brotherhood is far-flung and wildly miscellaneous. We all have one thing in common—perhaps only one. We all believe that man as he walks on this earth, can find no more engaging companion than that golden hearted clown, the Poodle."

Miss Lydia Hopkins with her Miniature bred Toy Poodle Ch. Sherwood Petite Mademoiselle.

OBSERVATIONS
VPON
PRINCE RVPERTS
WHITE DOG,
CALLED
BOY:

Carefully taken by **T. B.** *For that purpose im-ployed by some of quality in the City of* LONDON.

Printed in the Yeere,
MDCXLII.

Reproduction of the front page of a Parliamentary broadsheet dated 1642 picturing the famous white Poodle "Boy," owned by Prince Rupert.

2

Origin and History

THE POODLE is without doubt one of the oldest breeds known. Its true origins are so far back in history that it is impossible to pinpoint a specific place or time. What appear to be Poodles in lion trim were carved on Roman tombs in the time of Emperor Augustus, around 30 A.D. and appeared on ancient Greek and Roman coins. It is possible to imagine that these rather indistinct images are truly Poodles, but actually they could be almost any full coated breed. It is definitely known that the first printed reference to Poodles appears in the writings of Conrad Gesner, printed at Zurich in 1553. Paintings from the mid-15th Century from France, Holland and Italy depict dogs clipped in the manner characteristic of the breed.

It is now generally agreed among authorities that the three main sources for the modern Poodle as we now know him were Russia, France and Germany. Each country had a true Poodle representative, but they were very different types of dogs, differing mainly in coat and thickness of bone.

The Poodle first seems to have found favor in Russia, where they were large in size and black with white feet and markings. The Russian Poodle was most like the Greyhound in body type. A prize-winning Russian dog named "Posen" weighed 31 pounds and was just over 20 inches high.

The Germans were the first to distinguish the two types of Poodles, what we now call curly and corded. They also called them "Pudels," and when the popularity of the breed took them to Holland and Belgium, they were known as "Poedels." When they found their way to France, perhaps during the Revolutionary Wars, carried by German soldiers, they became "Barbet" and "Caniche."

The German Pudel, according to G. O. Shields in 1891, was long necked, long legged, straight stifled, and had a domed skull and a curled woolly coat. It

The Water Dog, woodcut by Gervaise Markham, 1621.

Woodcut dated 1643 showing Cavaliers encouraging Boy to attack Roundhead dog with the words "To him pudel," the first use in English literature of the word "Poodle."

20

was very closely allied to the German Water Spaniel, and in fact the very word Pudel means "to splash in water."

Although the Poodle's origin may be found in any or all of these countries, it was France that brought the breed to international prominence. The Poodle had occupied an honorable and unique place in French life—in court circles, on the battlefield, in the home—and had long been recognized as the French national dog.

The earliest portrayal of the Barbet, the recognized ancestor of the French Poodle, can be found in the Print Room of the British Museum in a fifteenth century engraving by an unknown French master titled *Je Suis Loyal Barbet Veillant*. However, the little dog pictured has the appearance of a Toy Spaniel. We should perhaps be broadminded enough today to agree that there must have been some affinity in those early days between not only the Poodle and the Spaniel, but the Maltese as well. The Barbet looks much the same in the famous painting *Petit Barbet* by Cima, around 1470. It was during this time that the French hunted a strange sort of duck with a beard-like growth on its bill, and both the duck and the dog used for hunting it became known as a Barbet (from the word *barbe* for beard in French).

The French also developed another duck-hunting dog, the Caniche, from the word *canard*, meaning duck. The Poodle is still known as a Caniche in France today. It is believed that the Caniche was produced by crossing the Barbet with another breed, probably our old friend the Spaniel. The present day Poodle and the Irish Water Spaniel look very much alike.

There was a third type of French Poodle that never got his feet wet on purpose, the truffle dog. This Poodle cultivated a strong sense of smell, in order to locate the illusive and aromatic fungi that grew under the soil of beech and oak groves, a delicacy much prized by the French in their gourmet cooking. He was taught to ignore all live game when hunting for the truffles. In no time at all this priceless dog was imported to England for the purpose and in 1867 the great historian John Henry Walsh, known as "Stonehenge," describes him as "nearly pure Poodle," though he doesn't look it in the illustration. In the personal papers of the Eli Collins family, great British truffle hunters for generations, there is evidence that their truffle dogs descended from some small Spanish Poodles brought over for John Stone of Stonehenge some 300 years ago.

In 1861 Meyrick wrote that in France the Poodle was the commonest dog there "except for the cur." He described the Poodle of that time as standing 15 to 18 inches high, with thick hair falling in curls or ringlets, the color either pure white or pure black, or a mixture of those two colors! From the reign of Louis XIV through that of Louis XVI Toy Poodles, so called, were very popular and were shaved and shorn. These very tiny Poodles were all the rage in court circles. It is not known how breeders managed to produce such small specimens, possibly by using the Maltese or a very tiny white Cuban dog that was imported into France for the purpose.

The earliest known picture to portray a Toy Poodle is an early seventeenth century German painting of a child (*see P. 182*) with what is undoubtedly an early variety of a white Toy Poodle. Between 1636 and 1678 Jan Steen painted his delightful *The Dancing Dog*, giving us the most charming representation of an early Miniature Poodle. As a young boy plays a flute, the Poodle dances on his hind legs in what appears to be a tavern courtyard, while those about him admire the scene. The dog's hindquarters are clipped and he sports a ring of hair and a pompon on his tail.

This instinct to perform was, of course, one of the main reasons for the Poodle's popularity. His keen intelligence set him apart from other breeds and provided unlimited opportunities. Early in 1700 a troop of performing Poodles known as "The Ball of Little Dogs" danced to music as an attraction at court. In London and Paris from 1814 through 1818 a Poodle named "Munito" played cards and solved mathematical problems (*see P. 32*). Poodles have been used as circus performers for centuries and the original French clowns always worked a Poodle or two into the act. There is a theory that the pompons on the wrists and ankles of the Poodles was evolved to match the larger poms on the clown's costume. Turn-of-the-century silent motion pictures from France and England show performing Poodles, and an early British film features a Poodle participating in a Punch and Judy show in Covent Garden. A colored lithograph engraved by J. J. Chalon and dated 1820 shows the equivalent of a modern grooming parlor, operated by the women barbers of France in the open marketplace, putting some Poodles into the lion clip. An engraving in *Harper's Weekly* of July 6, 1872 shows an old woman shaving Poodles on the Spanish Steps in Rome (*see P. 36*).

It is not known when Poodles or their ancestors were first introduced into England. They were probably imported as working and hunting dogs long before they were recognized as a distinct breed and assigned a name. It is important to realize that the Poodle was first known in Great Britain as the "Rough Water Dog" before the word "Poodle" came into general use in English literature. No one has ever claimed that the Rough Water Dog originated in England. Nevertheless, Dr. Johannes Caius, personal physician to Queen Elizabeth I, included them in his list of dogs to be found in Britain that he compiled for the famous naturalist Conrad Gesner, which was printed in the first known dog book, *De Canibus Britannicis*, published in London in 1570. Therefore, this is the first mention in literature of the Rough Water Dog, the undoubted ancestor of the Standard Poodle of today. It also contains the first known reference of the *lion-clip*. In 1621 Gervaise Markham published his *Hungers Prevention* in London, illustrated by a now famous woodcut of the Water Dog, holding a small bird in its mouth.

One of the earliest pictures of a dog which looks like a Poodle appeared on the front page of a parliamentary broadsheet of 1642, to be found in the British Museum. The wording says "Prince Rupert's White Dog Called Boy," and it was to become the first real step forward in English Poodle history. It was published in the first year of the Civil War between the Royalists and the

This "Water Dog" of 1803 painted by Philip Reinagle, R.A. for William Taplin's "The Sportsman's Cabinet" book is considered to be the ancestor of today's Poodles.

In comparison, the "Water Spaniel" by Philip Reinagle, R.A. for the same book shows how different this dog was from the Poodle's ancestor.

Parliamentarians and was intended to inflame both sides, which it did. Boy was a Poodle given to Prince Rupert by Lord Arundell, the British ambassador at Vienna, while the Prince was imprisoned in Linz after the siege of Minden. On his release Rupert came to England to join the Cavalier forces, and brought Boy with him. The Poodle became a great favorite with King Charles and was treated almost as one of the family at court. This was not lost on the puritanical Roundheads, looking for any opportunity to smear the royal family, and they issued the first of several pamphlets declaring among other things that Boy was possessed of supernatural powers in league with the Devil and maybe even the Pope! The second pamphlet in 1643 printed a crude woodcut of Cavaliers encouraging Boy to attack the Parliamentarians' dog with the words "*To him pudel,*" the first use in English literature of the word "Poodle," although still written in its German form. Another cartoon has Boy proudly telling the Roundheads he is "of a high German breed." We thus have the first formation of the word Poodle, the name of both the dog and his owner, and in Boy's own words the country of his origin. It is the fullest record known at such an early date of any breed of dog which actually existed. For the record, Boy died bravely defending his master at the Battle of Marston Moor in 1644, although the broadsheet had said that he would live forever.

In the National Gallery in London there is a painting of the *Patient Griselda* by Pinturrichio (1454-1513) in which a small shaven Poodle appears among the various spectators observing Griselda's many vicissitudes of fortune. It once again emphasizes the popularity of smaller versions of the Poodle as pets and lap dogs throughout history. The small white Toy is perhaps the most ancient of the Poodle varieties, always a separate branch of the family, even more closely associated with family life than his larger brothers. It was the British breeders who were clever enough to fix size, color and type which now tend to breed true. A popular painting by Sir Edwin Landseer dated 1840, entitled *Laying Down the Law*, shows a large white Standard Poodle in the role of judge, attesting again to the Poodle's wisdom, surrounded by dogs of various other breeds listening intently to his sage advice. It is the perfect satire of humanity in animal form. The original can be seen in the art collection at Chatsworth House in England.

In the history of the breed the first entry of Poodles can be found in 1874 in the second Stud Book of the Kennel Club (England), where six dogs are listed, each with one simple name. There was no Poodle Club at that time, and apparently little interest in purebred Poodles. Yet only two years later, in 1876, the Poodle Club was formed. This did not create an immediate demand for better specimens, since only two Poodles were entered in the Kennel Club Stud Book that year, but it was a move in the right direction. In 1886 a clear and definite printed Standard was laid down in England to unify and refine type. As the new century began the Poodle was well established not only as a companion and a hunting dog but also as a show dog to be reckoned with.

3

Poodle Popularity in America

THE POODLE was the most popular breed of dog in America for 23 consecutive years, an incredible record which will probably never be surpassed.

Poodle registrations (comprised of the three varieties—Miniatures, Standards and Toys) established the breed as one of the top ten in popularity in 1953, according to the American Kennel Club records. They rapidly increased in number and in 1960 replaced Beagles as the most popular breed in the United States. It is suggested that one reason for this registration explosion was that returning soldiers and tourists imported Poodles during the ten year period from 1944 to 1954, mostly from England, providing breeding stock for the pet population, which in turn brought about an acceptance of the breed by the public and made the Poodle "fashionable." At any rate Poodles continued to lead all other breeds in registrations until 1983 when the Cocker Spaniel moved into the top position in individual registrations. However, there are still more Poodle litters registered every year than in any other breed.

In 1984, Poodle registrations totaled 87,750. From 1890—when only one Poodle was registered by the American Kennel Club—until the end of 1984, more than four million Poodles have been registered in the United States.

In addition to quantity, quality has been most noticeable. The Poodle has been a formidable contender in the show ring. With his aristocratic bearing, an excellent specimen in top condition seldom fails to attract attention. Seven Poodles have won highest honors at Westminster, America's most widely publicized dog show. Early winners of Best in Show there were the white Standard Poodle Ch. Nunsoe Duc de la Terrace of Blakeen in 1935 and the black Miniature Poodle Ch. Pitter Patter of Piperscroft in 1943. More recent Best in Show winners at Westminster include: the white Toy, Int. Ch. Wilber

White Swan in 1956; the white Standard, Ch. Puttencove Promise in 1958; the black Miniature, Ch. Fontclair Festoon in 1959; the black Toy, Ch. Cappoquin Little Sister in 1961; and the white Standard, Ch. Acadia Command Performance in 1973. Three of these—White Swan, Festoon and Little Sister— were conditioned and handled by Anne Rogers Clark, who is credited by many with bringing Poodle presentation to its present high degree of excellence. The widespread publicity generated by these wins made the general public Poodle conscious and they soon learned that the Poodle was an ideal companion with his great intelligence, his desire to please, his non-shedding coat, lack of doggy odor and adaptability. In addition to all these virtues, he comes in a variety of solid colors and in three sizes.

Through the end of 1984 there have been 12,012 Poodle champions of record, 62 of which were Obedience Trial champions.

Ch. Acadia Command Performance, C.D., white Standard, shown going Best in Show at the 1973 Westminster Kennel Club Show under Mrs. Augustus Riggs IV, handled by Frank Sabella. Owned by Edward B. Jenner and JoAnna Sering.

4

Buying A Poodle Puppy

THERE are few greater joys in this world than owning a healthy, purebred Poodle puppy. Why purebred? There is always a feeling of pride and satisfaction in owning any top quality product. But more important, with a purebred dog one can safely predict how your Poodle will *look* when he grows up. You are profiting from years and years of careful breeding in order to keep bloodlines true.

When you buy a puppy from a reputable breeder, he or she can tell you not only how the puppy will eventually look but often what can be expected from the personality and temperament of their stock. This fact alone is reason enough to avoid puppy mills which breed indiscriminately or buy up litters in quantity for a quick turnover. This type of dealer invariably uses the cheapest food and housing, and the puppies are rarely inoculated properly and new owners rarely receive proper papers or any guidance at all on puppy care. The soundest advice that can be given any prospective puppy owner is this: Visit a reputable kennel, tell them if you want a pet or a show dog, then listen to what they have to offer and heed their suggestions.

Where do you find a reputable breeder? The American Kennel Club can provide you with a list of names in your geographical area. You will find kennels advertised in the various dog magazines. Attend a dog show and talk to breeders. Locate a local Poodle Club, which will have a list of members who have quality puppies available. Don't suddenly decide to buy a puppy and rush right out. Shop around, as you would for any item you plan to treasure for years.

When you visit the breeder or the kennel—always make an appointment first—leave the neighborhood children and your relatives at home. Take only those persons most interested. This way you can ask questions, without being confused by each child or adult liking a different puppy. It might be wise to ask

Ch. Ounce O'Bounce T.N.T. as a puppy.

an experienced breeder to assist you in your selection, if this can be arranged. He can best assess the value of the puppy's pedigree, especially if you find the arrangement of the names or the championship titles confusing. Temperament, conformation, soundness and the health of the puppy can also be judged by an experienced dog owner.

You should pretty much decide in advance exactly what you are looking for—the color, size, sex and age of the puppy in question. This will greatly help the breeder in selecting the correct dog to show you. Usually this means a young puppy, two to six months of age, who is more adaptable. But do not reject an older dog merely because of age, if you like him. Again, listen carefully to the breeder's advice. You might be passing up a loveable pet at a bargain price.

Do not take offense if the owner is at first wary of letting you handle each puppy. Understand that he has the best interest of the puppy at heart. You should not visit more than one kennel on any given day, as distemper virus and other diseases may be carried from kennel to kennel. Also a reliable breeder should not be offended if you ask to have the puppy examined by a veterinarian within a 24 hour period.

A healthy puppy will have bright eyes, a damp, cool nose, and be playful and outgoing. It is well to sit quietly for some time, watching puppies play, before deciding which of them is to be yours. If you pick up the puppy, lift it carefully and sensibly, with one hand supporting his hindquarters. Never grab for a puppy right off, but let him initially come to you.

Don't haggle or bargain over the price. A reputable kennel will be fair, and the chances are that you are getting full value for your money. All puppies are not worth the same price, and the breeder will take this into account. There are always some in a litter that are better than others, and occasionally one is a real standout. The exceptionally good puppy should bring a higher price than one with minor faults, meaning faults which according to the AKC standard of perfection for the show ring might prohibit the dog being shown in competition, but which actually do not detract from the health or appeal of the puppy. These puppies cost less than show stock and make excellent pets. You should remember that a kennel cannot afford to sell puppies cheaply and survive. The cost of raising a litter includes care and feeding of the dam, the stud fee, serum, veterinarian bills and care of the puppy itself. Even so, the cost of a pet from a reliable source will be much the same as that from anywhere else.

Make certain that you receive your puppy's pedigree from the breeder and also his litter registration certificate. This is a form from the American Kennel Club so that you can have him registered as an individual dog. If these papers are not ready on the day you take your puppy home, ask the breeder to specify on your receipt that he will mail them to you when he receives the litter registration from the AKC.

In choosing a show puppy, remember that a quality must be exaggerated at three months to remain fixed in maturity. To have a lean skull and a long head when older, a puppy's head must be almost too long and fine when about four

Chriscrest Jubilee and Chriscrest Jamboree at 10 weeks of age, by Duncount's Dauphin ex Ch. Chriscrest Franchonette. Both became champions and Top Producers. Bred by Christobel Wakefield.

Silver Toy puppies from the Rainforest Kennels.

months old, as heads tend to thicken and coarsen with age. Eyes never change in shape and rarely in color. Light eyes may even get lighter. Poodle puppies that are going to be very short backed are absurdly so in babyhood. A puppy that has the same measurement of height and length of back from shoulder to tail will not be too long of back, as a rule, but unless there are at least two inches difference, he will not be very short either. Feet seldom change. Tight ones come that way in the beginning and will remain so unless they are spoiled by being kept on too hard surfaced areas. Hindquarters should be good, well let down, and strong from the beginning. Structural defects increase rather than disappear. Puppy coats should be thick and curly to develop into the proper texture later, though of course they are always rather silky in babyhood. In the warmer climates there must be a super coat inheritance for the jackets to be thick, stiff and bushy and kept so generation after generation.

Choosing puppies is always a gamble, but they can usually be depended upon to be like their immediate family. Size is difficult to gauge. Miniatures very seldom grow much in height after six months, seldom over two inches at most, though sometimes a puppy that is outsized may keep right on growing, to its owner's dismay.

Carriage and stylish action are born in some puppies; but, if not born in them, these traits can, to some extent, be trained into puppies with praise, wise handling, and encouragement on the lead.

Who says that money can't buy love?

30

5

Home Training

BRING HOME your new puppy when there is no excitement to frighten him. He will require a little time to get used to his new environment and will prefer to do this at his own pace, exploring everywhere with great curiosity. Much has been written and said about the Poodle's intelligence and quickness of perception. Since they are not fawning dogs by nature, they must be inculcated with perfect trust in their master before they can develop the self-confidence they need. Poodles crave human companionship and understanding, and they must be loved, played with, sensibly talked to, and handled from their earliest age. They soon learn that they can depend upon you, not as a severe critic but as a friend. Once confidence is established, with a bit of patience on your part a Poodle can be taught almost anything a dog can learn. Although they are stubborn, Poodles never forget a lesson, once it is mastered.

If the puppy is a gift for a child, the child should be expected to care for it, and he must learn as well as the puppy what is and is not allowed. The parents should impress on the child that the puppy should be handled much as a small baby—that the puppy is not just another one of his playthings to be tossed casually about. You must realize that puppies are born without fear. Don't let them jump or fall from high places. Since they are dependent and trusting at first, all of their early experiences exert a strong influence on their disposition and, in fact, on their entire lives. Remember also that Poodles are notorious mimics. You need only convey to them what it is you desire them to do and they will usually accept this. In addition to the breed traits of character that Poodles have in common, they have individual personalities which the trainer must take into account and sometimes make allowances for. It is these quirks of temperament that make Poodles so interesting and their training at once a problem and a pleasure.

MUNITO,

OR

THE LEARNED DOG.

To be seen every Day at Mr. LAXTON's Room,

No. 23, NEW BOND STREET,

AT THE HOURS OF THREE AND SEVEN PRECISELY.

THIS WONDERFUL DOG understands the Alphabet, can read, copy Words, and cast Accounts. He knows all the playing Cards, and will select out of a Pack the Cards which any of the Spectators may be pleased to ask for. He plays at Dominos: is acquainted with the Principles of Botany and Geography: and exhibits many other astonishing Performances.

☞ *Admittance One Shilling.*

Munito, a famous performing Poodle, who startled audiences with his intelligence and tricks in London and Paris from 1814 through 1818.

Poodles are extremely sensitive and have a sense of justice that no trainer can override. They will comply with anything asked of them, but they refuse to be browbeaten or driven. Poodles tend to be set in their ways, so that care must be taken to teach them exactly what they are expected to do in exactly the way they are expected to do it for the rest of their days.

The trainer must never betray the loss of his temper or permit the dog to suspect his irritation. He must speak in a firm, emphatic tone of voice, but never an unkind or petulant tone. The same word or gesture of command must be employed without variation for a given response, and it must be repeated over and over again until the lesson is learned and perfectly mastered. When the Poodle at length perceives the command and responds to it correctly, his obedience should be rewarded with tidbits of food and lavish praise, after which the command is repeated and after the correct response the reward also should be repeated.

No Poodle should ever be punished for its failure to understand what is wanted of it. The routine should be gone over patiently time after time until he comprehends what is expected of him. However, once the trainer is sure that the dog understands, the pupil must feel the teacher's displeasure when he fails to obey a command. Punishment may take the form of scolding and grave expression of disapproval. Punishment must be prompt and absolutely just, or it will do more harm than good. A Poodle should never be whipped for any reason; a real whipping may ruin his temperament and disposition. But when one is absolutely sure a Poodle understands the meaning of a command, he should never be permitted to get away with disobedience. If it takes a week, the trainer must keep right at the task until the dog has made the correct response. The minute the dog obeys, he should be petted and praised and he should be given a respite from his work. The trainer's tact, gentleness, and patience are first requisites in the education of a Poodle.

Dogs, and especially young dogs, should not be tired with long, drawn out lessons. Ten or fifteen minutes a day are generally enough, provided the lessons are regular. They may be more frequently than daily, but in any event, the lessons should not be long and there should be considerable intervals between them.

One of the first things to teach a puppy is that "No!" means "No! Stop what you are doing at once!" When a puppy takes a bedroom slipper to chew upon, it should be taken from him gently with "No!" in a firm voice. When he starts to misbehave in the house, he should be told "No!" and taken outside immediately or shown that place in the house where he may safely relieve himself.

If it is not desired that your Poodle should get on any piece of furniture that he might wish, he should be given an old chair for himself, a covered new one, or a box or basket with a cushion or towel away from the drafts of the floor. He should have his own bed from the first day you bring him home. A cardboard box with sides so he feels secure, with half of one side cut part way down for an entrance and through which he can watch the activity about him, is fine. He should be taught that this is his, a refuge where he may go with his favorite ball and other cherished playthings. Poodles also have a keen sense of possession.

If convenient, place the box near your bed so that the puppy may be reassured, if lonely, by your dropping your hand into the box, caressing him and speaking softly. Remember at first he will be missing his mother and his littermates. Do not allow the puppy on the bed, as he may fall or jump off after you have gone to sleep, or he may relieve himself on the bed. Once he has experienced the warmth and comfort of your bed it will be very difficult to convince him to sleep any place else.

It is advisable to find out from his breeder exactly what your puppy has been fed, and to keep him on that diet for a few days, even if this is not what you have in mind for him. When he is quite settled you can introduce him to your own ideas of a good diet. The excitement of his new surroundings may put the puppy off his food for the first day, but be insistent that he eat regularly after that.

Housebreaking

Housebreaking your puppy is the most immediate problem of all. It can be effectively accomplished by following the three P's of house training—Planning, Patience and Praise. Keep in mind two more p's—prevention not punishment. Poodles are naturally clean dogs. Your puppy will not willingly foul his own box. You must provide a place for him to do his duty—Planning. Whether this is some spot outdoors or inside on papers is a matter of convenience and the puppy's eventual size. Big dogs, obviously, should be trained to the outdoors. Toy and Miniatures living in apartment buildings are often taught to eliminate on newspapers. Whichever you choose, be consistent. Don't confuse your puppy by switching from one to the other, at least in the beginning. And separate his sleeping and bathroom area to avoid confusion there. Take the puppy to the area chosen when you feel the time propitious, such as right after a nap, and be firm but gentle. As soon as he relieves himself, tell him he is a good boy and make a fuss over him—Patience and Praise.

There are three times of day when a puppy is most likely to have the urge—just after sleeping, just after eating or drinking and oddly enough, just as he starts to eat. He may start eating, suddenly stop to wet, and resume eating. Puppies will not eat if they are in discomfort and need relief. During any of these times, don't delay. Right after a nap, quickly and gently pick him up and place him on the newspaper or outdoor area. It is not of the slightest use to scold or smack him or put him out *after* he has made his puddle, as he simply will not understand what you mean.

Take him to the same spot each time he is taken out of the house and make sure he does what he is taken out for. He should never just be turned out and forgotten. It is wiser to stay with the puppy and make sure that he has emptied

his bladder or his bowels and when he does, praise him. Puppies, like children, are inattentive and if left alone will very often play only to come back into the house and soil the floor. But if it is insisted upon that they relieve themselves outdoors before they are readmitted to the house, this does not occur. Don't forget to praise him lavishly when the job is done. Soon he will learn what is meant when he is told, "Come on and be a good boy." When the Poodle puppy comes to know what he is taken outside for, half the battle is won, for the Poodle's desire is to comply with human wishes. The trainer must not relax, however, until the puppy responds each and every time he is taken out and the trainer must be right there to make sure of what the puppy does.

If the puppy misbehaves in the house and can be caught in the very act (no puppy remembers what he did fifteen minutes ago), he should be taken to the soiled spot and forced to listen to the riot act. In the course of such a lecture, the floor may be violently struck with a rolled newspaper several times. Then the dog should be taken out-of-doors immediately to the area where he is accustomed to relieve himself.

Spots on the rug or floor which the dog has soiled should be so thoroughly cleaned that no odor remains. This tends to prevent the repetition of the offense, since dogs are prone to relieve themselves in the same place time after time.

You should of course teach your Poodle to come to you whenever you call his name. Often he will run in the opposite direction, hoping this is a new game. Don't chase after him. Sit quietly and continue calling his name. You can hold out a bit of food or one of his toys to attract his attention until he catches on.

People love to spoil their Poodles. This is fine up to a point, but should not be overdone. Poodles are so intelligent that they can easily wreck a home, but if they do, almost invariably it is the owner's fault. If a puppy is so indulged and so spoiled that everything and everybody in the home is sacrificed to him, he soon catches on and uses this power in absolutely devious ways. He spoils a family meal by begging for food from the table. He is so noisy when callers visit that no one can make themselves heard. The owners start cancelling dinner dates, evenings out, even annual vacations because the dog "can't be left alone." This is all absolute nonsense and suddenly not funny. No one is really happy, least of all the Poodle, basically a sensitive animal which has become disturbed. He must be trained right from the start to stay quietly alone for periods of time, which should not be too long or too frequent, and should be given his familiar toys with which to amuse himself. A well trained Poodle knows how to behave and enjoys doing it. He revels in that special companionship he has with his owner through mutual understanding and discipline.

Shaving dogs on the Spanish Steps in Rome.

SHAVING DOGS IN ROME.

"In the good old time," says the artist to whose pencil we are indebted for the illustration on this page, "that's just a month ago, you could not descend the steps of the Trinita de' Monti without stopping before a very curious spectacle. You halted at a line of dogs tied to the stone-work in the sun, some shivering, some dripping, some dozing, some restless. Dogs they are, poodles, *lupettos*, Maltese; but jolly dogs no longer, and they look up at you with the most woe-begone expression. 'Yes, Sir,' they seem to say, 'you may well look at us. We are, indeed, objects of pity, deprived of coats, fleas, and liberty. The hand of Fate has been upon us—Fate in the person of that old woman who has ruthlessly washed and shaved us. If you have a heart, pray, oh, pray, to the dog-star to temper the wind to the shorn poodle.' You turn to the old woman, and find her bending low over a poodle patient, who lies under her scissors as if under chloroform. Queer old lady that! I sketched her the other day in the very act. At first she showed a coy reserve, a maiden modesty, and retired behind a slab. But I stood my ground, and time being valuable to her (Heaven knows how many dogs she shaved a day!), she reappeared, and set to work again. So did I; and in the midst of it she looked up, fixed me with her eye, smiled, and pointed to her mouth. I took the hint, and before I went left an offering on her altar beside the victim. And what a philosophic victim! Nothing of the Cynic about him, but the complete Stoic. He never snarls or flinches; he lies there perfectly resigned, turning his eyes up as he ponders why poodles should be allowed to wear hair only round the head, the stump or tip of the tail, and in anklets above the feet."

This originally appeared in *Harper's Weekly* of July 6, 1872.

6

Grooming, Bathing and Clipping

POODLES learn quickly. If grooming, which is a very important part of every Poodle's life, is presented as a natural and pleasant daily happening, then he will accept it cheerfully, and may even enjoy it. At any rate, it will not occur to him to make a fuss. It should begin in very early puppyhood, by teaching him to lie quietly on his side for a daily brushing, a minute or two at first, as soon as he begins to toddle. You must be firm during these sessions. At first he may squirm about, but speak quietly and reassuringly to him, and make him behave. Never slap or shout at him. Poodles are extremely sensitive to voice inflections. Use a firm tone of voice when making corrections. "No" is a magic word for almost all occasions, and always use this same word so that your dog understands what you want him to do, or not do. As soon as he does what you want, praise him lavishly! And be consistent yourself. Don't let him get away with something one day, then reprimand him for doing the very same thing the next day. Let common sense prevail. If you should lose all patience, abandon what you are doing and come back to it later. A Poodle should never associate brushing, clipping or bathing with an unpleasant experience.

Brushing is extremely important throughout a Poodle's life. It must be remembered that Poodles do not shed their hair as other breeds do and that dead hair remains in the coat and must be taken out. If it is not removed, mats will form. You should begin the brushing by making a part in the hair straight up the backbone. Have your Poodle lie with his feet toward you and brush a small area at a time. With your fingers part a section of the hair down to the skin and then brush it away from you. Always brush away from the skin, taking care not to scrape the skin. In this manner the entire coat will receive a thorough groom-

ing. The tangles and mats may be pulled apart with the fingers and then brushed carefully. The entire operation is repeated on the other side. Then the Poodle is allowed to sit up so that his chest may be brushed in the same manner.

Most groomers agree that the comb should be used only after the hair is free from tangles, and that you should never tug and tear at the coat at any time. With patience, tangles can be removed so that only the knot comes away without damage to the surrounding hair. Start at the bottom of the tangle and gently pull apart the hair until it is thoroughly separated; then gently brush out the loose hairs. Never start pulling apart tangles from the top, as this breaks the good hair and does not get to the bottom of the trouble.

The correct brush for a pet Poodle is a slicker. This is an oblong-shaped brush with a wooden handle, and has bent wire teeth set close together to help remove mats and dead hair. Slicker brushes come in three sizes, corresponding to the three sizes of Poodles. Slickers are not recommended for the long mane of a show Poodle, as the wire teeth will pull out the long hair and wreck the coat. For show grooming use a brush with long, pliable pins or bristles set in a cushioned rubber base. The finest of the pin brushes have long, polished stainless steel or chrome-plated pins with rounded ends to prevent scratching the skin. The pins should be flexible enough not to pull out long coat. Fine bristle brushes can also be used, though these tend to be a bit more expensive. They should have tufts of natural bristle set in a cushioned rubber base. The bristles in each tuft should be graduated in length to give even penetration through the show coat.

There are many different kinds of Poodle combs, the most popular having half-fine and half-medium teeth of metal with rounded tips. It is important to buy a good one. The best are made of chrome-plated solid brass and last a long time.

Brushing is really only the beginning of a full grooming session. A routine brushing on a daily basis should take from five to seven minutes, or until all tangles have been removed. Then you should check your dog's skin thoroughly for traces of external parasites, such as fleas or ticks, or for other problems. Check the ears and clean them if necessary. You may even need to clip the nails.

Use a steady table for grooming with a non-slip rubber top. Until your Poodle is thoroughly trained to sit quietly on the grooming table, *never* let him out of your reach as he may suddenly decide to jump off, perhaps breaking a leg or even worse. The room you are using must have adequate lighting. The light should come from above and behind you. Dark Poodles are difficult enough in the best light! The grooming area should be quiet. There must be no other dogs or loud noises to distract your Poodle. This is serious business and the dog must be made aware of this fact. Plan your time so that your Poodle will not have to stand still on the grooming table any longer than necessary. Remember that young puppies have short attention spans and fifteen minutes is long enough at first. Don't talk "baby talk" to the puppy. He is not there to play games with you. And reward him in some way after the grooming session. Lavish praise or a favorite treat will do nicely.

Your Poodle's ears should be cleaned out at least once a month, which should keep them in good condition and easy to maintain. The first step is to remove the long hair leading into the ear canal. Sit the dog firmly on the table, turn back the ear flap, and using your thumb and index finger, carefully pull out the excess hair leading into the canal. Never probe inside the ear with any sort of instrument. Remove a few hairs at a time, which will not hurt the dog. If the hair is difficult to grip, shake a little ear powder into the opening, which will give you a better hold. Once the hair is removed, moisten a piece of absorbent cotton with alcohol and carefully wipe the ear flap and the canal opening. Poodles are prone to severe and chronic ear infections. If there is a foul odor or a reddish-brown discharge from the ear canal, consult your veterinarian immediately. Excessive amounts of wax deep inside the ear should also be removed only by a veterinarian.

Toenails should be cut regularly. This improves the appearance of the feet and helps to tighten them up. Neglected nails may have a bad effect on the dog's posture and action. Walking becomes uncomfortable, even painful, and a dog can become lame. Do not be under the misapprehension that dogs naturally wear down their nails. The average Poodle spends most of his time indoors, and it becomes your job to trim his nails regularly. Unfortunately, most dogs detest having their nails clipped. They should be trained from puppyhood that this is part of the grooming routine, especially for show prospects. I have seen dogs draw back the foot when a judge examines it in the ring. A single injury to the sensitive quick of the nail can traumatize a dog for the remainder of his life, to the point where he will resent and resist having his feet handled. Especial care should be used to maintain the dog's confidence and to not hurt him. Take off very little of the nail at a time, while holding one of his feet in the palm of your hand, pulling it gently forward. If the dog pulls back during the trimming or tries to wiggle free, have someone steady him by placing a hand at the elbow as you trim the front feet and at the hock joint as you cut the nails on the back feet. If you should cut into the quick (that soft, fleshy area beyond the hard part of the nail), it will probably bleed. Immediately press a little Monsels Powder or nail clotting solution, available from a pet shop, against the nail for a minute or so until the bleeding stops. Various nail clippers are available. Some operate like a scissors, but the most effective works like a small guillotine. These are also available from a pet shop.

A Poodle's teeth should be kept free from tartar. Use a small dental scaler and operate from under the gum downward, using your thumb as a buffer between the sharp scaler and the lips and gums below. Feeding your Poodle Milkbones or other hard biscuits will help keep the teeth clean.

Most pet Poodles are bathed monthly, but there is no hard and fast rule about this. It really depends on how quickly he gets dirty, what color he is and therefore how dirty he looks, his coat texture, and even the temperature and humidity in your area. Show dogs that are groomed regularly do not require much bathing, and in fact a bath can easily wreck a heavy coat. But there comes a time, even in the lives of well groomed dogs, when a bath is absolutely necessary.

First of all the preparation for a bath is essential. Your Poodle must be very carefully groomed and every tangle or knot teased out of his coat before bathing him.

Choose a fine-quality shampoo that is correctly pH balanced for dogs. This has to do with the acid or alkaline content of the product. The pH range for a dog's skin and hair is not the same as that for humans, being slightly more alkaline. Manufacturers such as Lambert Kay, MBF, Wu Pi Products and House of An-Ju offer a range of shampoos correctly pH balanced for dogs and designed for general or specific uses. All-purpose shampoos, so called, clean beautifully and this is the type most used. There are also tearless shampoos for puppies or older Poodles with sensitive skin, medicated shampoos to help relieve itching and remove bacterial fungus, color shampoos (these are not dyes) to enhance specific colors or to remove yellow discoloration from white coats, and body building shampoos formulated to add body and texture to soft coats. Many dogs are allergic to detergents, and these should never be used.

Before bathing it is sometimes a good idea to put a drop of mineral oil in both the dog's eyes to protect him from the shampoo. You can also plug the ears with cotton before putting the dog into the tub. This is especially important if your Poodle has chronic ear trouble. Fill the tub with about three inches of warm water, testing for comfort with the inner elbow. Add the shampoo, and

A charming group of Miniature Poodle puppies at play from the Miradel Kennels in England.
—*Photo by Sally Anne Thompson*

then stand the dog in the water for bathing. Wet him down with a spray hose; then the sudsy water may be repeatedly scooped over the dog, using a plastic or metal scoop. Use warm water throughout the shampoo—cold water tends to make the coat limp. Give a brisk lathering with your fingertips. Your pet Poodle will love it!

Wash the head and ears last. A dog is less frightened of a bath if you do the body first. It takes two shampoos to really clean Poodle hair, so rinse lightly and shampoo a second time. Thorough rinsing is important, more important than soaping. Squeeze the excess water from your Poodle's coat, then let him shake well. Wrap him in a towel, take him out of the tub and stand him on the grooming table.

In the case of a puppy, dry the head and ears first while the rest of the puppy is wrapped in the warm towel. Blot the dog thoroughly with the towel, then dry him with an electric hair dryer set on "Warm." The old fashioned goose neck type of dryer that used to be seen in hairdressing shops is ideal, but a good brand small hand dryer does very well. Be certain that the chest is perfectly dry. Now groom your dog as usual, and by doing this while the hair is still damp you can train it in the desired direction.

There are four different Poodle clips which, according to the age group of the entry, are accepted by all Poodle clubs, including the Poodle Club of America. These are the "English Saddle" clip, the "Continental" clip, the "Puppy" clip, and the "Sporting" clip, all of which are discussed in detail in Chapter 8. There are, of course, many unorthodox clips which are not acceptable for the show ring, but popular with pet owners. One of these is the "Dutch" clip, in which the face is clipped close, leaving a moustache on the end of the nose, and the ears are clipped, leaving only a fringe at the bottom. The topknot is rounded sometimes to a ball. The chest, stomach and back of the dog are clipped, leaving the long hair on all four legs either squared off about four inches above the elbows or coming to a point higher up, something like a raglan sleeve. Feet and tail are clipped. A detailed description of fifteen other pet clips and their variations can be found in *The Complete Poodle Clipping and Grooming Book* by Shirlee Kalstone, published by Howell Book House.

The disqualification by breed clubs of dogs unconventionally clipped is not born of an arbitrary decision. There is a very definite purpose behind it. A trim such as the Dutch clip destroys the line of face and neck and, if persisted in by breeders, would soon make the breeding of good Poodle heads a thing of the past. The outline of the dog behind the head is also often destroyed. Fanciers have worked hard for generations to produce an elegant and attractive dog and realize that an indiscriminate trim could negate all their efforts.

Whatever the clip, the Poodle must be groomed and trimmed regularly. He should never, never be allowed to become a mass of matted, dirty hair. Since the Poodle does not shed, you must remove the excess hair. You will soon learn the use of the Oster Electric Animal Clipper, so much a part of the Poodle lover's equipment. Lessons from an experienced groomer can be a great help. For

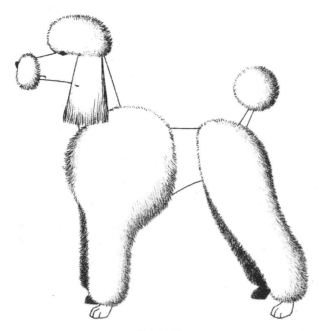

Dutch clip.

puppies or dogs unused to clipping, either the #10 or #15 Oster Clipper blade is best and safest. Older dogs can take a closer clip. The clipper blades should be kept clean, and the clippers themselves oiled and greased regularly. If you do not feel you can do the clipping yourself, or if you find it too time consuming for your schedule, there are Poodle trimming parlors in all towns of any size. Shop around and find one you like. If you see someone with a neatly groomed Poodle which you admire, ask where they have had it groomed. Be sure to check the hours when the shop opens and closes each day, to find if these times are convenient for you. But do have your Poodle groomed on a regular basis.

EARS set low: hanging close to head: leather long, wide, heavily feathered

NECK well-proportioned, strong: length to allow head carried high with dignity: skin snug at throat

SHOULDERS strong, muscular: should slope back from point of angulation at upper foreleg to withers.
Back short, strong, slightly hollowed

loins short, broad, muscular

TAIL straight: rather high set: length sufficient to insure balance: carriage up,

THIGHS well-developed, muscular: width in stifle region

STIFLES well-bent

HINDLEGS very muscular: turning neither in nor out

HOCKS well-let-down

CLIPS: "Puppy Clip" for Poodles under one year of age.
"Continental" or "English Saddle" for dogs over one year of age

COAT dense throughout: profuse: texture harsh

SIZE determines 3 varieties:
STANDARD, over 15" at withers:
MINIATURE, over 10" (to 15")
at withers: TOY,10" or under
at withers

SKULL moderately rounded

STOP slight but definite

EYES set far apart: very dark: oval appearance

NOSE sharp: nostrils well-defined: color (see COLOR)

MUZZLE long, straight, fine: slight chiseling under eyes: strong without lippiness: chin definite enough to preclude snippiness. Teeth white, strong: scissors bite

CHEEKS: Bones, muscles flat

CHEST deep, moderately wide

FORELEGS straight from shoulder: parallel: bone and muscle in proportion to size

RIBS well-sprung: braced up

PASTERNS strong

FEET rather small: oval: turning neither in nor out: toes arched, close: pads hard, thick, well-cushioned

COLOR even, solid at skin: in blues, grays, silvers, browns, cafe-au-laits, apricots, creams, coats may show varying shades of same color (ears, ruff, etc.): clear colors preferred. Browns, cafe-au-laits—liver-colored noses, eye rims, lips, dark toenails, dark amber eyes. Black, blue, gray, silver, apricot, cream, white Poodles— black noses, eye rims, lips, black or self-colored toenails, very dark eyes. Apricots—black preferred: liver-colored noses, eye rims, lips, self-colored toenails, amber eyes permitted

DISQUALIFICATIONS: Parti-colors where coat is not even solid color at skin but variegated in patches of two or more colors.Only specified clips allowed in show ring: only specified sizes for each variety permitted

VISUALIZATION OF THE POODLE STANDARD
Reproduced with permission from Dog Standards Illustrated.

7

Official AKC Standard for the Poodle

As approved by the American Kennel Club,
August 14, 1984.

GENERAL APPEARANCE, CARRIAGE AND CONDITION—
   That of a very active, intelligent and elegant-appearing dog, squarely built, well proportioned, moving soundly and carrying himself proudly. Properly clipped in the traditional fashion and carefully groomed, the Poodle has about him an air of distinction and dignity peculiar to himself.

HEAD AND EXPRESSION—
   (a) Skull—Moderately rounded, with a slight but definite stop. Cheekbones and muscles flat. Length from occiput to stop about the same as length of muzzle.
   (b) Muzzle—Long, straight and fine, with slight chiseling under the eyes. Strong without lippiness. The chin definite enough to preclude snipiness. Teeth white, strong and with a scissors bite.
   (c) Eyes—Very dark, oval in shape and set far enough apart and positioned to create an alert intelligent expression.
   (d) Ears—Hanging close to the head, set at or slightly below eye level. The ear leather is long, wide, and thickly feathered; however, the ear fringe should not be of excessive length.

NECK AND SHOULDERS—
   Neck well proportioned, strong and long enough to permit the head to be carried high and with dignity. Skin snug at throat. The neck rises from strong,

smoothly muscled shoulders. The shoulder blade is well laid back and approximately the same length as the upper foreleg.

BODY—

To insure the desirable squarely-built appearance, the length of body measured from the breastbone to the point of the rump approximates the height from the highest point of the shoulders to the ground.

(a) *Chest*—Deep and moderately wide with well sprung ribs.

(b) *Back*—The topline is level, neither sloping nor roached, from the highest point of the shoulder blade to the base of the tail, with the exception of a slight hollow just behind the shoulder. The loin is short, broad, and muscular.

TAIL—

Straight, set on high and carried up, docked of sufficient length to insure a balanced outline.

LEGS—

(a) *Forelegs*—Straight and parallel when viewed from the front. When viewed from the side the elbow is directly below the highest point of the shoulder. The pasterns are strong. Bone and muscle of both forelegs and hindlegs are in proportion to size of dog.

(b) *Hindlegs*—Straight and parallel when viewed from the rear. Muscular with width in the region of the stifles which are well bent; femur and tibia are about equal in length; hock to heel short and perpendicular to the ground. When standing, the rear toes are only slightly behind the point of rump. The angulation of the hindquarters balances that of the forequarters.

FEET—

The feet are rather small, oval in shape with toes well arched and cushioned on thick firm pads. Nails short but not excessively shortened. The feet turn neither in nor out. Dewclaws may be removed.

COAT—

(a) *Quality*—

(1) *curly:* of naturally harsh texture, dense throughout.

(2) *corded:* hanging in tight even cords of varying length; longer on mane or body coat, head, and ears; shorter on puffs, bracelets, and pompons.

(b) *Clip*—A Poodle under 12 months may be shown in the "puppy" clip. In all regular classes, Poodles 12 months or over must be shown in the "English Saddle" or "Continental" clip. In the Stud Dog and Brood Bitch classes and in a non-competitive Parade of Champions, Poodles may be shown in the "Sporting" clip. A Poodle shown in any other type of clip shall be disqualified.

(1) "*Puppy*": A Poodle under a year old may be shown in the "Puppy" clip with the coat long. The face, throat, feet and base of the tail are shaved. The entire shaven foot is visible. There is a pompon on the end of the

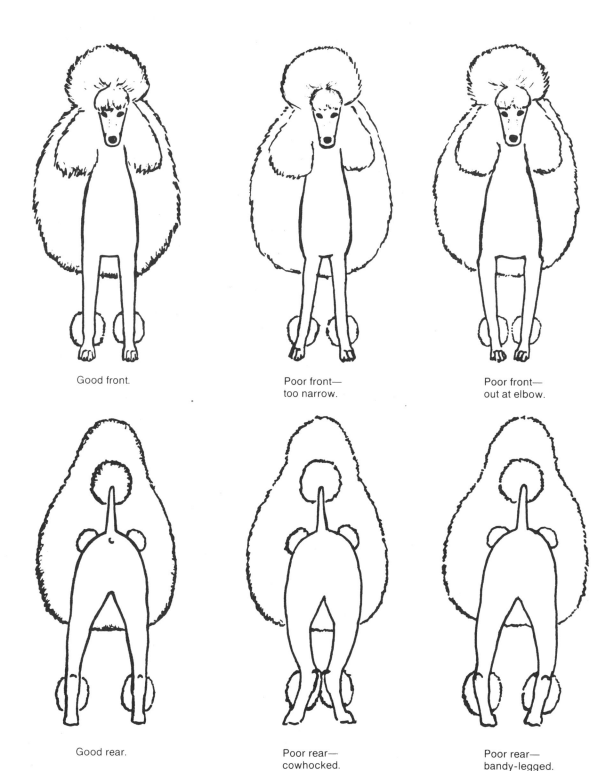

Good front.

Poor front—
too narrow.

Poor front—
out at elbow.

Good rear.

Poor rear—
cowhocked.

Poor rear—
bandy-legged.

Illustrated by Loraine L. Bush.

47

tail. In order to give a neat appearance and a smooth unbroken line, shaping of the coat is permissible.

(2) *"English Saddle"*: In the "English Saddle" clip, the face, throat, feet, forelegs and base of the tail are shaved, leaving puffs on the forelegs and a pompon on the end of the tail. The hindquarters are covered with a short blanket of hair except for a curved shaved area on each flank and two shaved bands on each hindleg. The entire shaven foot and a portion of the shaven leg above the puff are visible. The rest of the body is left in full coat but may be shaped in order to insure overall balance.

(3) *"Continental"*: In the "Continental" clip the face, throat, feet and base of the tail are shaved. The hindquarters are shaved with pompons (optional) on the hips. The legs are shaved, leaving bracelets on the hindlegs and puffs on the forelegs. There is a pompon on the end of the tail. The entire shaven foot and a portion of the shaven foreleg above the puff are visible. The rest of the body is left in full coat but may be shaped in order to insure overall balance.

(4) *"Sporting"*: In the "Sporting" clip a Poodle shall be shown with face, feet, throat, and base of tail shaved, leaving a scissored cap on the top of the head and a pompon on the end of the tail. The rest of the body and legs are clipped or scissored to follow the outline of the dog, leaving a short blanket of coat no longer than one inch in length. The hair on the legs may be slightly longer than that on the body.

In all clips the hair of the topknot may be left free or held in place by elastic bands. The hair is only of sufficient length to present a smooth outline. "Topknot" refers only to hair on the skull, from stop to occiput. This is the only area where elastic bands may be used.

COLOR—

The coat is an even and solid color at the skin. In blues, grays, silvers, browns, cafe-au-laits, apricots, and creams the coat may show varying shades of the same color. This is frequently present in the somewhat darker feathering of the ears and in the tipping of the ruff. While clear colors are definitely preferred, such natural variation in the shading of the coat is not to be considered a fault. Brown and cafe-au-lait Poodles have liver-colored noses, eye rims and lips, dark toenails and dark amber eyes. Black, blue, gray, silver, cream and white Poodles have black noses, eye rims and lips, black or self-colored toenails and very dark eyes. In the apricots while the foregoing coloring is preferred, liver-colored noses, eye rims and lips, and amber eyes are permitted but are not desirable.

Parti-colored dogs shall be disqualified. The coat of a parti-colored dog is not an even solid color at the skin but is of two or more colors.

GAIT—

A straightforward trot with light springy action and strong hindquarters drive. Head and tail carried up. Sound effortless movement is essential.

SIZE—

The Standard Poodle is over 15 inches at the highest point of the shoulders. Any Poodle which is 15 inches or less in height shall be disqualified from competition as a Standard Poodle.

The Miniature Poodle is 15 inches or under at the highest point of the shoulders, with a minimum height in excess of 10 inches. Any Poodle which is over 15 inches or is 10 inches or less at the highest point of the shoulders shall be disqualified from competition as a Miniature Poodle.

The Toy Poodle is 10 inches or under at the highest point of the shoulders. Any Poodle which is more than 10 inches at the highest point of the shoulders shall be disqualified from competition as a Toy Poodle.

As long as the Toy Poodle is definitely a Toy Poodle, and the Miniature Poodle a Miniature Poodle, both in balance and proportion for the Variety, diminutiveness shall be the deciding factor when all other points are equal.

VALUE OF POINTS—

General appearance, temperament, carriage and condition 30
Head, expression, ears, eyes, and teeth 20
Body, neck, legs, feet and tail 20
Gait 20
Coat, color and texture 10

MAJOR FAULTS—

Any distinct deviation from the desired characteristics described in the Breed Standard with particular attention to the following:

Temperament—Shyness or sharpness.

Muzzle—Undershot, overshot, wry mouth, lack of chin.

Eyes—Round, protruding, large or very light.

Pigment—Color of nose, lips and eye rims incomplete, or of wrong color for color of dog.

Neck and Shoulders—Ewe neck, steep shoulders.

Tail—Set low, curled, or carried over the back.

Hindquarters—Cow hocks.

Feet—Paper or splayfoot.

DISQUALIFICATIONS—

Clip—A dog in any type of clip other than those listed under Coat shall be disqualified.

Parti-colors—The coat of a parti-colored dog is not an even solid color at the skin but of two or more colors. Parti-colored dogs shall be disqualified.

Size—A dog over or under the height limits specified shall be disqualified.

Am. & Can. Ch. Wilber White Swan, white Toy, shown going Best in Show at 1956 Westminster Kennel Club show. Left to right: Paul Palmer, judge; William Rockefeller, club president; and Anne Rogers Clark, handler. Bred and owned by Mrs. Bertha Smith, Bermyth Kennels.

8

Clipping the Poodle for the Show Ring

by Anne Rogers Clark

THE SECTION headed "Coat" in the Standard of the Breed explains in detail the various allowed trims for the Poodle and the two allowed presentations of the coat itself—curly and corded. To prepare your Poodle's coat correctly for the show ring you must first read and understand what this section says. It is also best if you have some background knowledge of the breed, some basic knowledge of anatomy, plus an eye for symmetry and balance. You must also be able to visualize the Poodle which you are about to groom without hair, as it is on this form that you will work using one of the trims described here.

The Poodle to be trimmed should be freshly washed and dried. He should also be taught proper brushing manners from a very early age. He must learn to lie quietly on his side and to enjoy the whole process so that he will nap and not be a bother to the person who is brushing him. He will thus learn grooming table manners in preparation for that day when he is first clipped. Never use a clipper blade that becomes so warm that it is uncomfortable to hold against your own arm. It is best to have several blades as well as several heads so that you may change them when the blade becomes hot. Guard your scissors well. Dropping them or using them for cutting anything other than hair will dull them and make them impossible to use effectively.

Experiment with different table heights. Some people cannot trim sitting down, while others cannot trim well standing up. A table of the wrong height can cause undue fatigue for the groomer. Always try to finish scissoring with the dog on the ground—just the final touches. This is where he will be judged, so he must keep that special look he had on the table when he is put on the ground.

In the "English Saddle" clip the face, throat, feet, forelegs and base of the tail as shaved, leaving puffs on the forelegs and a pompon on the end of the tail. The hindquarters are covered with a short blanket of hair except for a curved shaved area on each flank and two shaved bands on each hind leg. The entire shaven foot and a portion of the shaven leg above the puff are visible. The rest of the body is left in full coat but should be shaped in order to insure overall balance.

With your dog sitting securely on a firm, rubber-topped or towel-spread table, begin with the front feet. Clip up to where the dewclaw is or was, using a #00 or #40 blade. Put a finger underneath each toe, one by one, to spread the foot for careful and meticulous clipping. When the feet are neat and clean, in between the pads, underneath as well as on top, use an electric buffer to shorten and round the nails. If the buffer is used between grooming sessions, the nails will be kept short and neat, without need for drastic measures. Attend to the hindfeet in the same manner, starting the clipped area just above the toes in front and just above the large back pad behind.

Next clip the front legs from just above the wrist to just below the elbow, using a #40, #30 or #15 blade against the growth of the coat. Leave the elbow joint just-covered. The front puff should cover the wrist of the dog with just a little to spare.

Now clip the belly with the #15 blade. The area to be clipped should extend from the navel back to the joining of the rear legs to the body. At the side it should follow the flap of skin in the loin and flank. Never push the clipper through the hair. Let it do its own work and it will remain cool longer and will not need sharpening as frequently. Try not to stretch the skin unduly when you are clipping as this may result in scrapes and clipper burns. Next do the base of the tail with the #30 blade, always clipping against the growth of the hair. The tail should have an adequately shaved area at its base to permit the tail bone to be visible. However, try to leave as much tail bone in the pompon as possible as it will give it body and firmness. Poodles clipped just after they are bathed will clip closer than if done before the bath, and the clipper blade will not dull as quickly.

Before beginning the pattern, get someone to set up the dog while you back off to get an overall picture and decide on the proper proportions for perfect balance. From now on, the individual interpretation of the Standard will apply.

Modern trimming practices dictate that the mane start at or near the last rib. It is safer to start just behind the last rib as the pack can be moved forward far more easily than the mane can be moved back. With the dog standing, carefully part the dog's coat at a point just behind the last rib, parting it the complete way around his body. Comb the mane forward of the part and scissor the hair on the hindquarters to about double the length of the finished pack.

52

Now place the straight edge of the #30 blade on the part between the mane and the pack with the clipper facing the rear of the dog. The middle of the clipper blade should be on an imaginary line drawn through the dog's side. Clip around in a half circle, with one sweep, and do the same on the other side. The area on a Toy Poodle should be somewhat smaller than on the Miniature and one of the smaller clipper heads may be used. The area on the Standard is larger in proportion to the size of the dog. However, the original half circle will place the shaved area in the correct position and it may then be enlarged.

On a long-backed dog, a short circle makes him look shorter. Squaring off the top of the pack will make the dog have greater continuity. The pack meets the mane on top without a line. This topline should be straight and level to give a put-together appearance. Let the judge discover whether or not the dog has a slightly hollowed topline as suggested by the Standard. This will also make the dog's tail look properly set, especially if the tail is not clipped precisely to the base.

If you are one-sided, do the most difficult side first.

Before beginning the shaved bands locate the sharp little bone that juts out in the middle of the dog's leg at the stifle. The top band should be located at this point or just below or above, depending on the individual dog. The band may be set first with the scissors and then clipped in with a #30 blade. With the dog standing in show pose this band should be straight across the width of the hind leg and must circle the leg completely. Its width depends on the size of the Poodle being patterned, from almost just the width of the scissors mark on a Toy, to an inch or more on a big Standard. The shaved band at the hock should once again be set with the scissors and later clipped. This band slants from just above the hock joint, forward and *slightly* downward. Once again the width of the band is dictated by the size of the dog and the band must encircle the leg.

Now have someone take the dog on a lead for you. You must watch him move from the front and from behind and equally important, from the side. Your project is now to trim with scissors, the bracelets, the pack, the hindquarters and the tail as well as shaping the mane coat to present a neat, attractive, soundly moving specimen of the breed. Remember that fashions in grooming change with the times. What is acceptable today may look very odd tomorrow. At this time a very tailored look is popular. The mane coat is hedged back, with a positive silhouette trimmed in. The coat goes from nothing at the beginning of the mane, and careful attention is paid to creating a tailored, long necked, sharp outline, that looks the same moving or standing. This aids in presenting the Poodle as an active athletic dog—one who may move around at will, without disturbing his look.

Shorten the hair on the pack to conform with the ideal for which you are striving, remembering that the Standard calls for a "short blanket of hair." The pack may be prepared for the show ring in two ways; either brushed dry under the dryer and then scissored for a "plush" look or shortened to about double the finished length carefully combed, washed and then allowed to dry naturally.

This will result in a "curly" pack, and requires arranging with a comb when dry and careful scissoring. The topline in profile, from the mane coat to the set of tail, should be straight. The hair covering the rear part of the quarters should not be so long as to give the dog a rotund look. Shape the hair where the curved, shaved area is placed so that it appears beveled from the longer pack into the shaven part. Bevel also the back hair into the shaven band at the stifle. Comb the bracelets up and then shake them or allow the dog to move around a bit so that the hair will assume a natural position before you scissor. Shape the middle bracelet to conform with the dog's hindquarters, rounding it somewhat on its forward edge and keeping the rear edge fairly straight. Once again, bevel the hair into the shaven band at the hock.

Rear bracelets are flat on the sides and between the legs and should resemble as closely as possible the anatomy that they cover. They require careful scissoring. The dog should be moved on a lead often to make sure you are doing him justice and not creating faults where none exist.

The front bracelets should be fairly round and neatly tapered at the bottom to reveal the "entire shaven foot." Too big bracelets, that appear to interfere with each other when the dog moves, should be avoided.

To shave the "face and throat" use your #40 or #30 blade to draw an imaginary line from the opening of the ear to the corner of the eye. Clip along this line, keeping it perfectly straight. Next clip the throat upwards from about an inch to an inch and a half below the Adam's apple, rounding the "necklace" and clipping cleanly the area just in front of the ear to join the area already clipped. The "V" between the eyes should neither be over or under done. It should enhance the stop on a good-headed dog and draw attention to a properly placed and shaped eye. If clipped up too far the dog will have a startled expression; if too low, a beetle-browed one. Start with it low and work it back to the desired place.

In the "Continental" clip, the face, throat, feet, and base of the tail are shaved. The hindquarters are shaved with pompons (optional) on the hips. The legs are shaved, leaving bracelets on the hindlegs and puffs on the forelegs. There is a pompon on the end of the tail. The entire shaven foot and a portion of the shaven foreleg above the puff are visible. The rest of the body is left in full coat but should be shaped in order to insure overall balance.

Shave the hindquarters using a #15 or a #30 blade against the grain about three days before a show, and before bathing. By show time any clipper lines or very bare places will have darkened to the color of the dog's coat. Or shave the hindquarters after bathing and just prior to the show with a #40 blade to give a dramatic contrast between the shaved and coated areas. The Poodle's skin must be conditioned for several months by close clipping weekly, to accept the #40 blade without it irritating the skin.

Whether or not to leave pompons on the hips is decided by the shortness of your Poodle's back. The shorter the Poodle, the less room or reason for

English Saddle clip.

Continental clip.

rosettes. If you wish pompons, center them over the hip bones, but have them far enough forward so that they do not appear to be falling off the rear and so that they do not cover the lovely muscle just near the tailset. Cut out the top and bottom of a tin can of the appropriate size, position the can on the hindquarters, hold or have held for you, and clip around the area. Tidy up lines carefully after removing can. Improve the rosette to a plush or curly button. The rear bracelets cover the hock as in the English Saddle Trim and are scissored in the same manner.

A Poodle under a year old may be shown in the "Puppy" clip with the coat long. The face, throat, feet and base of the tail are shaved. The entire shaven foot is visible. There is a pompon on the end of the tail. In order to give a neat appearance and a smooth unbroken line, shaping of the coat is permissible.

The Puppy Trim can be difficult to master. The feet, face, throat and tail are clipped as in the other trims. It is in the shaping of the coat that problems may occur. A heavily coated puppy that is trimmed to show any signs of having a break where the mane coat will start eventually may be correctly penalized. Remember the key phrases "neat appearance" and "smooth *unbroken* line." The feet should be quite visible. The very full coat on the rear and around the base of the tail should be shaped. The legs should be neat and trimmed to relieve the illusion that they are interfering with each other when the puppy is moving. If there is any doubt it is best to put a very heavily coated puppy into one of the adult show trims, generally the Continental, thus avoiding the risk of being penalized or the equal problem of showing a dog that is more "bearlike" than "Poodley".

The Poodle may be shown either brushed or corded. The "brushed" coat is when the "curly" coat is brushed dry under the dryer. The "corded" coat, as stated in the Poodle Standard, is "hanging in tight even cords of varying length; longer on mane or body coat, head, and ears; shorter on puffs, bracelets and pompons." The corded coat is not simply an unbrushed or matted coat, but derives from an intricate process of taking a coat with a natural tendency to cord and maintaining these cords with your fingers to keep them separate one from the other from the skin outwards. A special bathing technique is required in order to keep them in immaculate condition. It is suggested that before undertaking the care of a corded coat, you should seek the advice of someone who has had success with the corded Poodle or Puli or Komondor. Except for the maintenance of the coat itself, the same clipping practices apply to both the corded and brushed coats. It should be mentioned that a puppy is not usually kept in cords as it has been found that a mature coat is a key part of successful cording.

In the Stud Dog and Brood Bitch classes and in a non-competitive Parade of Champions, Poodles may be shown in the "Sporting" clip. In this clip the face, feet, throat, and base of tail is shaved, leaving a scissored cap on the top of the

Puppy Trim.

Sporting or
Kennel clip.

Ch. Fontclair Festoon, black Miniature import, shown going Best in Show at 1959 Westminster Kennel Club show. Left to right: William Rockefeller, club president; Anne Rogers Clark, handler; and Thomas Carruthers III, judge. Owned by Dunwalke Kennels.

Ch. Cappoquin Little Sister, black Toy, pictured going Best in Show at 1961 Westminster Kennel Club show. Left to right: William Rockefeller, club president; Anne Rogers Clark, handler; and Dr. Joseph Redden, judge. Owned by Miss Florence Michelson, Tropicstar Kennels.

head and a pompon on the end of the tail. The rest of the body and legs are clipped or scissored to follow the outline of the dog, leaving a short blanket of coat no longer than one inch in length. The hair on the legs may be slightly longer than that on the body.

In all clips the hair of the topknot may be left free or held in place by rubber bands. The hair is only of sufficient length to present a smooth outline. "Topknot" refers only to hair on the skull (from stop to occiput). This is the only area where rubber bands may be used. This hair should be attractively arranged; to ascertain the most pleasing effect, try sectioning the hair in several places and fastening each section with a rubber band. The topknot should enhance the Poodle's expression and leave a smooth unbroken line which extends up the back of the neck and over the top of the head. The topknot may also be left free (many puppies are shown this way until the hair is of sufficient length to be put up in an attractive topknot). Also the topknot may be left free and slightly scissored to fit the English Saddle or Continental trims.

Wrapping the ears and topknots protects them against crate rubbing, food, etc. Waxed paper, Saran wrap, or light-weight plastic may be used. Take the ears down at least twice a week and re-wrap, or you will get mats where the waxed paper stops. Remember that a topknot that is too long looks awkward, and should be trimmed to frame the head.

To roll the ear-feathers in paper, first comb out thoroughly. Take the feather in one hand, checking with your finger where the end of the leather is, so as not to catch the leather in the rubber band. Now roll the feather in paper, rolling along the length of the hair, not towards the ear. Then double up the paper roll and catch with a rubber band. Test with your comb to make sure the leather is free. Coat a bit of cotton with capsicum, which is liquid red pepper and procurable at any drugstore, and tuck it under the elastic to discourage chewing.

Ch. Puttencove Promise, white Standard, shown going Best in Show at 1958 Westminster Kennel Club show. Left to right: William Brainard, judge; Robert Gorman, handler; and William Rockefeller, club president. Bred and owned by Puttencove Kennels.

9

Showing the Poodle

IT IS GREAT FUN and an invaluable experience to show your Poodle yourself at local dog shows or sanctioned matches. The Poodle loves to perform, and with early and constant training you can bring out his best while in the ring. He is THE SHOW DOG par excellence. But in anticipation of this, many months of training and grooming are necessary. Many of the Poodles in competition at major shows across the country are shown by professional handlers. It is a breed that requires much preparation.

You must start training your puppy to the lead early. A soft slip lead is all that is necessary. Hold the lead straight and fairly tight in your left hand, and train your Poodle *always* to walk on your left side. Never allow him to walk on the right side, and teach him not to cross in front of you.

Start posing the future show dog on the table each time he is groomed. Teach him to allow you to place his four feet just the way you want them and to keep them that way. Then hold his head and his tail up and tell him to "Stay" or "Hold it," giving the command in a firm voice. If he does not obey and keeps moving, start all over from the beginning and keep at it until he understands just what you want; it will not take him too long. At first he should hold the pose for just a few seconds at a time; then gradually increase the time until he is standing still for five minutes and longer. Pet and praise him when he does this correctly or reward him with a tidbit. Sometimes counting helps, starting in with "one, two, three," said quickly, and allowing the dog to break his pose at three. Then gradually lengthen the time between the numbers, and still later add to them. In the end, the command to "Hold it" will be all that is needed. Then pose him on the floor, with people and other dogs moving around.

Open his lips and examine his front teeth and encourage members of the household to do so; then later, friends and strangers. Always be gentle. Have people lift up his front feet, run their hands along his spine and handle his hindquarters and hocks. Soon he will take this all as a matter of course.

You should of course attend as many dog shows as possible yourself to learn the procedure in the show ring in order to teach your Poodle exactly what to do. If your dog knows in detail just what you require of him and thoroughly understands the routine, he will do his utmost to please without any uncertainty or bewilderment. You must in turn remain calm and collected and have confidence in yourself and in your dog. A great many Poodles enter into the game of showing with zest and enjoyment and give of their very best. They seem to sense that the other dogs are rivals, and with confidence in and affection for their handler, do their best to out-show their competitors. You must do your best as well.

Watch the best handlers at the dog shows. Watch very carefully and see what they do and how they do it. Learn as much as possible of ring technique. Observe, for instance, that a good handler never comes between his dog and the judge, but always allows the judge a clear and uninterrupted field of vision. Standing or moving, you must always keep your dog in the judge's eye in the most advantageous manner. Learn how to avoid the too ambitious owners out to win at any cost and never permit them to push you and your dog into corners or to step on your heels in the walk around. If an exhibitor allows his dog to annoy yours and put it off its stride, quietly drop out of line and fall in again next to a more considerate handler.

The ring is no place to train or discipline your dog; all of that should have been done at home. The judge can see at a glance whether or not your dog knows the ropes. Do not try to show off how well trained he is, either, or give loud commands. Just go quietly along, doing what is required in a pleasant way and without trying to call attention to yourself or the dog in any undue manner.

Before you show your Poodle, make up your mind that you will meet other very good dogs in the ring. A knowledge of your dog's faults and virtues helps you to keep a balanced point of view. Study him against others in your own mind, study the printed Standard, study pictures of the best. Know just where your dog stands. Be fair enough to realize that, although your Poodle is a friend, and your affections are involved and you are justly proud of him, all the other exhibitors feel exactly the same way about their respective dogs. These natural sentiments, while giving everybody pleasure, have nothing to do with your Poodle's points as a show dog. The judge, expertly trained to see faults and virtues and weigh one against the other, is on this occasion invited to give his considered opinion about the dogs brought before him as they appear at that moment in the ring. He sees them but a brief time, and it is not his job to consider what they have won before and what they may win again, but only what he can see of them at the moment. He has but a short time to weigh every point as fairly as he can. No two of us see exactly alike, and all you can ask of the judge is that he give you his honest and expert opinion. Most judges try to be fair. They make mistakes, and who does not?

You may be sure, if you keep on showing, your Poodle will find his rightful level in the end; if he is really good, nothing can keep him down; if not, nothing can bring him up. And in the course of a long show career, you will be knocked down at times unjustly, and, on the other hand, you may win unjustly also. So unless you can cheerfully take whatever comes, make up your mind not to show. Be a modest winner and a good loser. It pays.

While in the ring, pay strict attention to the matter at hand. Concentrate on your own dog and on the judge. Obey the judge's commands, gestures, and even glances, promptly, and be alert for them. The ring is no place for conversation or dreaming, either for you or for your dog.

I have said nothing about conditioning your dog for the show ring, for the simple reason that if the directions for clipping and grooming are followed, and if the Poodle is in perfect health, it should always be in show condition, more or less. But it goes without saying that for the day of the show he must be expertly barbered and in full bloom. Never show a good dog out of coat, thin, or not in the pink of condition. A puppy may go to several shows in puppy classes for experience, but do not expect to go to the top with him until he is in full bloom and has a mature finish of body. The better the youngster is the more it pays to wait until he is just right before bringing him out.

Ch. Peeples Sahara shown winning the Toy Group at the 1975 Westminster Kennel Club Show under Henry Stoecker, handled by Richard Bauer. Owned by Marjorie Pearson.

Eng. Ch. Stanlyn Cleopatra at play with her daughter Miradel Parra. Owned by Patricia Rose, Miradel Poodles, London, England.

10

The Brood Bitch

IN POODLES, as in other breeds, the selection of the mother of coming winners is of the utmost importance. Not only should she be from a family noted for the production of winners, but her pedigree on both sides should be well balanced and she should be line-bred, if possible. Make up your mind which virtues are most important to you, for you cannot have them all, and which faults you find most objectionable, and choose your bitch's family accordingly, for the foundation of your breeding operations should be anything but haphazard. Your matron should have no glaring faults. In fact, the better a show dog she is, the better puppies she is likely to have. This is not always so, and there are cases in which the plainest one of a brilliant family turned out to be the best producer; but that cannot be known ahead of time, and to choose for good points is a wiser general rule. A bitch from a fine litter whose brothers and sisters, sire and dam, and grandparents were not only good themselves but also noted for production, is the wisest choice.

Disposition in a brood bitch is as important as show points, for a shy mother seems to infect her brood with alarms from which they seldom recover, having been taught, both by inheritance and example, to be distrustful. A very nervous and fidgety mother or one that is overanxious is seldom a good one, and she is prone to neglect or trample her puppies or to carry them around in her mouth so that they grow up undernourished and nervous, too. A calm, sensible, and intelligent mother is the best start any puppy can have in life. Puppies learn about living from their mother, and a level-headed mother can give them sense as well as health.

A definitely important requisite is robust health. No bitch that is thin, harboring worms, or in any way out of sorts can do justice to a bouncing family; and unless a bitch is in the pink of condition she should not be bred. Bitches that come from a long line of show dogs, well fed and well cared for and not overbred for many generations, inherit stamina; those that come from a line of puppy factories, with backyard care, without proper food for several generations, inherit deficiencies which they hand on to their puppies and which no amount of feeding and care can wholly cure. As Poodles have big families as a rule, one litter a year or, at most, two litters with six months rest before a third, should be the rule. In fact, one good, healthy litter a year, preferably in the spring, pays much better dividends in the end.

Poodle bitches are usually very good, patient and intelligent mothers. The pointed heads of the puppies at birth make their delivery easy; and, as a breed, Poodles are prolific.

Eng. Ch. Montfleuri Sarah of Longnor, black Miniature, winner of 19 Challenge Certificates with her 7½ weeks old son who became Eng. Ch. Tarka of Montfleuri, winner of 21 Challenge Certificates. Owned by Mr. and Mrs. P. Howard Price, Montfleuri Kennels, England.

66

11

The Stud Dog

In POODLES, it has been my experience that to be a super successful stud dog a male must, in addition to excellent breeding, show quality, and abounding health, have real vigor of personality and be aggressively masculine. It seems to take an exaggeration of every Poodle characteristic to successfully stamp Poodle character on the progeny. A jaunty action and a cocky carriage, as well as a fine head and expression, and good legs and feet are so much a part of Poodle character that the stud dog should possess these attributes in abundance. Also, a stud dog should be bold and friendly.

The stud dog, of course, should have no really serious fault and, above all, no serious inherited fault; but a well balanced dog with a fault is better than one with a single outstanding virtue but lacking in proper balance. I would say that structural soundness, sloping shoulders, strong hindquarters with well let down hocks, a long neck, good tight feet, a well ribbed body, and a straight back are the most important requirements for a stud dog. Texture and profuseness of coat are also essential, and for the warmer climates this must be especially excellent to be stamped on the progeny at all. We all want lovely lean heads with dark, oval eyes and low-set, long ear leathers.

Aside from the stud dog's pronounced individual virtues of type and balance, his pedigree should also be well balanced and, in my opinion, it should show line breeding to a strain produced with a definite purpose in mind. No dog has every virtue, and no strain can have every wanted quality either; but certain strains can be depended upon to produce certain definite good points just as other strains stamp other important virtues. But a dog with a pedigree that is a hodgepodge of many unrelated strains bred together haphazardly and without any predetermined intention will usually produce mediocre or even inferior stock.

Ch. Summercourt Square Dancer of Fircot, Miniature, shown winning the Stud Dog class at the 1958 Washington Poodle Club Specialty under the late Col. E. E. Ferguson, with two of his get: Tedwin's Two Step (left, with John Paluga handling) and Tedwin's Top Billing (right, with breeder Ted Young, Jr.). Square Dancer shown by Anne Rogers Clark. Two Step finished and became a Group winner. Top Billing developed into one of the top winners in the breed.

Can. Ch. Highlane Bonhomme Richard, shown winning the Miniature Stud Dog Class at the 1971 Poodle Club of America Specialty under Sue Chisholm Dreyer. Richard was shown by his breeder-owner Elaine Crawford, with his get Ch. Highlane Exclusive handled by Todd Patterson and Ravendune Sweet Baby James, handled by Eric Wagner.

There are two ways to stamp a virtue or virtues on stock. One of the most common methods is to breed together two related (cousins or closer) members of the same strain, both exemplifying that virtue. Even here to be successful the most rigid selection must be practiced. The second method is by pure selection to mate together unrelated dogs possessing the same virtue in a pronounced form for a number of generations. Such a pedigree is, of course, extremely rare; for such intelligent selection over a long period of years is very rarely practiced. The quicker way is through the mating together of related dogs who are themselves alike in the wanted quality to begin with and whose pedigrees indicate its inheritance.

The Poodle stud dog selected for your bitch should be as much like her as possible. If the two are related they probably have many of the same genes in common. At any rate, they should exhibit just as many virtues in common as possible, and none of the same faults. The mating of extreme opposite types is almost never successful.

The father of your coming family need not necessarily be a famous champion, though puppies sired by a well and favorably known dog bring better prices and find a readier sale. Often, a lesser known stud dog that is thoroughly suited to your bitch in pedigree and appearance will produce better puppies. A great dog that makes the show circuit, full of fatigue, suffering from nervous strain and lack of exercise, is often not in the pink of productive health and may be exhausted from over-use even when he is at home.

The health and vigor of a sire depend upon the care and handling given him by his owner. That he should have a complete diet high in its protein content, ample sunshine, exercise, and happy contentment, are all important. I have known of stud dogs whose productivity of superior progeny was exhausted when they were four or five years old, while others have lasted well into old age.

A charming trio of Meisen Toy puppies in black, apricot
and silver bred and owned by Hilda Meisenzahl, Meisen Kennels.

12

Color Breeding

BLACK

Black is the basic, dominant color in Poodles. When a dominant black is mated with any of the other colors, all the puppies will be black. And as a rule this pure dominant also carries the greatest perfection of type.

A black Poodle's coat should be absolutely dense and inky jet black. The skin should have a distinct bluish cast. To keep it this way, or to clear it if it is shaded, is relatively simple. The magic formula is simply to breed jet blacks to jet blacks and never allow the admixture of any other color. But outside of European countries, where it is obligatory, this is very seldom done consistently. Yet, without question it is the only way to get and keep inky black, practically unfading coats. A true black has no graying (or dilution) factor which causes the black to fade with age.

Only one cross is safe—that of black's own dilution, brown—which, if sparingly used, will not affect the purity of color. But, of course, such brown crosses must be used very sparingly and not too close together. Some breeders believe that although this cross does not affect the coat color, it may lighten the color of the eyes. The fact that brown does not affect the purity of black coats is a recognized fact, and even in countries where the mixing of colors is banned, such a mixture is permitted.

Many black strains, black-bred for many generations, carry a brown gene which causes browns to appear every now and then in an otherwise black litter. Such browns usually carry very dark eyes and pigmentation.

Blue, gray and silver crosses in a black strain are fatal for soundness of color and most difficult to breed out. They leave a most unpleasant grayish shading in the coat and are crosses that never should be used.

It is not definitely known whether eye color is part of the same gene for color, or whether it follows a pattern of its own. In countries where black must be bred only to black, the eyes are very dark, almost black. But nothing has been proven scientifically. Be that as it may, eye color, like any other point, can be fixed by selection. There is no doubt that light eyes have need of correction in many of our American blacks as well as in many English imports. A dark, velvety, oval eye plays an important part in the beautiful Poodle expression we all desire in our dogs. It is too valuable an asset to overlook or to lose carelessly. And in no other color does a light eye stand out as unpleasantly as in a black Poodle.

Standard and Miniature breeders are still finding it difficult to create pure non-fading jet black lines, due to the fading factor which appears in almost all American bred lines. The gray import Ch. Griseley Labory of Piperscroft was a major culprit in Standards as was the gray Ch. Misty Isles Algie of Piperscroft in Miniature lines. Since the graying gene is a recessive, it is particularly difficult to cope with in breeding. Two apparently good blacks may harbor the graying gene and when bred together will produce a proportion of blacks who will gray as they age.

Breeders have a better chance of stabilizing and enhancing a good black by using an older male who has held his color until nine or ten years of age. Breeding to an excellent colored young dog who grays in later years is another problem. Even worse is discovering you have used a beautiful colored jet black who has been dyed!

A male's true color may best be observed at home in his later years rather than in his glamorous show ring days. Unfortunately, almost all blacks fade to some degree and a true jet black at ten years is still a rarity. It has been observed that some of the best lasting blacks only gray around the muzzle rather than a gradual and steady all over graying with age.

BROWN

Brown is a recessive or dilution of black and closely related to it, although the color globules are different in shape. And if black is unharmed by a brown cross, brown is greatly benefited by a black cross to keep the color and pigmentation dark.

Like all recessives, brown bred to brown breeds true. Two browns, even when all black bred, when mated invariably throw an entire litter of browns. Of course, to produce even one brown puppy, both black parents must carry a brown gene.

On the Continent only the darkest shades of brown are recognized, such as the deepest shades of chocolate. But in England and in the United States, all the various shades are allowed, and there is no color that has as many charming color variations. These range from an almost black chocolate to the pale brown of cafe-au-lait and parchment shades. The beautiful reddish chestnut brown is brilliant, and there is a shade which is almost liver colored. There are cinnamon browns both light and dark. By the way, all brown puppies, no matter what shade they are going to be in later life, are born very dark.

The worst and commonest defect in browns is their marked tendency towards light eyes, pale yellow at their worst, with light pinkish eye-rims, lips and noses. This robs them of true Poodle outlook and expression and gives them either a bold or a vapid expression.

The eyes of all browns, dark or light, should be several shades darker than their coats and just as dark as it is possible to get them. Dark eyes are always surrounded by dark eye-rims, and the lips and nose are the same dark shade. One or two black crosses help to keep the eyes and pigmentation dark. A really dark-eyed brown is invaluable for the breeding of browns.

In the lighter dilute shades, it is possible to get actual dark eyes and correct pigmentation, which adds a hundred percent to the attractiveness of these charming colors.

Since blacks and browns are so closely related, it also holds that the dark browns bred from jet blacks or dark browns are more apt to hold their color than are browns from graying blacks or graying browns. The same inherited graying factor that fades blacks will also cause similarly bred browns to fade.

BLUE

A real blue Poodle, which is an even color throughout with a bluish cast, can be quite beautiful. Unfortunately blue has become a "catch all" name for Poodles who are not good blacks and yet too dark to be called gray. Most often the eventual blue color does not clear until two or three years of age. Blues seen in the ring are usually the result of a mixture of colors and so beautiful in conformation they are shown despite their color, not because of it.

Two of the most famous blues were Eng. Am. Ch. Frenches Blue Marvel who won the Group at Westminster and Ch. Jocelyene Marjorie who had a great career in the ring and was the dam of 18 champions. She was never bred to produce more blues. She was always bred to good blacks and most of her get were blacks.

SILVER

Silver is a most appealing color in Poodles. It may vary from a glistening light platinum to a light gray flannel, but a silver Poodle should be an even color all over with no shadings. Silvers should have black eyes, nose and toenails. To many people a pair of coal black eyes set in a frame of silver hair is almost irresistible. Silvers are favorites with exhibitors and pet owners.

Silver puppies are nearly always born jet black except for a frosting of white on the underpads of the feet. It is possible to tell the color of a silver puppy at six weeks of age when it is first clipped. The lighter the face the lighter the puppy will be at maturity. The puppy lightens gradually from dark to medium to its lightest mature color at about 18 months of age. Some breeders cut the coat back with a No. 10 blade to get rid of the softer dark puppy coat.

Silver is a recessive color. Pamela Ingram of Sassafras Kennels, who has bred more silvers than anyone else, states, "I have never known two silvers bred together to throw a color darker than silver—such as blue or black." Two silver mates can, however, produce silver-beige, cream or white. Those colors bred to each other respectively will breed true.

Silvers have existed in Miniatures almost from the beginning. Silver Toys have inherited the silver color factor through their Miniature ancestors. A few Standard Poodle breeders have tried to establish lines of silver Standards but have not as yet met with the success that silver Miniature and Toy breeders have achieved either as winners or producers. It is more difficult to breed good silvers than whites or blacks.

APRICOT

The apricot color has been known in Poodles for more than seventy years. The first Poodle to be registered as apricot was Whippendell Abricotinette, whelped October 11, 1912.

An apricot colored Poodle should be the color of a ripe apricot. The original apricots just happened, from the mixing of many different colors and they did not breed true consistently. It has taken many years to stabilize the color and finally apricot lines have been established which will produce true apricots generation after generation.

The apricot Miniatures and Toys in England and America for the most part are descended from a deep apricot dog named Aureolin of Toytown, whelped September 25, 1941. Aureolin was by the cream Whippendell Petit Eclair (Whippendell Duvet ex Nunsoe Sixpence) out of an apricot Bechamel of Toytown (Paul of Toytown ex Whippendell Bambinette). English breeders interested in apricots bred to Aureolin and this is the strongest continuing apricot line in existence today. The English apricots of Venda's, Frenches, Fircot, Puckshill, DeRegis and Greatcoats all trace back to Aureolin not once but many times. In this country the Aureolin influence has been spread in Toys through his linebred descendent Midas of Greatcoats as outlined in the Adam of Evesgarden male line chart. These include the American Toy kennels: Beaujolais, Little Bit, Secota, Spinnerin and Ounce O'Bounce.

Successful apricot breeders agree that apricots should be kept pure. The introduction of any other color presents problems. Breeding to blacks usually results in the apricot being covered completely. Breeding to browns introduces the danger of unattractive brown noses and points. Breeding to pure whites poses the problem of white chests and toe markings or even a dark apricot line down the back of a cream dog. Much is lost and little gained.

Hilda Meisenzahl's Meisen strain was one of the earliest and most successful in this country. She was emphatic in stating that apricots should only be bred to apricots, and that by doubling the apricot genes the color will deepen.

Mrs. Myles Dobson's Puckshill Kennels in England bred Eng. Ch. Oakington Puckshill Ambersunblush who won Best in Show at Crufts in 1966. She recommends, "Start with a good apricot bred apricot bitch, the purer the line the better. If you can stick to this color they will get deeper through each generation. All white should be eliminated."

Both Miss Meisenzahl and Mrs. Dobson have been most generous in sharing their own experiences for the betterment of this beautiful color.

In Miniatures the original Aureolin influence has been equally as great in the United States through Ch. Woodland Burning Bright, his son Ch. Marjoe's Tangerine Tiger, and his son Ch. Lyca's Dime Store Novel. Novel was the leading Poodle sire, all varieties, for 1983.

Only those persons who have actually bred apricots can appreciate the triumph of this accomplishment. And now having achieved so much and in the never ending quest for an impossible dream, a few apricot breeders have embarked on the task of breeding good quality reds. Evidently many of the same rules apply—breed color to color, always trying to improve type. They have already met with a degree of success. The solid red Toy Ch. Jodan's Red Pepper is a Best in Show winner and is a multiple champion producer.

WHITE AND CREAM

A beautiful white Poodle is a spectacular sight in the show ring. There are, however, two very different types of whites and they are often difficult to distinguish between at maturity. These are the true whites (ice whites or paper whites) and the cream whites which are so light (faded) as to appear totally white.

The two terms "white" and "cream" should not be used loosely and incorrectly as they so often are. It can be seen that they are absolutely different colors, though both recessive—the first the total absence of color, the other the furthest dilution of brown.

Professor David D. Whitney's summary and conclusion after extensive examination of hair samples of a number of white breeds, including white Poodles, stated "The Poodles with icy white coats belong to the black hair type, those with warmer tones in their white coats belong to the yellow hair type. Corroborated by microscopic examinations and breeding reports." The black haired type have dark eyes and black eye-rims, lips and noses. Those of the yellow type may have light eyes, and brown eye-rims, lips and noses in the case of apricots and creams. All creams and apricots with dark eyes, eye-rims, lips and noses have a predominance of black haired inheritance. Thus, scientific data confirms the experience of practical breeders. It is, of course, obvious that white dogs of colored breeding that carry even a tiny amount of color even in a few hairs of their coat are not genetically white, and undoubtedly carry cream and possibly apricot genes as well.

The late Commander T. Norman Hinton wrote in the English *Our Dogs* of considerable work done by him and other British breeders on this subject. His finding was that many white Poodles that look white are in reality faded creams and not genetically pure white at all. He believed, after a great many years of breeding whites exclusively, that the puppy that is whelped cream and later turns white is simply a faded cream and should be considered cream throughout life.

The fact that the color bred whites usually offered far superior genetic background for type (as in the cases of Ch. Snow Boy of Fircot and Ch. Summercourt Square Dancer of Fircot) made them popular at stud. In addition to superior type, the cream whites usually have dark skin pigment, black points and non-patterned skin. The cream whites, primarily through Square Dancer and his great influence, have dominated the Miniature show ring for years.

The glistening ice white Standards (as best exemplified by the earlier Alekais) are seen less frequently due to black crosses at Alekai and elsewhere. Cream or cream whites are often beautiful animals with excellent pigment. Ch. Acadia Command Performance, Best in Show at Westminster in 1973, was a beautiful example of a faded cream. The point being made is that there are two different types of whites and breeders should be aware of this fact.

Fortunately, two whites (or faded whites), irrespective of their backgrounds, will produce a whole litter of whites or faded whites with no mismarking problems.

MISMARKED POODLES

Perhaps this is as good a place as any to discuss a serious menace to the Poodle breed and one which apparently occurs not only from the mixing of white with the other solid colors but also from the use of too much silver blood in a black strain.

·One form of mismarking seems to show a definite pattern, either the complete "Airedale" markings or a broken pattern with the color on only some of the parts in which tan is found on the Airedale instead of on all of them. Blacks or browns may carry this design in any of the dilute colors, such as brown, tan, cream or any of the many shades of brown, or the markings may be silver or blue or even white. The off-color runs along the inside of the legs, back and front, across the chest, along the side of the face, under the tail, under the chin, and on the paws.

Scientifically, I believe, the mismarking is caused by an incomplete masking of the dilute color by a dominant one. In any event the result is a mismark, and the Poodle should be a solid color. The theory is that the puppy will in time change to the color of the markings, but this does not as a rule prove to be the case. Selling such a puppy as a pet does not end the matter, for if it is bred it will likely produce other mismarks like itself. The pattern is hereditary,

Three forms of mismarked Poodles:
Left, white spots; *center,* particolor; *right,* two-tone or "phantom."

and even solid colored dogs from a mismarked strain will produce mismarked puppies. This mismarking may skip a generation, or even two, only to recur. This is so recognized that many breeders in England, where mismarkings are more common than with us, refuse to mate mismarked bitches to their good studs or even a bitch of solid color known to have mismarked ancestry. Of course, such a strain should never be used for breeding, and any dog or bitch known to carry this inheritance should never be bred.

Experiments should be left in the hands of those who wisely limit the color-cross to one mating and who understand just what they are trying to do. White should not be bred to any other color except white. Of all the colors, it is the worst offender in producing mismarked solids.

SUMMARY OF COLOR BREEDING

To sum up briefly the known facts concerning the various colors:

The safest rule in color breeding is to breed like color to like color.

Black is heavily dominant over all the other colors and will overlay them in a Mendelian pattern. Mismarks come when the overlay is not complete. Black also carries the banner for true Poodle type.

Hybrid blacks may carry any number of colors recessively. These colors can only be determined by breeding, since the dog in appearance will be black.

Brown is a recessive. Brown bred to brown will produce only brown.

Apricot is a recessive. Apricot bred to apricot will produce apricot or perhaps some cream if this color appears close up in the background.

White is recessive, and bred to another white or cream will produce only whites or creams.

Pure silver to silver will produce only silver. However, two hybrid silvers may also produce whites, creams, or silver-beiges, if those genes are present.

In founding strains of the dilute colors, not only should the mating be to the same color, but also, a certain amount of line breeding is recommended.

Ch. Wavir Hit Parade winning Best of Breed at the 1984 Poodle Club of America Specialty. Shown with: Frank Sabella; Sterg O'Dell; Anne Rogers Clark; Frank Fretwell, Inter-Variety Judge; Doris Cozart; Harold Langseth, handler; Norma Strait; Virginia Milroy, owner, and Dr. Samuel Peacock. Owned by Virginia and Walter Milroy and Harold Langseth.

The Miniature Poodle

13

Foreword to Miniature
Male Line* Charts

IN the last ten years, 1575 Miniature Poodles have completed American Kennel Club championships. It is interesting to note that virtually all of the winners and producers of the variety today trace back to either one, or both, of two great male lines—the "Monarch" and the "Chieveley." It is even more surprising that these two lines, in spite of time and dilution, still breed fairly true.

Two other Miniature lines, the "Bodo von Kurpark" and the "Blue Boy," have gained some importance, but even of these the "Blue Boy" is an offshoot of the Monarch line.

To some degree, the Monarch and the Chieveley lines represent the two opposite types in nature. These types exist in all animals: the long-headed, long-bodied, light-boned type (Monarch), and the chubby, heavy-boned, short thick-headed type (Chieveley). Of course, in both cases these types have been modified to a great extent, depending on the skill of various breeders in using them, on the bitches brought to them, and on the amount of interweaving between the two lines. In Poodles, we go directly against Nature when we try to breed long, lean heads on short, cobby bodies. For this reason, it is the combination of the two lines that has been the classic recipe for success.

The Monarch line brings to the combination the beautiful heads and true Poodle expression. The Chieveley line contributes the short-back body type, tight feet and sound hindquarters. Here and in England, some fanciers have

---

*The word line as used here identifies the male descent from father to son.

made the mistake of completely discarding one line in favor of the other. Most breeders, however, have combined them to great advantage to produce the in-between type embracing the virtues of both lines, although even now, many years later, families and individuals still tend to resemble one line more than the other.

There even appear to be periodic swings in popularity from one type to the other. A particularly prepotent stud will appear on the scene and win a large and enthusiastic following, with result that almost everyone rushes in that direction, doubling and redoubling the line and type until it is carried to excess. This emphasis continues until it is so exaggerated that the followers begin to have doubts. Eventually the virtues of the opposite type become more attractive, and the pendulum swings in the other direction. Actually, all of this helps keep the variety in better balance, as it is the combined type that has proven the most desirable.

English Miniature imports have been an important source of supply for American Miniature breeders from the very beginning. Many of the top English winners or producers, or their sons, have been brought to this country to be utilized for showing and breeding. In recent years as American breeders have become more concerned with PRA and its prevention there have been fewer Miniature imports from England, as English breeders appear to be slower in dealing with this problem.

In studying the charts of the lines as presented here note that each indentation represents a new generation. The majority of the males which have sired 10 or more champions may be traced back to their original tail male origins on the charts. The color of each dog is stated in parentheses and the number following that indicates the number of champions the dog has sired.

Any male that has produced five or more champions, including foreign champions where known, is considered a Top Producer. You will also find many of these included on the chart, although it would be impossible to include every one. These numbers are of course constantly changing as new champions finish. Note that the general popularity of the blacks and whites have allowed them to accumulate much larger numbers of champions than apricots and silvers.

The charts serve as an outline to guide students of the breed in their search for bloodlines and pedigrees. Each chart is accompanied by a commentary that aims to point out the high spots of the line.

Two famous dogs from the Monarch line, Ch. The Laird of Mannerhead, and his litter brother, Ch. Limelight of Mannerhead, by Am. Ch. Sparkling Jet of Misty Isles, owned by Mrs. Campbell Inglis, Mannerhead Kennels, England.

14

The "Monarch" Family

THE MOST SUCCESSFUL early Miniature Poodle breeder in Great Britain was Mrs. Jack Taylor. She showed her first Poodle, Bizarre, as early as 1897 in Cork and won with him. He and another dog, Trillo, both won at Edinburgh in 1900.

When her husband was ordered to China, the Taylors were not allowed to take their Poodles with them, and Bizarre died of grief. Trillo, however, was bred to Ch. Orchard Minstrel, owned by Mrs. Leonard Crouch, and produced the famous Rio Grande. Rio Grande won 98 prizes and the championship certificate at Belfast in 1905, and from him are descended all the Taylor Miniatures, although he was a small Standard of Standard breeding.

The first champion was Ch. Mons, a grandson of Rio Grande, who finished his championship in 1914. Wisteria was the smallest in a Standard litter by Rio Grande ex Dolly Varden. Wisteria bred to Millie Bunker's Whippendell Corbillat produced Star Spangle, who in turn was bred to Moufflon Bleu at Whippendell to produce Joan of Arc. Joan of Arc was bred to Mickey Free (by Puck of Pre-Fleuri ex Star Spangle) to produce Ch. Arc Angel, who accumulated six Challenge Certificates before she was run over and killed. However, before her death she became the dam of Ch. The Blue Boy and Ch. Angel of Mine (by Chic of Watercroft), and of Ch. Angelica.

Ch. The Blue Boy bred to Ch. Angelica produced Ch. Somebody. The Blue Boy bred to The Sprite (by Whippendell Azor ex Babette Grise, the dam of Mrs. Tyndall's Leila) gave the undefeated silver Ch. The Silver Gnome. The Gnome's daughter, Ch. Fee D'Argent of Piperscroft, came to this country and finished her title here. Ch. Angel of Mine was bred to Hunningham Silver (by Ch. The Silver Gnome) to produce Venda's Arrow of Silver and Romance of Rio Grande. Venda's Arrow of Silver was bred to Leila to produce the famous

Ch. Misty Isles Algie of Piperscroft, the first Miniature Poodle to win Best in Show in America.

Eng. Ch. Angelica (by The Aide de Camp ex Eng. Ch. Arc Angel), bred by Mrs. Jack Taylor.

Blue Jewel of Misty Isles (by Romance of Rio Grande ex Eng. Ch. Angel of Mine), bred by Mrs. Jack Taylor, owned by Mrs. Byron Rogers.

Venda's Blue Masterpiece. Romance of Rio Grande was bred back to his dam, Ch. Angel of Mine, to produce Mrs. Byron Rogers' two foundation bitches, Blue Jewel of Misty Isles and Venda's The Silver Sylph, bought directly from Mrs. Jack Taylor. Handled in accordance with Mrs. Taylor's advice, these two bitches established the Misty Isles Miniature line with great success.

Ch. Angel of Mine was bred to The Diplomat to produce the Ch. The Monarch who heads one of the Great Miniature sire lines. The Monarch was whelped December 11, 1924. His registered color was mole but he was later described as blue. He finished his championship in 1928. The Monarch sired four champion sons: Am. Ch. King Johnny of Marcourt and Eng. Ch. Blue Zenith (ex Blue Love Bird, full sister of Ch. Angel of Mine and Ch. The Blue Boy), Am. Ch. Whippendell Picot (ex Bougee Bleue, daughter of Ch. The Blue Boy and Leila), and Eng. Ch. Spriggan Bell (ex Toy Bell).

The Monarch's sire, The Diplomat, was a black, as were his parents Mannifred and Campden Rena. The Monarch's dam, Ch. Angel of Mine, was registered as a blue. In these early days of color breeding the blacks, blues, and grays were of necessity bred together in order to use the best individuals produced up to that time. Many dogs registered as blacks turned gray in their later years. The graying genes which turned the blacks into blues and grays were also responsible for the production of the silvers when sufficiently concentrated. Although Mrs. Taylor and others combined these colors with success, she cautioned against the introduction of any white or brown into these lines. Breeders today are aware of the difficulty of breeding good jet non-fading blacks when gray genes are present in the pedigree.

The Monarch line is the most successful Miniature line of all, combining well with all others.

Through the years the Monarch line is noted for having produced the most beautiful heads in Miniatures. The skulls are lean, the forefaces long and not deeply hollowed out under the eyes. The eyes themselves are oval and of a velvety darkness, and the expressions beautiful and typical. Ears are well placed, the leathers sometimes long, sometimes not. The bone is rather fine as a rule, and the backs sometimes short, but not always so. Coats are profuse, and, if there is not too much blue blood, they are soundly black.

The faults include the one greatest defect, a definite tendency toward flat and open feet, varying in degree. The legs are sometimes too short. Bodies, as a whole, are not as short backed or as round ribbed as the Chieveleys. They are not always stylish movers. The hocks, while well bent and let down, now and then show a weakness which, at its worst, extends to the whole hindquarters. They are not generally as sound as the Chieveleys. They sometimes show a snipiness of head and general build, a sort of "Whippety" quality.

It must be remembered that this is the largest line, and there are many branches of it which differ in type somewhat from each other; what might be true of one branch would not, perhaps, apply to another. These variations result, without doubt, from the breeders' manipulations of it and from the bitches used to correct the faults in it.

Unlike the Chieveleys, this is not a purely black line, and there are a number of blues, silvers and whites in it.

In disposition, the Monarch dogs were sweet, gay, obliging and much easier to train and handle than the Chieveleys. Though rather bold, they were also much more the friends of all the world, more everybody's dogs. They were affectionate, and much more adaptable than the Chieveley line, but not nearly as single hearted.

15

The "Monarch" Line—
Eng. Ch. The Monarch

E NG. CH. THE MONARCH was an extremely well-bred dog and he was in demand at stud. He sired six sons who were to head sub-divisions of this famous sire line: Success of Piperscroft, Marcourt Carnot, Dare Devil Dink, Popinjay, Am. Ch. King Johnny of Marcourt and Eng. Ch. Spriggan Bell.

SUCCESS OF PIPERSCROFT

The largest and most widespread influence from the line has come through Success of Piperscroft. Success sired Conceit of Piperscroft, and he in turn sired the famous litter brothers Monty of Piperscroft and Ch. Misty Isles Algie of Piperscroft. Ch. Misty Isles Algie of Piperscroft was the first Miniature to go Best in Show in America. Algie sired five champions, and his sons and daughters were noted producers. Bred to his granddaughter he produced Bibelot of Misty Isles, who sired eight champions. Bibelot's son, Bibelot Cadet of Misty Isles, sired six champions including Hollycourt's Ch. Petit Pierre. Another Bibelot son was Ch. Clairwell Ce Soir, whose son Hollycourt Chevalier D'Argent sired Ch. Hollycourt Grillon Argente (sire of five champions). Due to the fact that the Misty Isles kennels were founded on Mrs. Taylor's silver bitches, most of the Algie descendents from this line were grays or silvers.

Although untitled, Monty of Piperscroft (Algie's brother) remained in England where he exerted a great influence and sired many English winners and two American champions—Ch. Jingle of Piperscroft, who was a force in Massachusetts, and Ch. Leader of Piperscroft of Blakeen. Leader went to the West Coast where he was owned by Gary Cooper of movie fame but later

Conceit of Piperscroft

Am. Eng. Ch. Braebeck Toni of Montfleuri

Ruffles of Piperscroft

Tri. Int. Ch. Pixholme Firebrave Gustav, Int. C.D.

Clipper of Piperscroft

Ch. Cappoquin Carriage Trade

ENG. CH. THE MONARCH

Success of Piperscroft (*blk*)
   Conceit of Piperscroft (*blk*)
      Ch. Misty Isles Algie of Piperscroft (*gr*) 5
         Bibelot of Misty Isles (*gr*) 8
            Bibelot Cadet of Misty Isles (*gr*) 6
               Ch. Petit Pierre (*gr*) 9
                  Ch. Hollycourt Manicamp (*si*)
               Ch. Clairwell Ce Soir (*gr*)
                  Hollycourt Chevalier d'Argent (*si*)
                     Ch. Hollycourt Grillon Argente (*si*) 5
   Monty of Piperscroft (*blk*)
      Ch. Jingle of Piperscroft (*blk*)
         Ch. Leader of Piperscroft of Blakeen (*blk*) 5
            Ch. Galcit's Priority of Ste. Elmo (*blk*) 5
            Ch. Leader's Brown Topper (*brn*)
               Ch. Tommy K (*brn*) 11
                  Am. Can. Ch. Norcrest Surrey Sahib (*brn*) 9
         Eng. Ch. Barty of Piperscroft (*blk*) 2
            Robin of Piperscroft (*blk*)
               Firebrave Alphonse (*blk*) 4
                  Int. Ch. Firebrave Pimpernel (*blk*) 6
                     Int. Ch. Pixholme Firebrave Gustav (*blk*) 23
                     Ch. Poodhall Gus (*blk*) 19
             Russet of Piperscroft (*brn*)
               Sienna of Piperscroft (*brn*)
                  Eng. Ch. Firebrave Gaulois (*blk*) 6
                     Firebrave Patapan (*blk*) 6
                        Int. Ch. Firebrave Sanka of Montfleuri (*blk*) 7
                           Int. Ch. Merrymorn Antoine (*blk*) 9
                      Firebrave Spiro of Braebeck (*blk*) 7
                         Int. Ch. Braebeck Toni of Montfleuri (*blk*) 6
                    Orsino of Eldonwood (*blk*)
                     Eng. Ch. Montravia The Trojan (*blk*) 6
         Ch. Sabu of Piperscroft (*brn*)
            Ch. Smilestone's Sirprise (*brn*) 5
               Ch. Hollycourt Bronze Knight (*brn*) 10
                  Ch. Hollycourt Ensign (*blk*) 5
                  Ch. Cappoquin Bon Fiston (*blk*) 17
                     Ch. Cappoquin Carriage Trade (*blk*) 8
         Ruffles of Piperscroft (*blk*)
            Eng. Ch. Top Hat of Piperscroft (*blk*)
               Ch. Busby of Piperscroft (*blk*) 15
            Tiptop of Piperscroft (*blk*)
               Tais-Toi of Piperscroft (*blk*) 6
               Voila of Piperscroft (*blk*)
                  Clipper of Piperscroft (*blk*)
                     Eng. Ch. Rudolph of Piperscroft
                        (*See Miniature Chart 2*)

became the property of Miss Freddie Weis, under whose affectionate care he gained his championship and fame as a sire. His first litter was from a lovely brown bitch, Ch. Round Table Constance, but all died from distemper except one exquisite small brown dog, Ch. Leader's Brown Topper. Topper, bred to a daughter of his sire, gave Geneva Christine and she, bred back to Topper, gave that well-known brown, Ch. Tommy K, sire of 11 champions including Am. and Can. Ch. Norcrest Surrey Sahib, a Best in Show winner and sire of nine champions. Ch. Leader also sired Ch. Galcit's Priority of Ste. Elmo, who sired five champions.

Eng. Ch. Barty of Piperscroft

Monty of Piperscroft also sired the famous black, Eng. Ch. Barty of Piperscroft. Although Alida Monro of Firebrave is listed as Barty's breeder, in actual fact she had purchased his dam, Manon of Piperscroft, from Grace Boyd's Piperscroft Kennels and bred Manon back to Monty of Piperscroft with the arrangement that Mrs. Boyd was to have her choice of litter in lieu of the stud fee. Both of Barty's parents and all four grandparents bore the Piperscroft affix so Mrs. Boyd deserves a large share of the credit. Mrs. Monro kept Barty's litter brother, Firebrave Cupidon, who was just starting to win when World War II cut short his show career. He achieved more lasting fame as a foundation sire of the Firebrave line. Phillipe Howard Price of Montfleuri Kennels commented that although many of the Firebraves were descended from the Monarch male line, they were usually more typical of the Chieveleys in type (from whom they were also descended) being more short backed and compact.

Eng. Ch. Barty of Piperscroft was in the final five for Best in Show at the last Crufts Dog Show to be held before World War II. Barty was a tremendous success at stud. His daughter, Ch. Pitter Patter of Piperscroft, was brought to this country and became the first Miniature to go Best in Show at Westminster, this in 1943. Barty had four important sons: Robin, Ruffles, Russet and Am. Ch. Sabu—all of Piperscroft. Robin of Piperscroft sired, among other winners, Blakeen's import Firebrave Alphonse. Alphonse sired, in England, Am. Can. and Eng. Ch. Firebrave Pimpernel (six champion get). Pimpernel sired the great black Am. Can. and Eng. Ch. Pixholme Firebrave Gustav, C.D., who had 23 champion get in all parts of the world. At Poodhall Kennels, in Texas, Gustav sired Am. and Can. Ch. Poodhall Gus. Gus was the top winning Poodle in Canada from 1957 through 1961, and was retired after winning his 100th Group first with a total of 26 Bests in Show. Gus sired 19 champions in Canada and the U.S.

Now to return to Barty. His son Russet of Piperscroft appears in many pedigrees as he was the sire of the brown Sienna of Piperscroft who produced one of England's most famous sires and winners, Eng. Ch. Firebrave Gaulois. Some breeders felt that although Gaulois descended from the Monarch tail male line he and many of his Firebrave descendants more closely resembled the

90

ENG. CH. BARTY OF PIPERSCROFT

Whelped August 3, 1936   Deceased

Bred by Alida Monro, Firebrave Kennels, England
Owned by Grace Boyd, Piperscroft Kennels, England

Success of Piperscroft (*blk*)
Conceit of Piperscroft (*blk*)
Harpendale Nippy (*blk*)
Monty of Piperscroft (*blk*)
Presto of Gotton (*blk*)
Eng. Ch. Vanity of Piperscroft (*blk*)
Black Beauty (*blk*)

ENG. CH. BARTY OF PIPERSCROFT—*Black*

Chieveley Chanter (*blk*)
Petiti Ami of Piperscroft (*blk*)
Eng. Ch. Chieveley Chess (*blk*)
Manon of Piperscroft (*blk*)
The Aide de Camp (*blk*)
La Pompadour of Piperscroft (*blk*)
Belinda Bleue (*blu*)

ENG. CH. RUDOLPH OF PIPERSCROFT

Whelped January 1951   Died 1964

Bred by Mrs. Grace Boyd, Piperscroft Kennels, England
Owned by Mrs. A.D. Jenkins, Fontclair Kennels, England

                        Tip Top of Piperscroft (*blk*)
            Voila of Piperscroft (*blk*)
                        Firebrave Black Beauty (*blk*)
    Clipper of Piperscroft (*blk*)
                        Firebrave Andre (*blk*)
            Steeplejack Mezali of Piperscroft (*blk*)
                        Monica of Piperscroft (*blk*)

ENG. CH. RUDOLPH OF PIPERSCROFT—*Black*

                        Eng. Ch. Barty of Piperscroft (*blk*)
            Ruffles of Piperscroft (*blk*)
                        Bijou of the Rigi (*blk*)
    Show Girl of Piperscroft (*blk*)
                        Cirrus of Piperscroft (*blk*)
            Pants of Piperscroft (*blk*)
                        Michou of Piperscroft (*blk*)

Chieveley type which Alida Monro so greatly admired for its smaller size, deep black color and general short backed compactness. Gaulois sired Firebrave Patapan (six champions), who in turn sired Eng. and Am. Ch. Firebrave Sanka of Montfleuri (sire of seven champions) and his full brother Firebrave Spiro of Braebeck. Sanka sired Am. and Eng. Ch. Merrymorn Antoine (sire of nine champions). Firebrave Spiro sired the great English winner of 17 Challenge Certificates, Eng. and Am. Ch. Braebeck Toni of Montfleuri (sire of six champions).

Another important brown son of Barty was Am. Ch. Sabu of Piperscroft. Sabu sired the brown Ch. Smilestone's Sirprise (sire of five champions), who in turn sired Ch. Hollycourt Bronze Knight (sire of 10 champions). Bronze Knight sired Ch. Cappoquin Bon Fiston (sire of 17 champions) and Ch. Hollycourt Ensign (sire of five champions). Bon Fiston sired Ch. Cappoquin Carriage Trade, winner of eight Bests in Show and sire of eight champions.

Barty's son, Ruffles of Piperscroft (full brother of Pitter Patter), sired Eng. Ch. Top Hat of Piperscroft. Top Hat sired Highland Sand Kennels' Ch. Busby of Piperscroft, who sired 15 champions. Another son of Ruffles, Tiptop of Piperscroft, gave Cartlane Kennels the valuable stud Tais Toi of Piperscroft. Tiptop also sired Voila of Piperscroft whose son, Clipper of Piperscroft, sired the great Eng. Ch. Rudolph of Piperscroft.

Eng. Ch. Rudolph of Piperscroft

In January of 1951 a black puppy was whelped at the famous Piperscroft Kennels of Grace Boyd in England. This puppy, Rudolph of Piperscroft, changed the direction and type of black and brown Miniature Poodles. Almost totally Piperscroft bred for three generations he excelled in features then sorely needed in Miniatures, particularly head qualities and refinement. Mrs. Boyd was reducing her kennels and luckily Mrs. A. D. Jenkins was searching for a male to improve heads in her Fontclair line. It was a history making arrangement and Rudolph went to a home where he was loved and appreciated for many years. Rudolph qualified as a Junior Warrant winner (based on a number of wins) as a youngster.

In July of 1953 the great breed authority Phillipe Howard Price awarded him the Challenge Certificate and Best of Breed over 300 entries and predicted he would be, "a great Miniature in the years to come." Mr. Price bred four of his Montfleuri champion bitches to Rudolph and the results were spectacular as winners and producers. All this did not go unnoticed by other Miniature breeders and soon Rudolph was in great demand at stud.

Two of Rudolph's five Top Producing sons are out of Montfleuri dams. Rudolph also had several Top Producing daughters. The sons were Eng. Ch. Baroque of Montfleuri (sire of eight champions), Eng. Ch. Rippwood Milord of Eldonwood (sire of six champions), New Hat of Montfleuri (sire of nine champions) and Eng. Ch. Moensfarm Mascot of Montfleuri (sire of 18 champions). New Hat came to the U.S. and although he never gained his title he was good enough to go Best of Winners at the 1957 P.C.A. Specialty. New Hat sired Surrey New Broom who sired five champions.

Rudolph's most famous offspring was Dunwalke Kennels' Ch. Fontclair Festoon, winner of numerous Bests in Show including Westminster 1959. Festoon was the dam of 10 champions. Festoon's full older sister, the blue Eng. Ch. Fontclair Fleur of Burdiesel, was the dam of three champions which included both blues and silvers and introduced the Rudolph line into silvers. Another full sister to Festoon and Fleur, Emmrill Lindabelle, produced three champions. Yet another Rudolph daughter, Seraphita of Montfleuri, bred to Mascot produced three champions.

Rudolph's influence even spread to Toys. His small daughter, Topper of Montfleuri, produced the Toy Eng. Ch. Tammy of Manapouri who won 12 Challenge Certificates. Another Rudolph daughter, bred to Wychwood Gatesgarth Monarch, produced Eng. Ch. Tophill Toyboy. A double Rudolph granddaughter, also bred to Monarch, produced Eng. Ch. Tophill Trotabout. Toyboy and Trotabout were both influential Toy sires.

Rudolph produced champions when outcrossed, linebred or inbred. He sired champions from his own daughters and granddaughters. Rudolph's get were easy to recognize by their beautiful heads and eyes and strength of foreface. His get excelled in coat texture and profusion and great showmanship. He was always sweet and unspoiled and a great pet. His owner refused several very generous offers for him. He was a dominant black and never produced a brown.

Anne Rogers Clark was interested in Rudolph because of her admiration for his daughter, Ch. Fontclair Festoon. "I saw Rudolph but once, and that was when he was well on in years, but I was struck by his exceptional head and eye—a strong masculine head with no hint of coarseness or commonness—lovely depth through the end of his muzzle—fine in back skull—and with an eye of super shape, size and placement. He was a tall dog—nicely proportioned, in nice balance. His head I would classify as extreme, but not exaggerated. As I walked down bench after bench of Poodles at the Windsor Championship Show in 1956, I could pick out the Rudolph get without fail. They had the head, eye and expression of their father that was unmistakable, plus a certain air about them that was unique. I believe he set a style in postwar Poodles for type and a quality that can best be described as a 'Rudolph type'—not seen before."

Montfleuri Kennels, always noted for its beautiful heads, continued its use of Rudolph's family. Rudolph's son, Willowbrae Gavotte of Montfleuri, sired Eng. Ch. Lochleal Guardsman of Montfleuri. His son, Bearskin of Montfleuri, sired Tricorne of Montfleuri. Tricorne sired three champions including Ch. Florontie Black Orpheus who came to the Clarion Kennels in California where he produced 27 champions. Tricorne also sired Eng. Ch. Patrick Casey of Montfleuri. Patrick Casey sired seven champions including Eng. Ch. Tarka of Montfleuri who won 21 C.C.'s. Tarka produced an even more outstanding winner in Eng. Ch. Mickey Finn of Montfleuri who won 29 C.C.'s. Mickey Finn

Eng. Ch. Mickey Finn of Montfleuri

Ch. Montfleuri Fennel of Burdiesel

sired 12 champions. Another Patrick Casey son, Ch. Montfleuri Fennel of Burdiesel, came to the U.S. where he produced 38 champions.

Rudolph's leading producing son was Eng. Ch. Moensfarm Mascot of Montfleuri who stayed at Montfleuri where he sired 18 champions. Mascot's son, Attenelmes Benedick of Montfleuri, sired Eng. Ch. Token of Montfleuri. Token's son, Jondalin Shah of Montfleuri, went to Australia where he became a champion and exerted great influence, siring 37 champions. Montfleuri sent another Mascot son, Ch. Dunwalke Lorenzo of Montfleuri, to the States to replace a puppy which had gone oversize. Lorenzo proved a potent stud force and produced 14 champions including the Group winner, Ch. Dunwalke Sweetwilliam (out of Rudolph's daughter, Ch. Fontclair Festoon). Sweetwilliam sired the beautiful headed, typy Ch. Dunwalke Aster (sire of eight champions) and the brown Best in Show winner Ch. Surrey Sequoia. Sequoia is the sire of the Top Producer Ch. Surrey Samurai and the multiple Best in Show winner and Top Producer, Ch. Villa Russe Bismarck. Lorenzo's most famous son was Can. Ch. Highlane Bonhomme Richard, sire of 65 champions.

Eng. Ch. Moensfarm Mascot of Montfleuri

Australian Ch. Jondalin Shah of Montfleuri

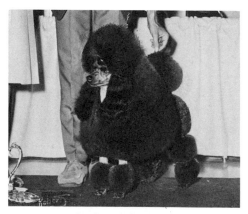

Ch. Surrey Sequoia

Ch. Aizbel The Imperalist

Ch. Gregella Some Spellbinder

Ch. Argosy Anchorman

ENG. CH. THE MONARCH LINE

Eng. Ch. Rudolph of Piperscroft (*blk*) 28
   Willowbrae Gavotte of Montfleuri (*blk*)
      Eng. Ch. Lochleal Guardsman of Montfleuri (*blk*)
         Bearskin of Montfleuri (*blk*)
            Tricorne of Montfleuri (*blk*) 3
               Ch. Florontie Black Orpheus (*blk*) 27
                  Ch. Cypress Hill Centurian (*blk*) 6
               Eng. Ch. Patrick Casey of Montfleuri (*blk*) 7
               Eng. Ch. Tarka of Montfleuri (*blk*)
                  Eng. Ch. Mickey Finn of Montfleuri (*blk*) 12
                     Ch. Clay-Mar Casanova des Jardins (*blk*) 10
               Am. Can. Ch. Montfleuri Fennel of Burdiesel (*blk*) 38
   Alistair of Eldonwood (*blk*)
      Eng. Am. Ch. Frederick of Rencroft (*blk*) 6
         Ch. Gay El's Christian (*blk*) 8
   Eng. Ch. Baroque of Montfleuri (*blk*) 8
   Eng. Ch. Rippwood Milord of Eldonwood (*blk*) 6
   New Hat of Montfleuri (*blk*) 9
      Surrey New Broom (*blk*) 5
   Eng. Am. Ch. Moensfarm Marcelle of Montfleuri (*blk*) 6
   Eng. Ch. Moensfarm Mascot of Montfleuri (*blk*) 18
      Attenelmes Benedick of Montfleuri (*blk*)
         Eng. Ch. Token of Montfleuri (*blk*) 2
            Aus. Ch. Jondalyn Shah of Montfleuri (*blk*) 37
      Ch. Dunwalke Lorenzo of Montfleuri (*blk*) 14
      Aus. Ch. Montmarne Mandingo (*blk*) 12
      Ch. Dunwalke Sweetwilliam (*blk*) 2
         Ch. Dunwalke Aster (*blk*) 8
         Ch. Surrey Sequoia (*brn*) 13
            Ch. Surrey Samurai (*blk*) 9
            Ch. Villa Russe Bismarck (*blk*) 16
      Can. Ch. Highlane Bonhomme Richard *(blk)* 65
      Temar's Attention Please (*blk*) 24
         Ch. Gregella Some Spellbinder (*blk*) 14
            Ch. Daktari Apogee Dakota (*blk*) 7
         Ch. Gregella Copyright Caliber (*blk*) 16
      Ch. Campbell's Raz-Ma-Tazz (*brn*) 40
         Ch. Rochambeau's Midnight Playboy (*blk*) 12
         Ch. Surrey Postmarc (*blk*) 36
            Ch. Fontella's Quick Brown Fox (*brn*) 7
      Ch. Campbell's Clansman (*blk*) 15
         Ch. Aizbel The Imperialist *(blk)* 13
            Ch. Penchant Paladin *(blk)* 54
               Ch. Praver's Watusi Warrior *(blk)* 7
               Ch. Wilhoit's Whoodeni *(blk)* 11
               Ch. Royal Look Winged Commander *(blk)* 7
            Ch. The Kinsman of Heatherly *(blk)* 11
            Ch. Cavalier Contraband *(blk)* 11
         Ch. Campbell's Cedric of Deshler (*blk*) 9
         Ch. Mulali's Sweet William (*brn*) 6
      Ch. Ravendune Sweet Baby James (*blk*) 11
      Ch. Argosy Anchorman (*blk*) 16
         Ch. Penchant Pinkerton (*blk*) 16
      Ch. Clay-Mar Peter Paul (*brn*) 5
      Monterosa Black Imp (*blk*) 6

CAN. CH. HIGHLANE BONHOMME RICHARD

Whelped: 1956   Died: 1972

Bred and owned by
Elaine Crawford, Highlane Kennels

Eng. Ch. Rudolph of Piperscroft (*blk*)
Eng. Ch. Moensfarm Mascot of Montfleuri (*blk*)
Moensfarm Mimi (*blk*)
Ch. Dunwalke Lorenzo of Montfleuri (*blk*)
· Gay Charmer of Ardian (*blk*)
Merrienda of Montfleuri (*blk*)
Montfleuri Claudette of Hockford (*blk*)

CAN. CH. HIGHLANE BONHOMME RICHARD—*Black*

Clipper of Piperscroft (*blk*)
Eng. Ch. Rudolph of Piperscroft (*blk*)
Show Girl of Piperscroft (*blk*)
Ch. Emmrill Lucky Charm (*blk*)
Eng. Ch. Rudolph of Piperscroft (*blk*)
Emmrill Lindabelle (*blk*)
Fontclair Fuschia (*blu*)

Can. Ch. Highlane Bonhomme Richard

The black Can. Ch. Highlane Bonhomme Richard was to become as potent a stud force in the United States and Canada as Rudolph had been in England. After Clarence Dillon of Dunwalke Kennels acquired Ch. Fontclair Festoon (by Rudolph) he arranged to have her full sister, Emmrill Lindabelle, bred back to Rudolph, her sire. This resulted in the Best in Show winner, Ch. Emmrill Lucky Charm, who was imported and campaigned by Dunwalke. Lucky Charm was placed with the Highlane Kennels of Elaine Crawford. She was bred to Ch. Dunwalke Lorenzo of Montfleuri and produced Ch. Dunwalke Annee of Highlane and Ch. Dunwalke Cadeau of Highlane—both Top Producers. A repeat breeding to Lorenzo in 1956 produced Can. Ch. Highlane Bonhomme Richard.

Richard was intensely linebred to Rudolph with three crosses in three generations. Richard was in the true Rudolph mold with a classically beautiful head and eye. He finished easily in Canada but was never seriously campaigned in the States. Nor was he heavily promoted at stud. As his list of champions grew, it was realized that only one of his first 17 champions was out of an American champion dam. It soon became evident to breeders that a new force had arrived on the scene.

Richard was bred to the imported Tophill Vista (linebred to Rudolph), owned by Mary Alice Campbell, and produced two important males in one litter whelped March 26, 1967. These were the black Ch. Campbell's Clansman and the brown Ch. Campbell's Raz-Ma-Tazz. Raz, a Best in Show winner, is the leading brown Miniature sire on the Top Producers list with 40 champions to his credit. Raz's get have been producers of note. He has several Top Producing daughters and two Top Producer sons, Ch. Rochambeau's Midnight Playboy and Ch. Surrey Postmarc. Postmarc, a Specialty Best in Show winner, gives every indication of topping his sire's record.

Raz's litter brother, Ch. Campbell's Clansman, a Best in Show winner at All-Breed and Specialty Shows, has been an important sire with three Top Producing sons—Ch. Aizbel The Imperialist, Ch. Cavalier Contraband and Ch. The Kinsman of Heatherly. The Imperialist sired Ch. Penchant Paladin, a multiple Group and Specialty Show winner. Paladin averaged better than a champion per litter in the first 25 litters he sired. Paladin's sons—Ch. Royal Look Winged Commander, Ch. Praver's Watusi Warrior and Ch. Wilhoit's Whoodeni—are all Top Producers.

Bonhomme Richard also sired the Top Producing males: Ch. Campbell's Cedric of Deshler, Ch. Clay-Mar Peter Paul, Ch. Ravendune Sweet Baby James and Ch. Argosy Anchorman. Anchorman is the sire of the Top Producer Ch. Penchant Pinkerton. Bonhomme Richard's daughters were also producers. His daughter, Ch. Rochambeau's Midnight Genie, is one of the leading Miniature dams with 11 champions to her credit. An untitled, oversize son of Bonhomme Richard, Temar's Attention Please, sired 24 champions including three Top

Ch. Campbell's Raz-Ma-Tazz   Ch. Campbell's Clansman

CH. CAMPBELL'S CLANSMAN

Whelped: April 25, 1967   Deceased

Owned by Hilayne & Charles Cavanaugh, Argosy Poodles

CH. CAMPBELL'S RAZ-MA-TAZZ

Whelped: April 25, 1967   Died: 1979

Owned by Nancy Cutler and Peggy Hogg

Both bred by Mary Alice Campbell

Eng. Ch. Moensfarm Mascot of Montfleuri (*blk*)
Ch. Dunwalke Lorenzo of Montfleuri (*blk*)
Merrienda of Montfleuri (*blk*)
Can. Ch. Highlane Bonhomme Richard (*blk*)
Eng. Ch. Rudolph of Piperscroft (*blk*)
Ch. Emmrill Lucky Charm (*blk*)
Emmrill Lindabelle (*blk*)

CH. CAMPBELL'S CLANSMAN—*Black*
CH. CAMPBELL'S RAZ-MA-TAZZ—*Brown*

Fontclair High Hat of Montfleuri (*blk*)
Simonet Sarraband of Battramsley (*blk*)
Willowbrae Tarantella of Simonet (*blk*)
Tophil Vista (*blk*)
Eng. Ch. Montfleuri Mick of Iniskeller (*blk*)
Serenade of Delmar (*blk*)
Gay Step of Rippwood (*blk*)

CH. PENCHANT PALADIN

Whelped June 18, 1975

Bred by Betsy A. Leedy, Penchant Kennels
Owned by Betsy Leedy and Margaret Durney

Can. Ch. Highlane Bonhomme Richard (*blk*)

Ch. Campbell's Clansman (*blk*)

Tophill Vista (*blk*)

Ch. Aizbel The Imperialist (*blk*)

Ch. Aizbel The One and Only (*blk*)

Ch. Aizbel All About Angels (*blk*)

Can. Ch. Escapade's Mistress O'Sigma Chi (*blk*)

CH. PENCHANT PALADIN—*Black*

Can. Ch. Highlane Bonhomme Richard (*blk*)

Ch. Campbell's Raz-Ma-Tazz (*brn*)

Tophill Vista (*blk*)

Ch. Fontella's Penchant Laurel (*blk*)

Ch. Edris Bet-A-Million (*blk*)

Ch. Edris Ooh La La (*blk*)

Challendon Fireflirt (*brn*)

CH. SURREY POSTMARC

Whelped: September 2, 1974   Died 1985

Bred by Mr. and Mrs. James Edward Clark, Surrey Kennels
Owned by Del Dahl, Fontella Poodles and Mrs. James Cutler

                                 Ch. Dunwalke Lorenzo of Montfleuri (*blk*)
                    Can. Ch. Highlane Bonhomme Richard (*blk*)
                              Ch. Emmrill Lucky Charm (*blk*)
            Ch. Campbell's Raz-Ma-Tazz (*brn*)
                              Simonet Saraband of Battramsley (*blk*)
                    Tophill Vista (*blk*)
                              Serenade of Delmar (*blk*)

CH. SURREY POSTMARC—*Black*

                                 Montmartre What-A-Boy (*blk*)
                    Ch. Dunwalke Boy (*blk*)
                              Ch. Dunwalke Marstella (*blk*)
            Dunwalke Marcy of Surrey (*blk*)
                              Montmarte What-A-Boy (*blk*)
                    Ch. Dunwalke Primrose (*blk*)
                              Ch. Fontclair Festoon (*blk*)

Temar's Attention Please

Producing sons: Ch. Gregella Some Spellbinder, Can. Ch. Gregella Ebony Executive and Ch. Gregella Copyright Caliber. Attention Please's daughter, Ch. Gregella Faultless Fanny, is also one of the leading Miniature dams with 11 champion get.

Another distinguished line descended from Success of Piperscroft through his black son Harpendale Little Tich through six generations to the blue Spotlight of Summercourt. Spotlight sired Fircot Silvafuzz of Summercourt and he, bred to a granddaughter of Ch. Hollycourt Platinum and Ch. Petit Pierre, gave the handsome Ch. Freeland's Flashlight. Flashlight possessed an exceptionally long well-made head, especially for a silver, and he was a success both in the show ring (Best of Variety at the 1961 Poodle Club of America Specialty) and at stud with five champions to his credit. Spotlight also sired one of the greatest stud dogs in the history of the breed, Am. Can. Ch. Summercourt Square Dancer of Fircot.

Miniature Chart 3

ENG. CH. THE MONARCH (continued)

Success of Piperscroft (*continued*)
    Harpendale Little Tich (*blk*)
        Harpendale John Brown (*brn*)
            Harpendale Admiration (*brn*)
                Chocolat of Swanhill (*brn*)
                    Eng. Ch. Cremola of Swanhill (*crm*)
                        Victor of Fircot (*apr*)
                            Spotlight of Summercourt (*blu*)
                              Fircot Silvafuzz of Summercourt (*si*)
                                Ch. Freeland's Flashlight (*si*) 5
                              Ch. Summercourt Square Dancer of Fircot (*crm*) 69
                              (*See Miniature Chart 4*)

Spotlight of Summercourt

Ch. Freeland's Flashlight

AMERICAN CANADIAN
CH. SUMMERCOURT SQUARE DANCER OF FIRCOT

Whelped March 7, 1956   Died: June 10, 1969

Bred by Miss S. A. Williams, England
Owned by Jewel Garlick, Gaylen Poodles

                            Eng. Ch. Cremola of Swanhill (*crm*)
                 Victor of Fircot (*apr*)
                           Cream Puff of Fircot (*crm*)
         Spotlight of Summercourt (*blu*)
                           Vendas Zante (*gr*)
               Vendas Falaise (*brn*)
                           Vendas Madame Bovary (*blk*)

AM. CAN. CH. SUMMERCOURT SQUARE DANCER OF FIRCOT—*Cream*

                            Eng. Ch. Toomai of Montfleuri (*blk*)
                 Pippo of Montfleuri (*blk*)
                             Eng. Ch. Philippa of Montfleuri (*blk*)
         Mistress of Pipers Lane (*blk*)
                           Mandarin of Mannerhead (*blk*)
               Mangeur of Bushill (*blk*)
                           Fifi of Swale (*crm*)

Am. and Can. Ch. Summercourt Square Dancer of Fircot

The cream Miniature, Am. and Can. Ch. Summercourt Square Dancer of Fircot, was bred in 1956 by Miss S. A. Williams and imported from England by Nigel Aubrey-Jones. He was owned by Jewel Garlick and was handled by Anne Rogers Clark to all of his wins. After his show career, he remained at Anne's Surrey Kennels for life.

On Thanksgiving Day, 1957 Dancer journeyed to Montreal, Canada to qualify for Westminster (this is no longer possible) and also gained his Canadian championship in one weekend. Making his debut in the U.S. at Westminster 1958, Dancer was Winners Dog and raced on to finish his championship in three more shows—undefeated for Winners and collecting two Best of Varieties and a Group first win along the way. In his 18 months of showing Dancer won three Bests in Show, 12 Group firsts, and 29 Bests of Variety. These wins were made under well known Poodle specialists and all-rounders.

A close look at Dancer's pedigree reveals that he was not bred along the conventional white lines and thus lacked their usual faults. The fact that he is a product of colored breeding is felt to account for his type, which is closer to that of the blacks than the whites. Fortunately Square Dancer was prepotent for his type and he changed the look and style of white, cream and apricot Miniatures. He had the ability to produce heads, style, rear angulation and showmanship in abundance.

Anne Rogers Clark describes Square Dancer as just under 15 inches, with bone in balance with his size. Dancer was a stallion of a dog, very masculine without being coarse; everything he had to give away he had in abundance. He had a thick, double, hard to grow and keep coat. He had a short back with a big rib and he loved to eat. He had high, hard round feet—almost too round for a Poodle foot. He was a high stationed, short backed dog, who could have been a touch more angulated at both shoulder and stifle. He had huge long thick ears. Dancer had a short, high placed, thick rooted tail. His head was masculine, very handsome with a beautiful, chiseled, strong foreface. His eye was very dark brown of a lovely size and shape, set a little too closely together. Dancer's pigment was very good. He had a very good mouth, but was missing three side teeth. His temperament was bold, domineering and kingly. He was a great character!

Most probably due to Dancer's own colored type, and his colored background, he bred remarkably true in producing his own type, temperament and showmanship. Dancer holds the record of 69 champion get, still the leading Miniature sire. Five bitches were to become Top Producers as a result of their liaisons with Dancer. And it was not just the numbers of champions that Dancer produced. His get were winners of the highest honors in the land. His son, from his first litter in the United States, Ch. Tedwin's Top Billing, was acclaimed by many as one of the greatest show specimens ever seen and confirmed this

Ch. Midcrest The Cosmopolitan

Ch. Tambodan's Special Edition

Ch. Cinbren's Glazier of Mi-Lyn

opinion with 56 All Breed Best in Show victories and 11 Specialty Bests in Show including P.C.A. 1963 and 1965. Dancer's daughter, Ch. Estid Ballet Dancer, won 30 All Breed and Specialty Bests in Show. Square Dancer's get numbered 10 Best in Show winners and 19 were Group winners.

Ch. Tedwin's Top Billing sired nine champions. Another son, Ch. Barbree Round Dancer, sired five champions. Square Dancer's son, the Group winner Ch. Lawson's High Flyer, bred to Ch. Midcrest The Cameo (a Square Dancer daughter) produced the Best in Show winner Ch. Midcrest The Tradewind who sired eight champions. Tradewind's son, Midcrest Daktari, sired the Best in Show winner Ch. Midcrest Touch of Magic (out of a Square Dancer daughter). Touch of Magic sired six champions and Woodcliff Madam I'm Adam. Adam's son, Woodcliff Magic Wind of Wavir, sired the Group winner Ch. Wavir Havoc. Havoc was intensely linebred to Square Dancer having fifteen crosses to him in six generations. Havoc sired 17 champions including the brothers Ch. Wavir Linus and Ch. Wavir Lucas. Linus sired the Top Producer Ch. Marais All Systems Go, who in turn sired the Top Producer Ch. Wavir Showboat. Showboat sired the Best in Show winner and Top Producer Ch. McKernan Redford of Valcopy. Ch. Wavir Havoc's Best in Show and Top Producing son, Ch. Wavir McBray, sired the lovely bitch Ch. Wavir Hit Parade who was Best in Show at the 1983 and 1984 Poodle Club of America Specialty Shows.

Square Dancer bred several times to Ch. Simloch Ice De La Fontaine (Rothara background) produced eight champions. Square Dancer bred to Ch. Midcrest The Vamp (also Rothara background) produced three champions in one litter: Ch. Midcrest The Cosmopolitan, Ch. Midcrest The Cameo and Ch. Midcrest Cleopatra—all became Top Producers. Although this breeding was an outcross, it brought Square Dancer's qualities to the Midcrest Kennels of Mr. and Mrs. Robert Middleton in Washington state. Cosmopolitan, a Best in Show winner, had an extreme long head, long neck, deep body and he was absolutely sound. He was a real showman and won eight Bests in Show at Specialties and All Breed Shows. Like his sire he produced champions when linebred, inbred or outcrossed. He sired 11 champions. Bred to his daughter he produced the Top Producer, Midcrest Haji Baba. Another son of Cosmopolitan, Ironwood Diogenes O'Hot Stuff, bred to Ch. Patroon's Taste of Honey (also by Cosmopolitan) produced Ch. Tambodan's Special Edition. He in turn sired the Top Producer Ch. Cinbren's Glazier of Mi-Lyn, who was the top winning Miniature for 1975 and 1976.

Square Dancer was bred only to whites, creams and apricots and never produced anything but those colors. His sons and daughters, in turn, when bred to whites, creams and apricots produced only those colors.

Ch. Midcrest Tradewind

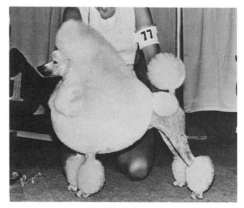

Ch. Wavir Linus

Ch. Wavir Havoc

Jap. Am. Can. Ch. Wavir McBray

Ch. Wavir Rampage

Ch. McKernan Redford of Valcopy

108

ENG. CH. THE MONARCH LINE

Am. Can. Ch. Summercourt Square Dancer of Fircot (*crm*) 69
    Ch. Tedwin's Top Billing (*wh*) 9
    Ch. Barbree Round Dancer (*wh*) 5
    Ch. Lawson's High Flyer (*wh*)
       Ch. Midcrest Tradewind (*wh*) 8
          Midcrest Daktari (*wh*)
             Ch. Midcrest Touch of Magic (*wh*) 6
                Ch. Doral's Viking The Magician (*wh*) 6
                Woodcliff Madam I'm Adam (*wh*)
                   Woodcliff Magic Wind of Wavir (*wh*)
                  Ch. Wavir Havoc (*wh*) 17
                     Ch. Wavir McCloud of Hiwood (*wh*)
                        Ch. Wavir Rampage (*wh*) 6
                   Ch. Wavir Linus (*wh*)
                     Ch. Marais All Systems Go (*crm*) 7
                       Ch. Wavir Showboat (*wh*) 7
                           Ch. McKernan Redford of Valcopy (*wh*) 6
                  Ch. Wavir Lucas (*wh*)
                   Aurora's Bobby McGee (*blu*) 5
                     Ch. Amity's The City Slicker (*blu*) 5
                Jap. Am. Can. Ch. Wavir McBray (*wh*) 22
      Ch. Midcrest The Cosmopolitan (*wh*) 11
         Ironwood Diogenes O'Hot Stuff (*wh*)
             Ch. Tambodan's Special Edition (*wh*) 11
                Ch. Charob's Charade (*wh*) 6
                Ch. Cinbren's Glazier of Mi-Lyn (*wh*) 18
             Midcrest Haji Baba (*wh*) 5
    Am. Can. Bda. Ch. Harmo Gay Prospector (*apr*) 6
    Ch. Woodland Burning Bright (*apr*) 15
      Can. Ch. Murwyn's Golden Guardsman (*apr*) 7
      Ch. Marjoe's Tangerine Tiger (*apr*) 4
         Ch. Lyca Dime Store Novel (*apr*) 28
             Ch. Lyca Clockwork Orange (*apr*) 5
             Ch. Orangecrest Happy Days (*apr*) 5

Ch. Woodland Burning Bright | Am. Can. Ch. Marjoe's Tangerine Tiger

Square Dancer's Apricot Influence

Just as it happened in whites, Square Dancer's influence helped to bring about much needed modern qualities in apricots particularly in head, style, coat and showmanship. Interestingly, Square Dancer is descended from England's famous deep apricot Aureolin of Toytown. Two of Square Dancer's apricot sons (both out of apricot dams) became Top Producers—Ch. Woodland Burning Bright and the Best in Show winner, Am. Can. Bda. Ch. Harmo Gay Prospector (six champion get). Burning Bright finished with four majors in just seven shows. He sired 15 champions including the Group winner Ch. Marjoe's Tangerine Tiger. Tiger sired four apricot champions including Ch. Lyca Dime Store Novel who was on the small side. Dime Store Novel's show career was not at all spectacular but he possessed the genes to produce tremendous improvements in apricots particularly in overall balance and refinement, carriage, rear ends and tailsets. His get had beautiful heads with soft expressions and they were Poodley. It was no longer necessary to say, "Beautiful quality—for an apricot." These apricots needed no apologies from anyone for their conformation and they won over the best of the blacks and whites. They performed so well they made Dime Store Novel the leading Poodle sire of all colors, all varieties, for 1983. And these were not just numbers, they included Group and Best in Show winners. Dime Store Novel is the most successful apricot sire in the history of the breed. Fortunately his influence is continuing. His inbred son, Ch. Lyca Clockwork Orange (out of a Dime Store Novel daughter) is a Top Producer. Another son, Ch. Orangecrest Happy Days, is also a Top Producer. Clockwork Orange's son, Ch. Stonecreek Tangerine Tiger, was the top winning Miniature for 1984.

CH. LYCA DIME STORE NOVEL

Whelped: December 8, 1975

Bred and owned by
Camille Lashley and Y. L. Meeks

                          Ch. Summercourt Square Dancer of Fircot (*crm*)
              Ch. Woodland Burning Bright (*apr*)
                    Woodland Paprika, U.D. (*apr*)
      Ch. Marjoe's Tangerine Tiger (*apr*)
                    Ch. Price's Pirates Gold (*apr*)
              Ch. Price Patrick's Marjoe's Ginger (*apr*)
                    Price Patrick's Golden Chip (*apr*)

CH. LYCA DIME STORE NOVEL—*Apricot*

                    Meridian Flambeau (*apr*)
              Ch. Karu The Sundowner (*apr*)
                    Dunham Adastra Doll (*apr*)
      Gregella Tempting Taffy (*apr*)
                    LeJoy's Burning Fire (*apr*)
              Gregella Fire Flirt (*apr*)
                    Darru Golden Sun Drop (*apr*)

POPINJAY

I will now connect Eng. Ch. The Monarch with another great English line. His son, Popinjay, sired Mannerhead Kennel's famous Eng. Ch. Eric Brighteyes, a big winner and sire of champions. Brighteyes' son, Harwee of Mannerhead (ex Eng. Ch. The Mistress of Mannerhead—Chieveley bred) sired Blakeen's famous Ch. Snow Boy of Fircot.

Ch. Snow Boy of Fircot

Earlier in this chapter we covered the great advancements in whites and creams through Ch. Summercourt Square Dancer of Fircot. In point of fact he was preceded 11 years by the great Ch. Snow Boy of Fircot (whelped April 28, 1945) who was the first great white Miniature and whose quality was an inspiration to those comparatively few breeders who were interested in breeding whites at that time. Snow Boy's sire was a black and his dam was a gray. There was no white in his pedigree for many generations, consequently Snow Boy did not possess or produce the faults that were so common in the whites of his day. Snow Boy was a big winner at important shows and exerted a great deal of improvement in the whites, both in England and the States. Before leaving England, Snow Boy sired Fircot Garcon de Neige who sired five champions.

At Blakeen, Snow Boy produced Blakeen Oscar of the Waldorf, who went to England where he completed his championship and became an important sire. Oscar sired 10 champions and several of his get came back to this country to win honors. One son, Eng. and Am. Ch. Adastra Magic Fame, became one of the greatest winners of the breed with 53 Bests in Show to his credit. Fame was the sire of 16 champions. An untitled son of Magic Fame, Silhou-Jette's Magic Fame, sired Ch. Woodland Snow Storm (ex Ch. Woodland Snow Fall, C.D.—also by Ch. Adastra Magic Fame). Snow Storm was the sire of seven champions including Ch. Woodland Fair Haired Boy who sired 14 champions. Another Oscar son, Ch. Rothara The Ragamuffin, won five Bests in Show and sired 11 champions. Another imported Oscar son, Ch. Wychwood White Winter, produced the Best in Show winner Am. and Can. Ch. Plaza-Toro Snow Fantasy who sired 10 champions.

This is just a brief resume of the influence of Snow Boy and his sons and grandsons on the whites. There were a number of bitches from these males that also made important contributions. Snow Boy was the single greatest influence on white Miniatures until the advent of Square Dancer, and Square Dancer benefited from the Snow Boy legacy in compiling his amazing record at stud.

Eng. Ch. Eric Brighteyes

Harwee of Mannerhead

Miniature Chart 5

ENG. CH. THE MONARCH (continued)

Popinjay (*blk*)
    Eng. Ch. Eric Brighteyes (*blk*)
        Harwee of Mannerhead (*blk*) 3
            Ch. Snow Boy of Fircot (*wh*) 10
                Fircot Garcon de Neige (*wh*) 5
                Eng. Ch. Blakeen Oscar of the Waldorf (*wh*) 10
                Ch. Rothara The Ragamuffin (*wh*) 11
                Ch. Wychwood White Winter (*wh*) 4
                    Ch. Plaza Toro Snow Fantasy (*wh*) 10
                Eng. Am. Ch. Adastra Magic Fame (*wh*) 16
                  Silhou-Jette's Magic Fame (*wh*)
                    Ch. Woodland Snow Storm (*wh*) 7
                      Ch. Woodland Fair Haired Boy (*wh*) 14
            Eng. Ch. Toomai of Montfleuri (*blk*) 2
            Man About Town of Rosvic (*blk*)
                Jervis of Rosvic (*blk*)
                    Wychwood Gatesgarth Monarch (*Eng. Toy*) 8
                    (*See Toy Chart 7*)

Ch. Snow Boy of Fircot

Eng. Ch. Blakeen Oscar of the Waldorf

ENGLISH, AMERICAN, CANADIAN
CH. ADASTRA MAGIC FAME

Whelped October 3, 1951   Deceased

Bred by Mr. and Mrs. L. H. Coventon, England
Owned by Maxine Beam

Harwee of Mannerhead (*blk*)
Ch. Snow Boy of Fircot (*wh*)
Solitaire of Piperscroft (*gr*)
Eng. Ch. Blakeen Oscar of the Waldorf (*wh*)
Ch. Blakeen Minnikin (*wh*)
Ch. Blakeen Christable (*wh*)
Blakeen Alba (*wh*)

ENG., AM. CAN. CH. ADASTRA MAGIC FAME—*White*

Eng. Ch. Adastra Magic Beau (*blu*)
Adastra Magic Gold (*wh*)
Adastra Cocotte (*si*)
Adastra Magic Glitter (*wh*)
Eng. Ch. Adastra Magic Beau (*blu*)
Adastra Magic Snow (*wh*)
Popipoupa (*wh*)

Mrs. Campbell Inglis' black Miniature, Dare Devil Dink (Eng. Ch. The Monarch ex Bonny Forget Me Not), and his son Am. Ch. Sparkling Jet of Misty Isles (ex Crystal Bell).

DARE DEVIL DINK

Eng. Ch. The Monarch also sired the black Dare Devil Dink, who was the sire of the famous black Ch. Sparkling Jet of Misty Isles. Before Jet left England he was bred to his granddam Bonny Forget Me Not, and produced the famous brothers Eng. Ch. The Laird of Mannerhead and Eng. Ch. Limelight of Mannerhead. Jet sired 11 champions and with Ch. Misty Isles Algie of Piperscroft dominated the world of Miniature Poodles for many years. Jet's son, Ch. Demon of Misty Isles, sired three champions including Ch. Clairwell Him Especially. Him Especially sired six champions including Ch. Periwig Surrey Peter Pan who sired Ch. Touchstone Top Kick, who is the sire of five champions. Ch. Demon of Misty Isles also sired Ch. Barrack Hill Bomber. Bomber sired Ch. Hollycourt Philippe, the sire of 20 champions. Philippe is the sire of Ch. Hollycourt Phillipson, who has eight champions to his credit, including Ch. Hollycourt Blackamoor. Blackamoor's son, Ch. Hollycourt Black Bobbin, is the sire of the magnificent brown Ch. Cappoquin Bon Jongleur. Bon Jongleur was considered by many the finest brown Miniature in the history of the breed. He had a great show career and won 21 Bests in Show. He was the sire of 23 champions.

Chriscrest and Aizbel

Ch. Clairwell Him Especially also sired Ch. Diablotin Onyx who sired seven champions. Onyx sired Duncount's Dauphin who sired Am. Can. Ch. Chriscrest Jamboree, a Best in Show winner. Jamboree sired eight champions including the Best in Show winner Ch. Chriscrest The Fiddler.

The Fiddler was intensely black bred and American bred for many generations based on the old Diablotin, Blakeen and Sherwood Hall lines. The Fiddler was 14 inches high at the shoulder, refined in head and sound with an excellent coat and disposition. He sired 18 champions including Ch. Fiddler's Green Pied Piper.

Ch. Chriscrest The Fiddler (by Ch. Chriscrest Jamboree ex Ch. Chriscrest Flirtation) bred by Christobel Wakefield and Phyllis Tworuk, owned by Phyllis Tworuk Greer, Fiddler's Green Kennels. Sire of 18 champions.

Pied Piper sired the Group Winner, Am. Mex. Can. Ch Logan's Ebony Coup de Vent. He, bred to Hardy High The Piper's Charm (also by Pied Piper), produced the sound, showy Ch. Mi-Bar's Devil Wind. Devil Wind finished in Canada in three shows. He finished in Mexico with five consecutive Groups and a Best in Show. He won over 100 Bests of Variety and 10 All Breed and Specialty Bests in Show. Like his ancestor The Fiddler, who lived to be 17 years of age, Devil Wind was active right up to his death at 14 years. Devil Wind had a strong brown gene. He produced 25 champions including two Top Producing sons, Ch. Pamper's Midnight Marauder and Ch. Firethorne Devil's Advocate.

One of the most important Miniature families is the Aizbel line which was founded on the strongly American-bred Chriscrest family. Ch. Chriscrest The Fiddler bred to his dam's litter sister, Int. Ch. Chriscrest Jubilee (both Best in Show winners) produced the 13¼ inch brown Ch. Aizbel Collector's Item. Collector's Item won seven All Breed and one Specialty Bests in Show, making him the top winning dog to come from the Chriscrest line. Collector's Item was bred back into the Chriscrest line to produce Ch. Aizbel The One and Only. The One and Only, bred by Luis and Maria Aizcorbe, was to serve as a fountain source for spreading the virtues of type, elegance and soundness of the Chriscrest-Aizbel lines. The One and Only's eyes and hips were checked normal at over 10 years of age. The early Aizbels offered an alternative to the Eng. Ch. Rudolph of Piperscroft-Can. Ch. Highlane Bonhomme Richard lines which were flooding the country. In the latter part of the 1970's and the 1980's breeders were combining the two lines with excellent results. The One and Only was an exceptional producer with four Top Producing sons: Ch. Aizbel Headstudy In Black, Ch. Aizbel The Aristocrat, Ch. Gemwood's Black With Envy and Ch. Firethorne Brass Band. The One and Only's daughter, Ch. Aizbel All About Angels, was the dam of six champions.

116

CH. AIZBEL THE ONE AND ONLY

Whelped: November 13, 1965   Died: March 23, 1979

Bred and owned by:
Mr. & Mrs. Luis Aizcorbe Jr.

                     Int. Ch. Chriscrest Jamboree (*blk*)
            Ch. Chriscrest The Fiddler (*blk*)
                     Ch. Chriscrest Flirtation (*blk*)
        Ch. Aizbel Collector's Item (*brn*)
                     Duncount's Dauphin (*blk*)
            Tri. Int. Ch. Chriscrest Jubilee (*blk*)
                     Ch. Chriscrest Franchonette (*blk*)

CH. AIZBEL THE ONE AND ONLY—*Black*

                     Ch. Icarus Prince de Parma (*blk*)
            Tophill Topcard (*blk*)
                     Tophill Tressor (*blk*)
        Chriscrest No Trumps (*blk*)
                     Int. Ch. Chriscrest Jamboree (*blk*)
            Chriscrest Lulubelle (*blk*)
                     Chriscrest Rhythm (*blk*)

Ch. Cappoquin Bon Jongleur

Ch. Sparkling Jet of Misty Isles

Ch. Diablotin Onyx

Ch. Mi-Bar's Devil Wind

Ch. Hollycourt Philippe

Ch. Pamper's Midnight Marauder

118

ENG. CH. THE MONARCH (continued)

Marcourt Carnot (*blk*)
   Ch. Marcourt Tricot (*blk*) 5
Dare Devil Dink (*blk*)
   Ch. Sparkling Jet of Misty Isles (*blk*) 11
      Ch. Demon of Misty Isles (*blk*) 3
         Ch. Barrack Hill Bomber (*blk*) 2
            Ch. Hollycourt Philippe (*blk*) 20
               Ch. Hollycourt Blackamoor (*blk*) 5
                  Ch. Hollycourt Black Bobbin (*blk*)
                     Ch. Cappoquin Bon Jongleur (*brn*) 23
               Ch. Hollycourt Phillipson (*blk*) 8
         Ch. Clairwell Him Especially (*blk*) 6
            Ch. Perriwig Surrey Peter Pan (*blk*)
               Ch. Touchstone Top Kick (*blk*) 5
         Ch. Diablotin Onyx (*blk*) 7
            Duncount's Dauphin (*blk*) 3
               Ch. Chriscrest Jamboree (*blk*) 8
                  Ch. Chriscrest The Fiddler (*blk*) 18
                     Ch. Fiddler's Green Pied Piper (*blk*) 4
                     Ch. Logan's Ebony Coup de Vent (*blk*) 4
                       Am. Can. Mex. Ch. Mi-Bar's Devil Wind (*blk*) 25
                       Ch. Pamper's Midnight Marauder (*blk*) 7
                       Ch. Firethorne Devil's Advocate (*blk*) 7
              Ch. Aizbel Collector's Item (*brn*) 5
                 Ch. Aizbel The One and Only (*blk*) 30
                    Ch. Aizbel Headstudy In Black (*blk*) 18
                     Ch. Aizbel The Knockout (*blk*) 19
                       Ch. Vanguard Noah It All (*brn*) 5
                       Ch. Delnor's Chairman of the Board (*blk*) 5
                    Ch. Aizbel Sunday Punch (*blk*) 8
                 Ch. Aizbel The Aristocrat (*blk*) 34
                  Ch. Aizbel The Heir Apparent (*blk*) 11
                  Vanguard Vandal of Valcopy (*blk*) 1
                    Ch. Gardencourt's Apache Brave (*blk*) 5
              Patti's Sparks A Fly 'N of Padot (*blk*)
                 Ch. Carsted Johnny America (*blk*) 6
              Ch. Gemwood's Black With Envy (*blk*) 9
              Ch. Firethorne Brass Band (*blk*) 9

MARCOURT CARNOT

Marcourt Carnot, a son of Eng. Ch. The Monarch, sired Sherwood Hall's Ch. Marcourt Tricot, the sire of five champions.

Ch. King Johnny of Marcourt, and Eng. and Am. Ch. Chieveley Chump. This is a rare old snapshot from the Marcourt Kennels.

Ch. Whippendell Picot (by Ch. The Monarch ex Bougee Bleue).

Whippendell Garconette Bleue, by Ch. The Monarch ex Leila. Most American champions come through Garconette, bred by Mrs. Tyndall.

CH. KING JOHNNY OF MARCOURT

Among Eng. Ch. The Monarch's earliest American sons were two dogs that exerted a great influence upon the Miniatures of their day: the silver Ch. Whippendell Picot and the black Ch. King Johnny of Marcourt, considered by many the best Marcourt of his period. King Johnny was bred to Whippendell Garconette Bleu to produce Ch. Marcourt Armand, who was bred to the gray Marcourt Mimi of Meredick (by Ch. Whippendell Picot) to produce the silver Ch. Talon's D'Argent of Meredick. Talon's D'Argent in turn sired Ch. Aucassin, who was an important early day sire in silvers. His son, Ch. Smilestone's Silvern, sired six champions including Ch. Hollycourt Light of Star Tavern (sire of 12 champions), Ch. Hollycourt Platinum (sire of 13 champions) and Ch. Hollycourt Ozmium of Paragon (sire of four champions). Light sired the beautiful Best in Show winner on the West Coast, Ch. Barclay Summer Smoke. Smoke was noted for his lovely head and excellent balance, and he sired 10 champions. Ozmium sired Ch. Paragon Dorien of Hollycourt and he in turn sired the Best in Show winner, Ch. Round Table's Avocat (sire of five champions).

ENG. CH. SPRIGGAN BELL

Eng. Ch. The Monarch also sired the black Eng. Ch. Spriggan Bell. A son of Spriggan Bell went to France, where his name was changed from Kinsoe Dapper to Footit de Madjige. Footit finished his championship and became an important Miniature sire on the continent. Footit sired French Ch. Illico de Madjige and Am. Ch. Moutit de Madjige, who came to the Blakeen Kennels where she produced Ch. Blakeen Tito and Ch. Blakeen Paper Doll. Spriggan Bell bred to the silver Hunningham Virginia produced Smoke Ring of Eathorpe. Smoke Ring sired Am. Ch. Grayling of Eathorpe-Carillon and Gunmetal of Eathorpe. Gunmetal was the sire of Silda of Eathorpe, who in turn sired the silvers Eng. Ch. Frenches Comet, Frenches Silverstar and Eng. Ch. Vendas Silver Pickles. Silverstar sired Poodhall Kennels' Am. Ch. Frenches Mercury, who was a Group winner and sire of Ch. Bayou Breeze L'Argent Puppet (dam of four champions). Eng. Ch. Vendas Silver Pickles sired Swandora Gypsyheath Silver Sequins, who in turn sired Eng. Ch. Gypsyheath Silver Wings (sire of four champions). Another Silda of Eathorpe son, Berinshill Patta Pouf of Ronada, sired the Best in Show winner Am. Ch. Wychwood Peroquet of Blakeen (sire of three champions).

The Monarch line is the largest and most successful in the Miniature variety. A study of the foregoing will show that it has exerted tremendous influence in blacks, and even in the whites and silvers, although The Monarch himself was a blue. And, of course, in the intervening years not only color, but type as well, has been affected by the bitches that breeders have brought to the line.

Ch. Smilestone's Silvern

Ch. Hollycourt Platinum

Ch. Kimbeney's Clipper Boy

Ch. Hollycourt Blue Ice

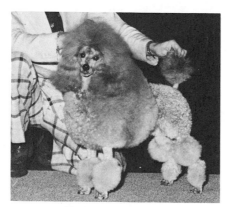

Ch. Fontenac's Florin

Ch. Brandywine's Beau Brummel

ENG. CH. THE MONARCH (continued)

Ch. King Johnny of Marcourt (*blk*)
   Ch. Marcourt Armand (*blk*)
      Ch. Talon's D'Argent of Meredick (*si*) 4
         Ch. Aucassin (*gr*)
            Ch. Smilestone's Silvern (*si*) 6
               Ch. Hollycourt Light of Star Tavern (*si*) 12
                  Ch. Barclay Summer Smoke (*si*) 10
               Ch. Hollycourt Ozmium of Paragon (*si*) 4
                  Ch. Paragon Dorien of Hollycourt (*si*)
                     Ch. Round Table's Avocat (*gr*) 5
               Ch. Hollycourt Platinum (*si*) 13
                  Ch. Hollycourt Blue Ice (*si*)
                     Ch. Hollycourt Montaigne (*si*)
                        Ch. Brandywine's Beau Brummel (*si*)
                         Ch. Kimbeney Clipper Boy (*si*)
                            Int. Ch. Fontenac's Florin (*si*) 4
Eng. Ch. Spriggan Bell (*blk*)
   Int. Ch. Footit de Madjige (*France*) 2
      Ch. Illico de Madjige (*France*)
   Smoke Ring of Eathorpe (*gr*)
      Ch. Grayling of Eathorpe-Carillon (*si*)
      Gunmetal of Eathorpe (*si*)
         Silda of Eathorpe (*si*) 2
            Eng. Ch. Frenches Comet (*si*)
            Frenches Silverstar (*si*)
               Ch. Frenches Mercury (*si*)
            Eng. Ch. Venda's Silver Pickles (*si*)
               Swandora Gypsyheath Silver Sequins (*si*)
                  Eng. Ch. Gypsyheath Silver Wings (*si*) 4
            Berinshill Patta Pouf of Ronada (*si*)
               Ch. Wychwood Peroquet of Blakeen (*si*) 3

Ch. Barclay Summer Smoke

Four generations from the Chieveley Kennels: Eng. Ch. Harcourt Jack, Eng. Ch. Chieveley Choufleur, Chieveley Clarence and Chieveley Chub (as a puppy).

Eng. Ch. Chieveley Chintz

Eng. Am. Ch. Chieveley Chopstick

16

Chieveley Kennels

THE CHIEVELEY LINE is the only one of the old black Miniature lines to come directly down to the dogs of this time. It is, of course, because of the merits of the Chieveley dogs more than because of their numbers that their blood has survived. At the time of the death of Miss Mary Morehouse and the dispersal of the inmates of her Chieveley Kennels in 1924, the institution housed some eighty Poodles, and had won more prizes up until that time than any other kennel with any breed of dogs.

A bitch named Jill, of whose pedigree there is no record, a gift to Miss Morehouse, was the foundation of the kennel that was soon to become famous as Chieveley. Jill was the dam of Eng. Ch. Harcourt Jack (whelped November 23, 1905), the first of Miss Morehouse's many distinguished champions. Harcourt Jack, mated to Harcourt Bijou, produced Chieveley Bunty, who, as a result of her union with Whippendell Petit Chou, was to produce the sensational Eng. Ch. Chieveley Choufleur.

However, of the earlier Chieveleys, old breeders are almost unanimous in considering Choufleur's son, Eng. Ch. Chieveley Cheeky Boy, to be the best. From pictures of Cheeky Boy, we may judge his length of foreface, body type and wealth of coat to be quite up to our modern concepts. He was by the small Choufleur out of Desdemona of Monte Christo, a small Standard Poodle of a well-known line. Desdemona was also the dam of Chieveley Gypsy, by Ch. Harcourt Jack. Gypsy was another with an excellent head, cobby body and magnificent coat.

Ch. Chieveley Cheeky Boy died of distemper while he was yet a young dog and left few progeny. However, included was a bitch called Chieveley Charmeuse (who became the dam of the great Eng. and Am. Ch. Chieveley Chopstick) and Eng. Ch. Naughty Boy. It was her admiration of Cheeky Boy that prompted Mrs. Audrey Tyndall, owner of the famous Venda's Kennels, to mate Belinda Bleue to Aide de Camp—both were by Ch. Naughty Boy. The resultant litter justified its breeder's judgment, for it included two of the most famous brood bitches of their time, La Pompadour of Piperscroft and Bonny Forget Me Not.

La Pompadour was the dam of Eng. Ch. Louis of Piperscroft (by Ch. Pronto of Gotton), and of Manon of Piperscroft (by Petit Ami of Piperscroft, who was by Chieveley Chanter ex Ch. Chieveley Chess). Manon was Mrs. Alida Monro's first Poodle. She was the dam of the great foundation sire, Eng. Ch. Barty of Piperscroft, and of Am. Ch. Leader of Piperscroft and Blakeen.

Bonny Forget Me Not went to Mrs. Campbell Inglis' Mannerhead Kennels, where she produced four champions. Bonny bred to Venda's Blue Masterpiece produced Eng. Ch. Flashlight of Mannerhead. Bred to Popinjay (by Eng. Ch. The Monarch), Bonny produced Eng. Ch. Eric Brighteyes. Bonny bred to Eng. Ch. The Monarch produced Dare Devil Dink. Dink bred to Crystal Bell gave Eng. Ch. The Ghost and Am. Ch. Sparkling Jet of Misty Isles. Sparkling Jet, bred to his granddam Bonny Forget Me Not, produced Eng. Ch. The Laird of Mannerhead (sire of three champions) and Eng. Ch. Limelight of Mannerhead.

Shortly after the end of World War I, Miss Morehouse died and her brother, Sir Henry Morehouse, saw fit to disperse the many dogs in her kennel, retaining Chieveley Cheepress (by Chieveley Chopstick) as a pet. Cheepress, when mated to Eng. Ch. Spriggan Bell, produced the famous winner and International Ch. Footit de Madjige. Sir Henry presented two of the Chieveleys to Mrs. Grace Boyd: Chieveley Chatty and Petit Ami of Piperscroft, both out of the tiny Eng. Ch. Chieveley Chess (by Chieveley Chaps ex Eng. Ch. Anita).

The cream of the Chieveley Kennels at its dispersement went to Mr. Charles Price's Marcourt Kennels in Boston, Massachusetts, the most notable being the three Chieveley champions Chopstick, Chess and her son Chump. Chopstick and Chump soon added American championships to their English titles, and were the first two Miniature Poodles to attain this double distinction. Chess was bred again to Chopstick to produce Ch. Marcourt Andre. This was a repeat of the breeding that had produced Chieveley Chatty, who remained in England. Chump was bred to Marcourt Justine (a Chopstick daughter) to produce Ch. Marcourt Petit Pierre. Chump's English son, Jambo, was the sire of Ch. Venda's The Black Imp of Catawba.

Perhaps the most famous of all the Chieveleys was the black Eng. Am. Ch. Chieveley Chopstick. Chopstick was by Chieveley Chaps (by Eng. Ch. Chieveley Choufleur ex Sue) out of Chieveley Charmeuse (by Eng. Ch. Chieveley Cheeky Boy ex Chieveley Charlotte). Chopstick was the sire of four champions: Eng. Ch. Caddy of Wymering, Ch. Marcourt Andre, Ch. Marcourt Sabot (dam of four champions at Sherwood Hall) and Ch. Marcourt Julia (dam of Sherwood Hall's Ch. Marcourt Tricot, sire of five champions). Chopstick's son, Tinker of Marcourt, sired Cartlane Augustin, the sire of five champions. In the Venda's Kennel, in the Wymering Kennels, in the Harpendale Kennels, in the Piperscroft Kennels, and elsewhere in England, bitches by Chopstick were treasured and bred from to produce notable Poodles.

Although most of the Chieveleys were black, there were occasional browns due to the influence of the brown Sue, who was from small brown French stock. Bred to Ch. Chieveley Choufleur, Sue produced Chieveley Peggy (dam of Eng. Ch. Naughty Boy) and Chieveley Chaps. Chaps was the sire of Am. Eng. Ch. Chieveley Chopstick and Eng. Ch. Chieveley Chess. Chess was the dam of Am. Eng. Ch. Chieveley Chump and Petit Ami of Piperscroft (by Chieveley Chanter, a double grandson of Choufleur). Petit Ami proved of tremendous worth to the Piperscroft Kennel, and through his son, Petit Morceau of Piperscroft, of equal value to the Venda's line. Chess bred to Ch. Chieveley Chopstick produced Am. Ch. Marcourt Andre and the 12-inch Chieveley Chatty, whose daughter was to found the world-famous Firebraves of Alida Monro in 1938.

Mrs. Monro was a great admirer of the Chieveleys and her Firebrave Kennel contained the strongest concentration of these bloodlines to be found anywhere. Chieveley Chatty bred to Francois of Piperscroft produced Firebrave Mam'selle. Mam'selle was bred to Firebrave Copperfield to produce the Eng. Ch. Firebrave Nicolette, dam of four champions. Nicolette bred to Firebrave Alphonse produced Eng. Am. Can. Ch. Firebrave Pimpernel (sire of six champions). Nicolette bred to Firebrave Patapan (by Eng. Ch. Firebrave Gaulois ex Firebrave Mam'selle) produced Eng. Ch. Firebrave Olympia, Eng. Ch. Firebrave Marie, Eng. Am. Ch. Firebrave Sanka of Montfleuri (sire of seven champions) and Firebrave Spiro of Braebeck (sire of seven champions). Mam'selle bred to her grandson Eng. Ch. Firebrave Gaulois produced Firebrave Patapan (sire of six champions). Mam'selle bred to another grandson, Ch. Firebrave Pimpernel, produced Eng. Am. Can. Ch. Pixholme Firebrave Gustav, C.D. (sire of 23 champions). As can be seen by the foregoing Mrs. Monro carefully interwove and concentrated her precious Chieveley blood through Mam'selle and Nicolette.

In the nineteen years (1905 to 1924) of the Chieveley Kennels, Miss Morehouse set out to create a uniform type of Poodle which appealed to her and to a large measure she succeeded. As a rule the Chieveleys had beautiful, short bodies, were straight backed and round ribbed with high set tails. The feet were high arched and tight-toed. At their best the heads were refined but did not have the length of head and muzzles (nor length of back) that the Monarch line had. There was a tendency to skulls that were too thick with short forefaces and eyes sometimes too round and too light. Some lacked shoulder and rear angulation. The Chieveleys at their best were lovely typey Poodles who could be counted on for color and size and they won in the best competition. They were predominantly black with a few browns. They tended to the smaller size and were particularly useful in breeding to large Miniature bitches who in the early days had small Standard blood close behind them—often with excellent results. This same small size factor was later used at Firebrave and elsewhere in creating the black English Toy. The short bodied, compact Chieveley type then, as

Ch. Venda's The Black Imp of Catawba

Ch. Blakeen Eldorado

Ch. Highland Sand George

Ch. Magic Fate of Blakeen

Petit Ami of Piperscroft

Ch. Highland Sand Magic Star

128

ENG. CH. CHIEVELEY CHOUFLEUR

Eng. Ch. Chieveley Cheeky Boy (*blk*)
Chieveley Chaps (*blk*) 2
    Eng. Am. Ch. Chieveley Chopstick (*blk*) 4
        Tinker of Marcourt (*blk*)
            Cartlane Augustin (*blk*) 5
Chieveley Challenger (*blk*)
    Chieveley Chanter (*blk*)
        Eng. Am. Ch. Chieveley Chump (*blk*)
            Jambo (*blk*) 1
                Ch. Venda's The Black Imp of Catawba (*blk*) 8
                    Ch. Blakeen Eldorado (*brn*) 7
                        Ch. Diablotin Demi-Setier (*blk*) 5
                    Ch. Blakeen Bitzie Boy (*blk*) 5
                    Blakeen Chieveley (*blk*) 5
                    Ch. Black Magic (*blk*) 2
                        Am. Can. Ch. Magic Fate of Blakeen (*blk*) 13
                            Am. Can. Ch. Highland Sand Magic Star (*blk*) 23
                              Ch. Highland Sand George (*blk*) 17
                              Ch. Highland Sand Star Baby (*blk*) 6
                    Bric A Brac Barker (*blk*) 5
                      Ch. Bric A Brac Best Man (*blk*) 5
                        Hollycourt Excalibur II (*blk*) 5
             Petit Ami of Piperscroft (*blk*)
                Petit Morceau of Piperscroft (*blk*) 2
                    Vulcan Champagne Muscatte (*blk*)
                      The Chocolate Tin Soldier of Toytown (*brn*) 3
                      The Elfin Boy of Toytown (*blk*) 1
                        Eng. Ch. Toy Boy of Toytown
                      (*See Miniature Chart 9*)

today, was a much needed alternative to the longer headed, leaner Monarch type. The modern day Miniature owes its great improvement to the combination of these two lines and types and the most successful breeders have been those who have appreciated and used the two types as a counterbalance.

ENG. CH. CHIEVELEY CHOUFLEUR

Whelped May 23, 1914   Deceased

Bred and owned by Miss Mary Morehouse
Chieveley Kennels, England

Whippendell Marzipan
Whippendell Mouche (*blu*)
White Pearl
Whippendell Chou (*blk*)
Moufflon Bleu
Whippendell Midinette (*blk*)
Whippendell Toto

ENG. CH. CHIEVELEY CHOUFLEUR—*Black*

Meg's Sambo
Eng. Ch. Harcourt Jack (*blk*)
Jill
Chieveley Bunty (*blk*)
Peter
Harcourt Bijou (*blk*)
Dinah

17

The "Chieveley" Line— Eng. Ch. Chieveley Choufleur

THE KEY DOG in the Chieveley tail male line was Eng. Ch. Chieveley Choufleur who was whelped May 23, 1914. Choufleur was the sire of five champions. Choufleur's most important sons were Eng. Ch. Chieveley Cheeky Boy who died early, Chieveley Chaps and Chieveley Challenger. Chaps was the sire of the famous Eng. Am. Ch. Chieveley Chopstick who was the sire of four champions. Chopstick's son, Tinker of Marcourt, produced Cartlane Augustin who was a stud force in the early days. Chieveley Challenger bred to Chieveley Chatterer (also by Choufleur) produced Chieveley Chanter. Chanter produced two sons, full brothers, which were to be of great importance to the breed—Am. Eng. Ch. Chieveley Chump and Petit Ami of Piperscroft. These were out of Eng. Ch. Chieveley Chess who was a granddaughter of Choufleur.

Before going to America, Chump sired a black dog called Jambo, who was bred to Venda's Maid of Honor to produce Ch. Venda's the Black Imp of Catawba. The Black Imp was a truly great sire. His main contributions were an excellent body type, the good feet of the Chieveley line, and a profuse stiff-textured coat. There were some that were too light in the eye, some that were too heavy-boned, and some could have been finer in the skull but the appearance of these faults and virtues depended to a degree on the bitches to which he was bred. There is no doubt that he was a great sire, and his appearance on the American scene was well-timed.

The Black Imp sired eight champions including Ch. Blakeen Eldorado. Eldorado was probably the greatest brown Miniature in America up to his time, and he had a sensational career with seven Bests in Show to his credit. Eldorado in turn sired Ch. Diablotin Demi-Setier who sired five champions.

The Black Imp also sired Ch. Blakeen Bitzie Boy (sire of five champions) and Sherwood Hall's Blakeen Chieveley (sire of five champions). Another Black Imp son, Ch. Black Magic, was bred to Bric A Brac Ballerina, to produce the great winner, Am. Can. Ch. Magic Fate of Blakeen, who won 25 Bests in Show. Magic Fate went to Ernie Ferguson's Estid Kennels in California where he made his record in the ring and at stud and produced 13 champions. Magic Fate was the sire of another top winner (11 Bests in Show) and producer, Am. Can. Ch. Highland Sand Magic Star. Magic Star was the sire of Ch. Highland Sand George who was a notable winner in the Mid-West with five Bests in Show to his credit. George sired 17 champions. Another Magic Star son, Beaujeu Kennels' Ch. Highland Sand Star Baby, was the sire of six champions. Ch. Black Magic's son, the non-titled Bric A Brac Barker, was the sire of five champions, including Ch. Bric A Brac Best Man (sire of five champions). Best Man's son, Hollycourt Excalibur II, also sired five champions.

Eng. Ch. Toy Boy of Toytown

A full brother of Ch. Chieveley Chump, Petit Ami of Piperscroft remained in England to perform great service to the breed. His daughter, Manon of Piperscroft, produced three important sires: the great Eng. Ch. Barty of Piperscroft, Am. Eng. Ch. Leader of Piperscroft and Blakeen, and also Firebrave Cupidon. Petit Ami also sired the champion producer Petit Morceau of Piperscroft who in turn produced Vulcan Champagne Muscatte. Muscatte sired The Chocolate Tin Soldier of Toytown (three champion get), who sired The Elfin Boy of Toytown. The Elfin Boy sired the famous Eng. Ch. Toy Boy of Toytown.

Toy Boy was whelped September 2, 1941. Toy Boy, a Best in Show winner, was described as "full of quality from his nicely-proportioned and quality head, dark eyes and thick ears to his well-muscled hindquarters, and thick harsh coat." His owner reportedly refused an offer of 2,000 pounds for him, and this was in the days when the pound was worth a great deal more than it is today. Philippe Howard Price, of the famous Montfleuri Kennels, described Toy Boy as "a small, very smart and ultra-compact little dog with a huge, dense black coat." Toy Boy sired Eng. Ch. Jacqueline Jegu, Eng. Ch. Braeval Bobo and Eng. Ch. Glendoune Dapper. In addition to these, three of Toy Boy's sons and six of his daughters were producers of champions.

The breeding of Eng. Ch. Toy Boy of Toytown to La Poupee of Heatherton produced (in May 1946) Eng. Ch. Braeval Bobo, a dog who was to exert a tremendous influence on the breed. Phyllis Austin-Smith of the Braeval Kennels, one of Britain's most successful breeders, acclaimed Bobo as having "the perfect Poodle head." Bobo sired six champions. Bred to his own double granddaughter, Braeval Burnt Grass, he produced Eng. Am. Can. Ch. Braeval Boomerang who went to the Beaujeu Kennels in Texas where he produced 15 champions, including the Best in Show winning brothers Ch. Beaujeu Royal and

ENG. CH. TOY BOY OF TOYTOWN

Whelped: September 2, 1941   Deceased

Bred by Miss B. Lobban
Owned by Mrs. Sine Fordham, Toytown Kennels, England

Vulcan Champagne Muscatte (*brn*)
The Chocolate Tin Soldier of Toytown (*brn*)
Nunsoe Merry Miss (*blk*)
The Elfin Boy of Toytown (*blk*)
Paul of Toytown (*si*)
Philosell of Toytown (*blk*)
Whippendell Bambinette (*brn*)

ENG. CH. TOY BOY OF TOYTOWN—*Black*

Eng. Ch. Barty of Piperscroft (*blk*)
Robin of Piperscroft (*blk*)
Michelle of Piperscroft (*blk*)
Seething Duchess (*blk*)
Eng. Ch. Barty of Piperscroft (*blk*)
Belinda of Piperscroft (*brn*)
Lola of Piperscroft (*blk*)

Ch. Beaujeu Regal. Regal in turn sired the Best in Show winner Ch. Crikora Commotion (sire of five champions). Bobo bred to Braeval Brighteyes (by Harwee of Mannerhead) produced three important individuals: Eng. Ch. Braeval Bolero, Eng. Ch. Braeval Brioche (dam of five champions) and Braeval Brown Bella (dam of four champions). The Braevals were noted for their showy temperaments, solid bodies, excellent coat texture and good rear movement. Fronts and feet were sometimes a problem. Bolero was a multiple Best in Show winner with 10 Challenge Certificates to his credit. Bolero sired 21 champions including Eng. Ch. Braeval Barty and Eng. Ch. Braeval Brave. Barty sired five daughters who finished in America (all out of Aspen Arraminta—a double granddaughter of Montmartre What-A-Boy). Eng. Ch. Braeval Brave, bred to his half sister Eng. Ch. Braeval Brown Venus (also by Bolero), produced Braeval Bingo. Braeval Bingo bred back into the Braeval line produced four champions including the 13-inch Group winner in the U.S., Ch. Braeval Busker. Busker left behind a son, Eng. Ch. Braeval Bentley, who won 10 Bests in Show. Bentley, whose parents and grandparents were all Braevals, was bred to Bartat Montmartre Lilly-Marlene, who was solidly Montmartre bred but also went back to Eng. Ch. Toy Boy of Toytown.

This breeding produced the next key dog, Eng. Ch. Montmartre Bartat By Jingo, England's Miniature of the Year for 1963 and winner of 14 C.C.'s. Erna Conn of Montmartre Kennels, who had acquired By Jingo from his breeder Mrs. J. W. G. Tompkins, would not part with By Jingo until she felt she had a suitable son as a replacement. She chose Eng. Ch. Montmartre Michel Andre. By Jingo won 52 Groups and seven Bests in Show in the States, and added Canadian and Mexican titles to his laurels. He had a beautiful head, strong rear action and a remarkable disposition, all of which he passed on to his get. By Jingo sired 27 champions, mostly in the United States, but oddly enough two sons sired prior to his departure became his most important contribution to the breed. And just as By Jingo had been a culmination of two of the great kennels of the past, Braeval and Montmartre, from his loins were to emerge two of the most important kennels of the future—Beritas and Lochranza. These two By Jingo sons were Eng. Ch. Beritas Bonaparte and Lochranza Piero. Bonaparte followed his sire as England's Miniature of the Year in 1964 and won 12 C.C.'s. Bonaparte sired 23 champions including Eng. Ch. Beritas Banacheke (sire of the Top Producer Ch. Baretta of Beritas) and Ch. Beritas Ronlyn Danger Man. Danger Man, at Peter Federico's Petwill Kennels in Massachusetts, produced 27 champions including two Top Producers, Ch. Beritas Balboa (Best in Show winner) and Ch. Grancourt's Johnny Hurrah.

Int. Ch. Montmartre Bartat By Jingo's untitled son, Lochranza Piero, was the key sire at the Lochranza Kennels where he produced the lovely headed, upstanding, well bodied and strong reared Eng. Ch. Lochranza Hell For Leather (7 Challenge Certificates). Hell For Leather sired 11 champions. Hell For Leather bred to his double granddaughter, Am. Ch. Lochranza Tamura, prior to her export produced the Top Producer Am. Ch. Loubelle's Hell Fire. Another

Eng. Ch. Braeval Bobo

Eng. Ch. Braeval Bolero

son of Hell For Leather, Lochranza Moccasins, produced the brown Ch. Lochranza Rumbaba who became a Top Producer through his stud work at Beaujeu and Daktari-Apogee Kennels in the States. Eng. Ch. Lochranza Hell For Leather bred to his half sister, Eng. Ch. Lochranza Desdemona (also by Piero) produced Ch. Lochranza Hell's Fire who, after finishing his English title, went to Australia where he won 27 Bests in Show including the 1975 Sydney Show over 3800 entries. Hell's Fire sired 32 champions, including Eng. Am. Ch. Tiopepi Typhoon. Typhoon won 12 C.C.'s and was England's Top Miniature for 1976. Typhoon came to the U.S. for a limited time for showing and stud work. He finished here and was a Group winner as well. He returned to England where he continued to win C.C.'s although no longer young and produced more champions. Typhoon's son, Ch. Tiopepi Tornado, came to the Round Table Kennels in the U.S. where he gained his title and became a Top Producer.

Eng. Ch. Toy Boy of Toytown produced another son equally as important as Eng. Ch. Braeval Bobo, already discussed. This was Eng. Ch. Glendoune Dapper. These two males have laid the foundation for the modern Miniature Poodle in England. Bred to his granddaughter, Braeval Brown Bella, Eng. Ch. Toy Boy of Toytown produced Eng. Ch. Glendoune Dapper. Dapper bred back to his dam, Brown Bella, produced Eng. Ch. Glendoune Dazzle, Eng. Ch. Glendoune Dinah and Am. Ch. Glendoune Brunetta. Dapper produced a total of six champions. Dapper's son, Faskine Velutina, sired Faskine Talpatina. Talpatina was a Best in Show winner with two Challenge Certificates. Talpatina bred to Eng. Ch. Braveal Betta (a granddaughter of Ch. Braeval Bobo and Ch. Toy Boy of Toytown) gave the Best in Show winner in England, Montmartre What-A-Boy. What-A-Boy was used extensively at Montmartre before coming to the Dunwalke Kennels in America. He sired 16 champions—seven of them out of Dunwalke's Ch. Fontclair Festoon. This was a prime example of the wisdom of combining the Chieveley-Monarch lines.

In the United States What-A-Boy bred to his daughter, Ch. Montmartre

Eng. Ch. Beritas Bonaparte

Am. Eng. Ch. Braeval Boomerang

Ch. Beritas Ronlyn Danger Man

Eng. Ch. Braeval Barty

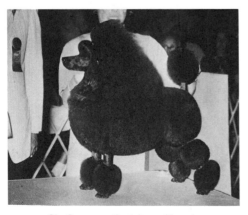

Ch. Grancourt's Johnny Hurrah

Aus. Eng. Ch. Lochranza Hell's Fire

ENG. CH. TOY BOY OF TOYTOWN

Eng. Ch. Toy Boy of Toytown (*blk*) 3
   Eng. Ch. Braeval Bobo (*blk*) 6
      Int. Ch. Braeval Boomerang (*blk*) 15
         Ch. Beaujeu Regal (*blk*) 7
            Ch. Crikora Commotion (*blk*) 5
      Eng. Ch. Braeval Bolero (*blk*) 21
        Eng. Ch. Braeval Barty (*blk*) 5
        Eng. Ch. Braeval Brave (*blk*)
           Braeval Bingo (*blk*) 4
              Ch. Braeval Busker (*blk*) 6
                Eng. Ch. Braeval Bentley (*blk*)
                   Eng. Am. Ch. Montmartre Bartat By Jingo (*blk*) 27
                   Eng. Ch. Beritas Bonaparte (*blk*) 23
                     Eng. Ch. Beritas Banacheke (*blk*)
                       Ch. Baretta of Beritas (*blk*) 8
                   Ch. Beritas Ronlyn Danger Man (*blk*) 27
                     Ch. Beritas Balboa (*blk*) 5
                     Ch. Grancourt Johnny Hurrah (*blk*) 8
                 Beritas Texet Tycoon (*blk*)
                   Beritas Beware (*blk*)
                     Am. Eng. Ch. Tranchant Statesman (*blk*) 9
                       Villa Russe Best Man (*blk*) 11
             Lochranza Piero (*blk*) 3
               Eng. Ch. Lochranza Hell For Leather (*blk*) 11
                 Ch. Loubelle's Hell Fire (*blk*) 12
               Eng. Aus. Ch. Lochranza Hell's Fire (*blk*) 32
                 Eng. Am. Ch. Tiopepi Typhoon (*blk*) 17
                   Ch. Tiopepi Tornado (*blk*) 10
               Lochranza Moccasins (*blk*) 2
                 Ch. Lochranza Rumbaba (*brn*) 8
               Eng. Ch. Aesthete Hot As Blazes (*blk*) 8
  Eng. Ch. Glendoune Dapper (*blk*) 6
    Faskine Velutina (*blk*)
      Faskine Talpatina (*blk*) 1
        Montmartre What-A-Boy (*blk*) 16
          Ch. Dunwalke Marcellus (*blk*) 32
           Eng. Ch. Montmartre Marksman (*blk*) 8
             Eng. Ch. Montmartre Marco Polo (*blk*) 23
               Eng. Ch. Tranchant Montmartre Best Man (*blk*) 4
                 Eng. Ch. Tranchant Philismar Pablo (*blk*) 6
                   Eng. Am. Ch. Foreman of Tranchant (*blk*) 6
                     Eng. Am. Ch. Tranchant Mantoman (*blk*) 9
             Eng. Ch. Beritas Bosun (*blk*) 10
               Eng. Ch. Beritas Ronlyn Rockafella (*blk*) 15
                 Eng. Ch. Gosmore Beritas Talked About (*blk*) 8
                 Ch. Bentwater Beritas Shiloh (*blk*) 8
               Ch. Bentwater Aztec (*blk*) 11
           Aus. Ch. Montmartre Mighty Tiny (*blk*) Eng. Toy 1
          Montmartre Louis Miguel (*brn*) Eng. Toy 2
             Eng. Ch. Montmartre Mastersinger (*blk*) Eng. Toy 3
               Montmartre Ring-Master (*blk*) Eng. Toy 5
                 Montmartre Minute Man (*blk*) Eng. Toy 2

Marcella, produced Ch. Dunwalke Marcellus, who sired 32 champions. Marcellus' son, Ch. Highlane Hocus Pocus, sired the Top Producer Ch. Honey Hill's Royal Rogue. What-A-Boy left in England a Best in Show son, Eng. Ch. Montmartre Marksman. Marksman, bred to a litter sister of his sire, Eng. Ch. Montmartre Little Mo, produced Eng. Ch. Montmartre Marco Polo, who was the sire of 23 champions. At Montmartre, Erna Conn considered Marco Polo the best Poodle she ever bred. Marco Polo was elegant with a refined head, black almond eyes, a straight front with beautiful feet and a great showman. Marco Polo's daughter, Eng. Am. Can. Ch. Tranchant Annabelle, was considered one of the great Miniature show bitches. In the U.S. she won 19 Bests in Show at All Breed and Specialty shows. Marco Polo also sired Eng. Ch. Tranchant Montmartre Best Man (four champion get), whose son Eng. Ch. Tranchant Philismar Pablo produced seven champions. Pablo's son, Eng. Am. Ch. Foreman of Tranchant, and his son Eng. Am. Ch. Tranchant Mantoman are both Top Producers.

Eng. Ch. Montmartre Marco Polo also sired the influential Eng. Ch. Beritas Bosun who produced 10 champions. Bosun's son Eng. Ch. Beritas Ronlyn Rockafella won 16 C.C.'s under 16 different judges. Prior to coming to the U.S. Rockafella sired the Top Producers Eng. Ch. Gosmore Talked About and Ch. Bentwater Beritas Shiloh. Shiloh finished in the U.S. as did his imported son, Ch. Bentwater Aztec, who sired 11 champions.

Starting with Montmartre What-A-Boy and passing father to son to Ch. Bentwater Aztec there are seven consecutive generations of all black males and all are Top Producers (sire of five or more champions). This is the strongest black bred Miniature line in the world. There have been innumerable crosses back and forth with the Monarch line but always the return to the Chieveley heritage. The present day specimens whose success has been outlined attest to the quality inherent in this line and represent many, many crosses to the Chieveley line other than just through the male tail line. Alida Monro's Firebraves, Phyllis Austin Smith's Braevals, Erna Conn's Montmartres, Rita Gee's Beritas, Trudy Edge's Tranchants and Sheila MacKenzie-Spencer's Aspens—all British kennels are rich in Chieveley breeding, however distant at the point in time, and have rewarded their breeders for their faith in this great family line.

And the influence is not limited just to the Miniature variety; Montmartre What-A-Boy, who was only 13½ inches tall, possessed a small gene. His Toy-sized daughter, Eng. Ch. Montmartre Miss Muffet, was the dam of three Toy champions. What-A-Boy also heads an English tail male Toy line. One of his sons, Eng. Ch. Montmartre Marksman (mentioned above) sired the Toy Aus. Ch. Montmartre Mighty Tiny. His Toy sized brown son, Montmartre Louis Miguel, sired the black Toy Eng. Ch. Montmartre Mastersinger. Mastersinger sired three Toy champions and the non-titled black Montmartre Ring Master who sired five champions including the multiple champion producing Montmartre Minute Man. Through him the lines influence continued, spread through a number of English and American Toy champions.

ENG. AM. CAN. MEX.
CH. MONTMARTRE BARTAT BY JINGO

Whelped November 27, 1960   Died January 14, 1976

Bred by Mrs. J. W. G. Tomkin, England
Later owned and shown by Mrs. Erna Conn, Montmartre, England
Last Owner: Mrs. Robert Tranchin, Beaujeu Poodles

Braeval Bingo (*blk*)
Ch. Braeval Busker (*blk*)
Braeval Bright Show (*blk*)
Eng. Ch. Braeval Bentley (*blk*)
Braeval Bingo (*blk*)
Braeval Boleyn (*blk*)
Braeval Best Bet (*blk*)

ENG. AM. CAN. MEX. CH. MONTMARTRE BARTAT BY JINGO—*Black*

Montmartre What-A-Boy (*blk*)
Eng. Ch. Montmartre Marksman (*blk*)
Montmartre Monica (*blk*)
Bartat Montmartre Lilly-Marlene (*blk*)
Montmartre What-A-Boy (*blk*)
Montmartre Black Beauty (*blk*)
Montmartre Beatrice of Innisfail (*blk*)

ENG. CH. LOCHRANZA HELL FOR LEATHER

Whelped May 16, 1969   Deceased

Bred by Mrs. French
Owned by Miss J. MacMillan and Mrs. Gillespie
Lochranza Kennels, England

Eng. Ch. Braeval Bentley (*blk*)
Int. Ch. Montmartre Bartat By Jingo (*blk*)
Montmartre Bartat Lilly-Marlene (*blk*)
Lochranza Piero (*blk*)
Eng. Ch. Montmartre Marksman (*blk*)
Lochranza Mantilla (*blk*)
Lochranza Lucia of Longnor (*blk*)

ENG. CH. LOCHRANZA HELL FOR LEATHER—*Black*

Eng. Ch. Montmartre Marksman (*blk*)
Lochranza Matador (*blk*)
Lochranza Lucia of Longnor (*blk*)
Lochranza Kristina (*blk*)
Eng. Ch. Montmartre Marco Polo (*blk*)
Lochranza Clorinda (*blk*)
Lochranza Antonia (*blk*)

CH. LOUBELLE'S HELL FIRE

Whelped: September 30, 1977

Bred by M. MacMillan and J. Gillespie
Owned by Louis Goldman and Diane Flanagan

<pre>
                    Int. Ch. Montmartre Bartat By Jingo (blk)
          Lochranza Piero (blk)
                    Lochranza Mantilla (blk)
   Eng. Ch. Lochranza Hell For Leather (blk)
                    Lochranza Matador (blk)
          Lochranza Kristina (blk)
                    Lochranza Clorinda (blk)

CH. LOUBELLE'S HELL FIRE—Black

                    Eng. Ch. Lochranza Hell For Leather (blk)
          Lochranza Moccasins (blk)
                    Lochranza Fredrika (blk)
   Ch. Lochranza Tamura (blk)
                    Eng. Ch. Lochranza Hell For Leather (blk)
          Lochranza Pandora (blk)
                    Lochranza Prunella (blk)
</pre>

AM. ENG. CH. TIOPEPI TYPHOON

Whelped: December 19, 1973

Bred and owned by Clare Coxall
Tiopepi Kennels, England

Lochranza Piero (*blk*)
Eng. Ch. Lochranza Hell For Leather (*blk*)
Lochranza Kristina (*blk*)
Eng. Aust. Ch. Lochranza Hell's Fire (*blk*)
Lochranza Piero (*blk*)
Eng. Ch. Lochranza Desdemona (*blk*)
Lochranza Ramona (*blk*)

AM. ENG. CH. TIOPEPI TYPHOON—*Black*

Int. Ch. Montmartre Bartat By Jingo (*blk*)
Eng. Ch. Beritas Bonaparte (*blk*)
Eng. Ch. Beritas Holly of Eldonwood (*blk*)
Eng. Ch. Vernlil Angela from Conersk (*blk*)
Eng. Ch. Gay Charmer of Ardian (*blk*)
Katrina from Conersk (*blk*)
Pelsinora Romance (*blk*)

Eng. Ch. Montmartre Marksman

Eng. Ch. Beritas Bosun

Eng. Ch. Montmartre Marco Polo

Eng. Ch. Beritas Ronlyn Rockafella

Ch. Foreman of Tranchant

Ch. Bentwater Aztec

Ch. Fircot L'Ballerine of Maryland

Berinshill Dancing Boy (white Miniature) by Berinshill Polar ex Berinshill Dancing Shoes, bred by Berinshill Kennels.

18

The "Bodo" Line—
Bodo Von Kurpark

THE IMPORTANCE of this line is greater than its size indicates. It has its origins in the white German dog, Bodo Von Kurpark. The foundation dogs were unrelated to either the Monarch or Chieveley lines, although in later generations other lines were added through the bitches brought to it. The line is primarily white, cream and apricot in descent in the tail male line. Bodo Von Kurpark sired Whippendell Perce Neige Deux who in turn sired Whippendell Duvet. Duvet sired Whippendell Petit Eclair who was the sire of Petit Jean of Toytown and of Aureolin of Toytown, an important foundation sire of apricot Miniatures and Toys particularly in England. Petit Jean bred to the silver Storyval Maree of Fircot (sister of the great white Ch. Snow Boy of Fircot) produced the white Berinshill Polar. Polar bred to a granddaughter of Whippendell Petit Eclair produced the silver Am. Ch. Berinshill Tarrywood Silver Glow (Best in Show winner) and Berinshill Dancing Boy.

In England, the 13 inch creamy-white Dancing Boy was a Best in Show winner and won two Challenge Certificates. He was a popular stud, and a number of his sons came to this country and were outstanding winners. These include Ch. Fircot L'Ballerine of Maryland, Ch. Icarus Duke Otto (Best in Show winner and sire of nine champions), Ch. Nikora of Manapouri (Best in Show winner), Ch. Pita of Manapouri and Ch. Berinshill Silver Nickle. Another son, Eng. Ch. Kannishon Venda's White Lancer, remained in England. When Diana Waugh moved to Canada she brought Dancing Boy with her. Upon her return to England she felt Dancing Boy was too old to be put through the six-month quarantine period, so she left him in the care of the Harbridge Kennels in Michigan, where he lived to an advanced age, siring right up to the

Ch. Icarus Duke Otto

Ch. Rothara The Cavalier

Ch. Calvinelle Dandy Gow

Ch. Andechez Tristan

Ch. Timijon's Town Crier

Ch. Light N'Lively Lil Awful Andy

BODO VON KURPARK

Whippendell Perce Neige Deux (*wh*)
  Whippendell Duvet (*apr*)
    Whippendell Petit Eclair (*apr*)
      Petit Jean of Toytown (*apr*)
        Berinshill Polar (*wh*)
          Berinshill Dancing Boy (*crm-wh*) 8
            Rothara the Rake (*wh*)
              Ch. Rothara The Cavalier (*wh*) 5
            Ch. Icarus Duke Otto (*wh*) 9
            Ch. Fircot L'Ballerine of Maryland (*lt. crm*) 2
            Bric A Brac Ballet Master II (*wh*)
              Bric A Brac Bright N Handsome (*wh*)
                Ch. Calvinelle Dandy Gow (*wh*)
                  Calvinelle Fine N Dandy (*wh*)
                    Ch. Timijon's Town Crier (*wh*) 9
            Am. Can. Ch. Calvinelle Jolly Roger (*wh*) 2
              Chelle's Jolly Prince of M (*wh*) 4
              Ch. Snow Prince of P (*wh*)
              Ch. Andechez Tristan (*wh*) 9
                Ch. Light N' Lively Lil Awful Andy (*wh*) 8
      Aureolin of Toytown
      (*See Miniature Chart 11*)

end of his long life. On this side of the Atlantic, he sired Ch. Silhou-Jette's Dancing Shoes and Can. Ch. Tarna's Vanessa.

Dancing Boy's most famous son was Ch. Fircot L'Ballerine of Maryland who finished his title undefeated by any dog of any breed. He won two Specialties and 12 All Breed Best in Shows. He went Best in Show at the famous Morris and Essex Kennel Club Show 1957 and at the 1955 Poodle Club of America Specialty. L'Ballerine sired Ch. Bric A Brac Ballet Star and Am. and Mex. Ch. Hawesdown Blanche Neige. The L'Ballerine influence continues through his sons Bric A Brac Ballet Master II and Am. Can. Ch. Calvinelle Jolly Roger. Ballet Master was the grandsire of the Best in Show winner Ch. Calvinelle Dandy Gow. His son Calvinelle Fine N'Dandy produced the refined, beautiful headed Top Producer Ch. Timijon's Town Crier. Ch. Calvinelle Jolly Roger sired Chelle's Jolly Prince of M who produced four champions including the Top Producer Ch. Andechez Tristan. Tristan sired seven conformation and two O.T. champions including the Specialty Best in Show winner and Top Producer Ch. Light N' Lively Lil Awful Andy. An untitled English son of Dancing Boy, Rothara The Rake, sired Am. and Can. Ch. Rothara The Cavalier who was a Best in Show winner in England and the States. The Cavalier was the sire of five champions. This line has combined well with the descendants of Ch. Snow Boy of Fircot, Ch. Summercourt Square Dancer of Fircot and Ch. Round Table Cognac.

147

BODO VON KURPARK LINE

Aureolin of Toytown (*apr*)
   Frenches Lil Goldsmith (*apr*)
      Fircot Sunshine of Zizi Pompom (*apr*)
         Tio Pepe of Greatcoats (*apr*)
            Puckshill Amberglister (*apr*)
               Puckshill Amberbloom (*apr*)
                  Puckshill Ambersunfire (*apr*)
                     Puckshill Ambersunslant (*apr*)
                        Puckshill Ambersunrock (*apr*)
                           Aus. Eng. Ch. Tiopepi Puckshill Amber Nightlife (*apr*) 2
                           Dutch Ch. Tiopepi Red Rebel (*apr*)
                           Tiopepi Red Blaze Away (*apr*) 2
                             Am. Braz. Ch. Tiopepi Trendy (*apr*)
           Puckshill Amberglaze (*apr*)
             Puckshill Ambersuncrush (*apr*) 1
             Puckshill Marmalade of Greatcoats (*apr*)
               Eng. Ch. Rhosbridge Golden Shred (*apr*) T

Aureolin of Toytown

Returning to the apricot (later cream) Whippendell Petit Eclair, he also sired the deep apricot Aureolin of Toytown (whelped September 25, 1941). Interestingly Aureolin's pedigree traces back to Whippendell Abricotinette, born in 1912, the first Poodle to be registered as an apricot. Aureolin was the best and most influential apricot to appear on the scene up to that time. His unusual color attracted much attention and breeders rushed to use him. His greatest influence comes down through Rita Price-Jones' Frenches line in both Miniatures and Toys. Aureolin's son, Frenches Lil Goldsmith, sired Fircot Sunshine of Zizi Pompom and he in turn produced the beautiful Tio Pepe of Greatcoats for Kay Edwards' Greatcoats Kennels. Elaine Dobson of Puckshill bred her best apricot bitch, Puckshill Amberglimmer, to Tio Pepe and produced in one litter: Puckshill Amberglister (a force in apricot Miniatures), Puckshill Amberglaze and the Toy-sized bitch Puckshill Ambersunspeck. These three ladies, Rita Price-Jones, Kay Edwards and Elaine Dobson, were all pioneers and devotees of the apricot color and they continually selected for both type and color.

Passing through several generations, Puckshill Amberglister's great, great grandson Puckshill Ambersunrock sired Eng. Ch. Tiopepi Puckshill Amber Nightlife, who went to Doreian family's Brumina Kennels in Australia where he finished his championship and produced additional champions. Prior to his

148

Eng. Ch. Oakington Puckshill Ambersunblush (Toy)
Best in Show at Crufts, England 1966

Eng. Ch. Rhosbridge
Golden Shred

export, Nightlife produced Dutch Ch. Tiopepi Red Rebel and Tiopepi Amber Tanya who came to Mrs. Gardner Cassatt's Beaufresne Kennels where she won 15 Bests in Show and was the top winning Miniature for 1977 and 1978. Red Rebel's son, Tiopepi Red Blaze Away, sired Tiopepi Barbrella Collette who also came to the States where she finished and produced five champions for Martha Dull and Dorothy Bates. In England, Red Blaze Away bred to Tanya's daughter Tiopepi Amber Glowingly produced the Best in Show winner and champion producer Brazilian and Am. Ch. Tiopepi Trendy.

Puckshill Amberglaze, mentioned above, sired the 13-inch deep apricot Puckshill Ambersuncrush who just hours before being exported to the States was bred to produce a litter which contained the exquisite little showgirl, Eng. Ch. Oakington Puckshill Ambersunblush. After several litters Sunblush was acquired by Clare Coxall's Tiopepi Kennels where she was owner-handled to Best in Show at the 1966 Crufts Dog Show in London. Another son of Puckshill Amberglaze named Puckshill Marmalade of Greatcoats sired Eng. Ch. Rhosbridge Golden Shred who was England's first apricot Toy male champion.

Aureolin greatly influenced apricot Miniatures and Toys in England and later in the United States. Kay Edwards of Greatcoats made extensive use of the Aureolin line in producing her apricot Greatcoats Toy family although they trace back in male tail line to the black Toy, Adam of Evesgarden. In the U.S. Dorothy Gooch and now Bob Fry's Ounce O'Bounce, Vicki Dobbs' Spinnerins, Jean Wallace's Secotas, Peggy Patrick's Entre Nous, Beverley Valerio's Beaujolais and Domenick Nappi's Little Bit apricot Toys all trace back many times to Aureolin, but not in the tail male line of descent.

ENG. CH. THE BLUE BOY

Eng. Ch. The Silver Gnome (*si*)
    Hunningham D'Argent (*si*) 2
        Ch. Platinum of Eathorpe of Blakeen (*si*) 4
    Hunningham Silver (*si*)
        Venda's Arrow of Silver (*si*)
            Venda's Blue Masterpiece (*gr*)
                Eng. Ch. Flashlight of Mannerhead (*gr*)
                    Francois of Mannerhead (*gr*) 2
                        Roadcoach Qui Vive (*si*) 3
                        Ch. Hollycourt Venture (*si*) 5
                            Ch. Hollycourt Mercure (*si*)
                                Ch. Hollycourt Vaillant (*si*) 8
                                    Ch. Hollycourt Talent of Silver (*si*) 10
                                    Ch. Touchstone Silversmith (*si*) 5
                Kirkby Flashback (*gr*)
                    Camlad Silverlight (*si*)
                        Frankie of Hockford (*si*)
                          Freeland's Ecru
                            Freeland's Gunsmoke (*si*)
                              Frankie of Freeland (*si*) 4
                                  Ch. Char-K Touch of Class (*si*) 8
                                      Ch. Manorhill's Classic Touch (*si*) 10
        Bari of Mannerhead
            White Fuzz of Fircot (*wh*)
                Michel of Piperscroft (*wh*)
                      Bubbles of Piperscroft and Blakeen (*wh*) 5
                        Ch. Cricket of the Valley (*wh*)
                          Ch. Round Table Conte Blanc (*wh*) 2
                            Ch. Round Table Cognac (*wh*) 14
                            (*See Miniature Chart 13*)

Eng. Ch. The Silver Gnome

19

The "Blue Boy" Line—
Eng. Ch. The Blue Boy

T HE "BLUE BOY" SIRE LINE, although not directly descended from Eng. Ch. The Monarch, is very closely related. Chic of Watercroft sired Eng. Ch. Angel of Mine (dam of Eng. Ch. The Monarch) and her full brother Eng. Ch. The Blue Boy (whelped October 10, 1922). Blue Boy sired Eng. Ch. The Silver Gnome, who in turn sired Am. Ch. Fee D'Argent of Piperscroft and the silver full brothers Hunningham D'Argent and Hunningham Silver (ex Hunningham Rikki-Tikki, a silver). Hunningham D'Argent was bred to Griz Nez of Eathorpe (by Eng. Ch. Spriggan Bell ex Hunningham Virginia—a full sister to Hunningham D'Argent) to produce Am. Ch. Blue Streak of Eathorpe-Mansard and Am. Ch. Platinum of Eathorpe of Blakeen. Platinum sired Ch. Blakeen Hi Ho Silver, Ch. Blakeen Quicksilver, Ch. Snappy Morn and Hollycourt Kennels' great foundation bitch, Ch. Platina. Hunningham Silver was bred to Ch. Angel of Mine to produce Venda's Arrow of Silver (who later went to Misty Isles). Arrow of Silver was bred to Leila to produce England's great silver foundation sire, Venda's Blue Masterpiece (2 Challenge Certificates, 2 reserve C.C.'s).

Blue Masterpiece bred to the blue Bonny Forget Me Not (dam of four champions) produced Eng. Ch. Flashlight of Mannerhead. Flashlight won 9 C.C.'s. His color was described as being a rich, even, almost Persian-cat blue. Flashlight was bred to Eng. Ch. The Mistress of Mannerhead to produce the gray Francois of Mannerhead, who came to the States. Francois sired Roadcoach Qui Vive (sire of three champions), Ch. Dunwandrin Pepe Le Moko, and Ch. Hollycourt Venture (sire of five champions). Venture in turn was bred to Ch. Hollycourt Aure de Montalais to give Ch. Hollycourt Mercure.

Ch. Platinum of Eathorpe of Blakeen   Venda's Blue Masterpiece

Mercure was bred to Hollycourt Iridium (ex Ch. Platina) to give Ch. Hollycourt Vaillant who was the sire of eight champions including Ch. Hollycourt Talent of Silver (sire of 10 champions) and Am. and Can. Ch. Touchstone Silversmith (sire of five champions).

Eng. Ch. Flashlight of Mannerhead also sired the gray Kirkby Flashback who was the sire of the silver Frankie of Hockford who was imported by Hollycourt Kennels. Frankie sired the silver-beige Freeland's Ecru. Ecru's son, Freeland's Gunsmoke, sired the untitled Frankie of Freeland who produced four champions—all silvers and all sons. Frankie sired the Group winner and Top Producer Ch. Char-K Touch of Class. Touch of Class is the sire of the Top Producer Ch. Manorhill's Classic Touch, a popular sire at Hermscrest Kennels. Classic Touch's son, Manorhill's Keep In Touch, produced Char-K Travelling Man, who produced Ral-Lea's Little Maverick, who produced Ch. Freeland's Falstaff. Touch of Class, Classic Touch and Falstaff are all influential silver Miniature sires.

A third important son of Eng. Ch. Flashlight of Mannerhead was Bari of Mannerhead. Bari sired White Fuzz of Fircot and he in turn produced Michael of Piperscroft whose son, the white Bubbles of Piperscroft of Blakeen, came to the U.S. where he produced five champions and was a vital link in a winning family of whites. Bubbles, bred to a daughter of the great Ch. Snow Boy of Fircot, produced the lovely, sound Ch. Cricket of the Valley who founded Mrs. Alden (Caroline) Keene's famous whites at Round Table Kennels. Cricket's son, Ch. Round Table Cloche de Neige, sired that kennel's first homebred Best in Show winner, Ch. Round Table Conte Blanc, winner of three Best in Shows. Conte, bred to a Square Dancer daughter, sired the noted Ch. Round Table Cognac.

152

CH. CHAR-K TOUCH OF CLASS

Whelped December 6, 1972

Bred and owned by
Kathleen Brown, Char-K Kennels

Freeland's Ecru (*si-beige*)
Freeland's Gunsmoke (*si*)
Ivardon Cicely Neville (*wh*)
Frankie of Freeland (*si*)
Ch. Freeland's Flashlight (*si*)
Freeland's Finesse (*si*)
Ch. Hollycourt Vida de Plata (*si*)

CH. CHAR-K TOUCH OF CLASS—*Silver*

Silcresta Silver Smoke (*si*)
Tophill Silver Glint (*si*)
Montravia Silver Lace (*si*)
Chanteclair Classi Chassis (*si*)
Ch. Brandywine's Beau Brummel (*si*)
Chanteclair Nicolette (*si*)
Frenchie of Ottawa (*gray*)

CH. ROUND TABLE COGNAC

Whelped: December 11, 1961   Died: March 19, 1974

Bred and owned by
Mrs. Alden V. Keene, Round Table Kennel

Ch. Cricket of the Valley (*wh*)
Ch. Round Table Cloche De Neige (*wh*)
Heathermaid of Fircot and Round Table (*wh*)
Ch. Round Table Conte Blanc (*wh*)
Ch. Braebeck Esmond of Round Table (*blk*)
Ch. Round Table Elise (*blk*)
Round Table Bout Noire (*blk*)

CH. ROUND TABLE COGNAC—*White*

Spotlight of Summercourt (*blu*)
Ch. Summercourt Square Dancer of Fircot (*crm*)
Mistress of Pipers Lane (*blk*)
Surrey Dancer of Round Table (*wh*)
Berinshill Bonny Boy (*wh*)
Winelist Surrey Mrs. McThing (*wh*)
Ch. Winelist Angelica (*crm*)

Ch. Round Table Cognac

Even as a puppy Ch. Round Table Cognac had that special something that denotes greatness. Not only was his conformation superb but he had a special cockiness that attracted immediate attention. He won 12 Specialties, 24 Bests in Show All Breed and 80 Group Firsts including Westminster 1966. Cognac was a "laster" with a beautiful clean head and dark eye. He came out of retirement to go Best of Opposite Sex in his variety at the P.C.A. Specialty at 11 years of age.

Although from an outcross breeding, Cognac had the ability to contribute importantly to white Miniatures. He sired 14 champions, and that was only the beginning of his influence. His son, Ch. Round Table Loramar's Yeoman, won 16 Bests in Show. Yeoman's daughter, Ch. Tally Ho Tiffany, was the top breed winner for 1970 with many Bests in Show. She followed this with Group wins at Westminster in 1971 and 1972. Another Group winning son of Cognac, Ch. Round Table Brandy Sniff, went to England as a gift to Rita Price-Jones' Frenches Kennels, where he became England's greatest winning white Miniature with 24 C.C.'s to his credit.

Cognac, bred to Ch. Woodland Angel Face, produced Ch. Ralann's Count Monti. Count Monti sired two Top Producing sons—Ch. Ralann's Mr. Smart, an important sire at Manorhill Kennels, and the Best in Show winner Ch. Karelea's What's Happening. What's Happening sired 11 champions including the lovely headed, sound moving Ch. JLC Critique. Critique, a Top Producer, was the top breed winner for 1979 and 1980. He won the Group at Westminster in 1979 and again in 1981. Another son of Ch. Karelea's What's Happening, the Top Producer Ch. Ralann's Goodtime Charlie, sired Ch. Woodland That's More Like It—who died at just four years of age, but still sired 13 champions including the Group and Specialty Best in Show winner, Ch. Karelea Master Key of Alcala. Master Key, a Top Producer, sired Ch. Alcala Salutation of Karelea who won the Group at Westminster 1982. Starting with Cognac's win, he and his descendants have fared very well in the hot competition at the Westminster show.

Cognac was in the tradition of, and a continuation of, his great ancestors Ch. Snow Boy of Fircot and Ch. Summercourt Square Dancer of Fircot. His type, showmanship and ring career caught the attention of white Miniature breeders. Cognac and his descendants have made important contributions to his home kennel, Round Table, and at the late Ann Nucelli's Ralanns, Nancy and Douglas Adams' Woodlands, Elaine and Tim Ross' Manorhills, Karen and Philip Leabo's Karelea and Jordan Chamberlain's JLC Kennels. In the 1970's and 1980's these lines are important factors in white Miniatures. Fortunately they appear to be blending well with the Midcrest and Wavir lines from the Pacific Northwest. The Midcrest and Wavir lines, which are strongly linebred to Square Dancer, prove once again how one dog can change the direction in type and quality.

Eng. Am. Ch. Round Table
Brandy Sniff of Frenches

Ch. Karelea's What's Happening

Ch. Ralann's Mr. Smart

Ch. Ralann's Good Time Charlie

Ch. Manorhill's One Smart Son

Ch. Karelea's Master Key of Alcala

156

ENG. CH. THE BLUE BOY (continued)

Ch. Round Table Cognac (*continued*)
    Eng. Am. Ch. Round Table Brandy Sniff of Frenches (*wh*) 6
    Ch. Ralann's Count Monti (*wh*) 2
        Ch. Ralann's Mr. Smart (*wh*) 7
            Ch. Manorhill's Walkin Tall (*wh*)
            Ch. Manorhill's One Smart Son (*wh*) 7
        Ch. Karelea's What's Happening (*wh*) 11
            Ch. Ralann's Goodtime Charlie (*wh*) 5
                Ch. Woodland That's More Like It (*crm*) 13
                    Ch. Karelea Master Key of Alcala (*wh*) 11
            Ch. JLC Critique (*wh*) 6

Ch. JLC Critique

Ch. Gregella Faultless Fanny

Ch. Fontella's Alpine Savory

Ch. Rochambeau's Midnight Genie

158

20

Leading Miniature Dams

THE GREAT producing bitches are relatively unknown, and never receive the recognition given the more popular stud dogs. A noted stud may sire hundreds of offspring during his lifetime, but a bitch—even the most prolific, properly rested between matings—can produce but a limited number of puppies. In the case of Miniatures, it is generally not more than 20 or 25. Because of this limitation, it is unlikely that a bitch will ever approach the production records of the leading sires, although some bitches actually have a much higher percentage of champion offspring.

Whereas the genetic influence of the sire and dam are of approximate equal importance at the time of mating, the dam's role becomes the greater in the development of the puppies. For here her health and maternal instinct become significant. A litter of puppies from a poor "doer" with a nervous temperament will rarely live up to its full potential. Breeders of livestock are well aware of the virtues of vigor and maternal instinct, and females lacking in these qualities are promptly weeded out of a breeding program.

There are few breeds, if any, in which the bitches have to overcome so many handicaps to a show career as in Poodles. The growing of a full show coat on a Poodle takes considerable time and effort, and it is almost impossible to maintain a show coat on a bitch while raising a litter from her. For this reason, maternal duties are usually deferred until after the chance in the show ring. By the time the bitch wins the coveted title she may be well past her peak years as a producer. Studies have shown that the younger bitches have less trouble during gestation, whelp easier and produce larger litters.

Despite all this, it is amazing to learn that the champion Poodle bitch more than holds her own in competition with the vastly greater number of non-champion producers in the breed. In a study of the Miniature bitches that have

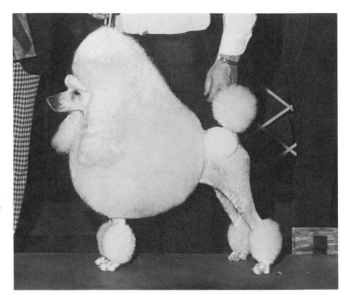

Ch. Wavir Legacy

Hooper's Merry Red Robinette, C.D.X.

Ch. Silverette of Ledahof

been Top Producers (that is producers of three or more champions) it was discovered that of the 240 total, 122—or just over half—were champions.

Many breeders, myself among them, believe that once a fine bitch line is firmly established in a kennel, the battle for successful production of show dogs is more than half won.

Four black bitches tie for top honors in Miniatures as dams of 11 champions and three of these are champions themselves. Ch. Diablotin Star of Elblac (Ch. Diablotin Onyx ex Diablotin Dryad, both Top Producers) accomplished all of her producing records at Dorothy Thompson's Highland Sand Kennels. Ch. Gregella Faultless Fanny (Temar's Attention Please ex Ch. Cutler's Ebony Pansy, both Top Producers) was the dam of 11 champions at Beverley Bellamy's Bell-Aire Kennels. Am. Can. Ch. Rochambeau's Midnight Genie (Can. Ch. Highlane Bonhomme Richard, Top Producer ex Rochambeau's Midnight Fancy) produced six champions at Lorraine Waldron's Cavalier Kennels before moving on to Bonnie and Dean Ramsey's Vanguard Kennels where she produced five more champions. Firethorne Flower Drum Song (Ch. Firethorne Devil's Disciple ex Firethorne Flower Power) was a stellar producer at Esther Hurst's Elissian Kennels.

The leading producing brown bitch Ch. Fontella's Alpine Savory (Ch. Dunwalke Aster ex Ch. Cutler's Ebony Wysteria, both Top Producers) was the dam of seven champions at Aileen Tobias' Sangueree Kennels.

The leading apricot Miniature dam was Hooper's Merry Red Robinette, C.D.X. (Merriwood Red Raider, U.D. ex Harper's Lady Suzette). Robinette was the dam of six champions at Lucille Hooper's Gardencourt Kennels.

Two bitches share top honors as leading silver dams. Ch. Hollycourt Aure de Montalais (Ch. Hollycourt Manicamp ex Frisette de Gris of Blakeen) was the dam of seven champions at Ruelle Kelchner's Hollycourt Kennels. Ch. Silverette of Ledahof (Smilestone's Spinner ex Starlet of Ledahof) was the dam of seven champions at Betty Van Sciver Atkinson's Perrevan Kennels.

The leading producing white Miniature dam was Am. Can. Ch. Wavir Legacy (Ch. Wavir Havoc ex Can. Ch. Wavir Amorous Amy, both Top Producers). Legacy was the dam of nine champions at Virginia and Walter Milroy's Wavir Kennels.

It is interesting to note that of the nine leading bitches above, eight are champions themselves and one has a C.D.X. degree. Most of these Poodle ladies proved their worth in competition before moving on to become outstanding producers.

Ch. Fontclair Festoon (by Eng. Ch. Rudolph of Piperscroft ex Fontclair Fuchsia), English import, owned and campaigned to a great show career by Dunwalke Kennels. Dam of many champions.

Ch. Emmrill Lucky Charm

Ch. Dunwalke Aster

21

Dunwalke Kennels

THE DUNWALKE KENNELS of the late Clarence Dillon were located in the lovely rolling hills near Far Hills, New Jersey. Dunwalke specialized in black Miniature Poodles. The most famous member of this kennel was the beautiful black bitch Ch. Fontclair Festoon, who was Best in Show at the Westminster Kennel Club in 1959.

In establishing the kennel Mr. Dillon selected the best individuals and lines that England had to offer. From Braeval Kennels came Ch. Braeval Baroness (Eng. Am. Ch. Braeval Boomerang ex Hygea Hanora). From Emmrill Kennels came Ch. Emmrill Psyche and Ch. Emmrill Lucky Charm (both ex Emmrill Lindabelle, a full sister of Festoon). From Montmartre Kennels came Eng. and Am. Ch. Montmartre Miranda and her daughter, Ch. Montmartre Marcella. Festoon was acquired as a puppy from Mrs. A. D. Jenkins, who owned her sire, the great Eng. Ch. Rudolph of Piperscroft. Ch. Braeval Baroness produced Ch. Dunwalke Heroine (by New Hat of Montfleuri) and Ch. Challendon Gay Deceiver (by What-A-Boy). Ch. Montmartre Marcella produced Ch. Dunwalke Marstella (by Ch. Beaujeu Regal) and Ch. Dunwalke Marcellus (by her own sire What-A-Boy). Marcellus first went to Challendon and then to Highlane, where he became one of the top sires of the breed with 36 champions to his credit.

To complement this stellar collection of bitches Mr. Dillon required the best male possible. He found his answer in Montmartre What-A-Boy, but What-A-Boy's owner, Mrs. Erna Conn, felt that he was too valuable to her Montmartre Kennel and would not part with him. What-A-Boy was a Best in Show winner in England, and with his litter sister, Eng. Ch. Montmartre Little Mo, founded the Montmartre line. After breeding a number of litters by What-A-Boy, which included Eng. Ch. Montmartre Marksman (sire of seven

163

champions), Mrs. Conn decided he could go to Dunwalke. What-A-Boy made important contributions in England and in the States with 16 champions to his credit.

Anne Rogers Clark described What-A-Boy: "I saw What-A-Boy shown at Windsor in 1956. He was considered a small dog in those days, not quite 14 inches, and I thought at the time he would be difficult to put over in the show ring in this country, because of the size factor. He was a showy, extremely short backed dog, with big ribs, a level topline, and moved quite well, particularly behind. As the years crept up on him, after he came to this country to be used so successfully at stud, his very short back, his great spring of rib, and his addiction to his feed pan, caused him to broaden in front, and move wider than is socially acceptable. He was a brown-eyed dog, pleasing though not extreme in head, good mouth. Not tremendous in length of neck, but bore himself proudly and well so that he was more than adequate in balance, of neck to length of back. A good footed dog, marvelous personality—more a country gentleman type— preferring long, rugged walks and checking the stock to sitting on a silk pillow. His color in later years became a very dark banker's grey. What-A-Boy's greatest successes, of course, were in his matings to Ch. Fontclair Festoon, which resulted in seven champions including two Best in Show winners, Ch. Dunwalke Carnation and Ch. Dunwalke Black Tulip. He invariably produced his good body and sturdy build, amenable temperament, coat quality and texture. He can best be described as the perfect example of what Montmartre strove for in breeding, at least in those days. An honest leg at each corner dog with good body, level topped, and carrying himself proudly. He produced these kind of puppies, and it was a joy to breed a good bitch to him, for the puppies often came out looking like the dam in head type and size, and with What-A-Boy's body, shape and steadiness."

In 1961 Ch. Dunwalke Lorenzo of Montfleuri (by Eng. Ch. Moensfarm Mascot of Montfleuri) joined the Dunwalke stud force. Lorenzo proved to be a most effective sire producing a total of 14 champions. Lorenzo's most successful breeding was to the Best in Show winner, Ch. Emmrill Lucky Charm. Lucky Charm had resulted from a mating Mr. Dillon planned, breeding Festoon's sister back to her sire, Ch. Rudolph of Piperscroft. Charm was bred several times to Lorenzo. This combination was extremely successful, producing Ch. Dunwalke Cadeau of Highlane (five champions), and six months later Ch. Dunwalke Annee of Highlane (three champions). This combination also produced Evening Charm (four champions). Ch. Emmrill Lucky Charm went to Highlane where she produced the leading black Miniature sire Can. Ch. Highlane Bonhomme Richard—sire of 65 champions.

Dunwalke was proud of the great show and producing records set by Ch. Fontclair Festoon. She won 16 Bests in Show including Westminster 1959. Retired from the show ring after her Westminster triumph, she became one of the breed's greatest producing bitches. In her first litter was the Group winner Ch. Dunwalke Tione (by Ch. Ardian Girlie's Son). From her three litters by

Ch. Dunwalke Lorenzo
of Montfleuri

Ch. Dunwalke Marcellus

Ch. Dunwalke Black Tulip,
Best in Show winner.

Ch. Aizbel The Aristocrat shown winning Best in Show at the 1978 Poodle Club of America Show handled by Luis Aizcorbe, Jr.

What-A-Boy came seven champions: Ch. Dunwalke Carnation (Best in Show winner), Ch. Dunwalke Black Tulip (Best in Show winner), Ch. Dunwalke Garland (Group winner), Ch. Dunwalke Primrose, Ch. Dunwalke Daffodil, Ch. Dunwalke Bouquet and Ch. Dunwalke Boutonniere. Festoon's last litter was whelped in 1963 by Ch. Dunwalke Lorenzo of Montfleuri and produced the Group winning bitch Ch. Dunwalke Sweetbrier and her Best in Show brother, Ch. Dunwalke Sweetwilliam. Sweetwilliam was the sire of Ch. Dunwalke Aster and Ch. Surrey Sequoia—both Top Producers.

In 1961, after seeing Festoon's early ability as a producer, it was decided to center all attention on her and her children. Of Festoon's 14 children by three sires, 10 were champions—a remarkable record. Both sons, Sweetwilliam and Boutonniere, produced champions, and five of the daughters have champion descendants.

When the decision was made to disband Dunwalke in 1967, it was Mr. Dillon's wish that all the stock go to Anne and James Edward Clark. As the Clarks keep no stud dogs at Surrey, the males—including Ch. Dunwalke Aster and Ch. Dunwalke Sweetwilliam—went to Richard Bauer, who had also been closely linked to Dunwalke and its aspirations.

Despite its relatively small size, Dunwalke through its imports and breedings, has had a considerable influence on the black American Miniature Poodle.

22

Aizbel Kennels

THE AIZBEL prefix of Luis and Maria Aizcorbe of Miami, Florida has been recognized for top winning and producing black Miniature Poodles for 25 years. As a boy in Cuba, Luis had imported Miniatures as a hobby, but the true beginning of the Aizbel Miniatures as they are known today began with the purchase in 1956 of Int. Ch. Chriscrest Jubilee from Mrs. Christobel Wakefield. Jubilee was not Aizbel's first champion, but she is the basis of the breeding program which they have followed and all the Aizbel champions, without exception, are descended from Jubilee. This line has sustained successive generations of Best in Show winning dogs, each one also a Top Producer, right up to the present. In addition, the Aizbel dogs have been owner-handled to the great majority of their wins.

Jubilee was bred to her Top Producing, Best in Show winning nephew, Ch. Chriscrest The Fiddler, and produced the Group winning Ch. Aizbel Imperial Imp and Ch. Aizbel Collector's Item, one of the all time top winning brown Miniatures. This was the first litter the Aizcorbes bred in the United States after coming here from Cuba in 1959. There were three males, one black and two browns. The black seemed exceptional from the beginning and became Ch. Aizbel Imperial Imp.

Of the two browns, Luis preferred the short backed, good moving, cocky little puppy he called Hector. Everyone else liked the other one. The Aizcorbes had just married and were living in an apartment, so it was decided Hector would go to a pet home. Within the month he was given away not once, but twice, and somehow managed on both occasions to get himself returned to the newlyweds. It was time for the Florida Circuit, so all three dogs were entered. At Palm Beach, Hector defeated both of his brothers and went Winners Dog for two points. At Miami he again placed above both brothers and ended Reserve in a five-point entry. In time he became Ch. Aizbel Collector's Item, and they decided to keep him! Luis Aizcorbe's early confidence in him was later justified by seven Bests in Show, a Specialty, and 30 Group Firsts. In very limited stud use, he became a Top Producer and two of his five champion progeny, Ch. Aizbel The Dauphin de Usher and Ch. Aizbel The One and Only, became multiple Best in Show winners.

One and Only was out of Chriscrest No Trumps, who was from the last Miniature litter bred at Criscrest Kennels. His name, One and Only, denoted the fact that he was the only male puppy in a litter of four. In One and Only we have the original blending of American and English bloodlines which have evolved into the typical Aizbel dog of today, inasmuch as his mother was sired by Tophill Topcard, a grandson of the famous Eng. Ch. Rudolph of Piperscroft. One and Only was winner of three Bests in Show, three Specialties and 20 Group Firsts, but he became best known as the sire of 30 champions, including at least seven Top Producers. In retrospect his most successful breeding at home was to Can. Ch. Escapade's Mistress of Sigma Chi, a bitch with several crosses to Eng. Ch. Rudolph of Piperscroft, who was purchased by the Aizcorbes not only for her many excellent attributes, but also because she complemented One and Only so well. This combination produced the multiple Group and Specialty Best in Show winner, Ch. Aizbel Headstudy In Black, and the Specialty Best in Show winner, Ch. Aizbel All About Angels. This brother-sister team has been an important link in strengthening their family's chain of producers.

Headstudy In Black is the sire of 18 champions to date. All About Angels was the dam of six champions, three of them Top Producers. Three champions resulted from inbreeding these two, all in turn champion producers: Ch. Aizbel The Knockout, an all breed and multiple Specialty Best in Show winner and Best of Variety at the 1975 Westminster Kennel Club Show, has sired 19 champions to date; Ch. Aizbel On Record won several Groups and Specialties for owner Marjorie Gans; and Ch. Aizbel Slick Chick is the dam of Ch. Aizbel Price-Patrick's Cha Cha, who has won several Specialties and numerous Groups.

All About Angels' highly successful breeding to Ch. Campbell's Clansman produced two other Top Producers. Ch. Aizbel The Imperialist sired 13 champions including several Best in Show winners at Barbara Ireland's Danlieri Kennels. His son, Ch. Penchant Paladin, is the current leading Miniature sire in the country. Imperialist's litter sister, Ch. Aizbel Impetuous, a Group winner for Clyde and Arlene McKernan of Seattle, is the dam of seven champions, including Ch. Aizbel The Aristocrat (by her grandsire, One and Only).

Aristocrat has attained a record of two Bests in Show, four Specialty Bests in Show—including the 1978 Poodle Club of America show, and twenty Group firsts. Thirty-four of his offspring have completed their championships to date. Ch. Aizbel The Heir Apparent, an Aristocrat son out of a Headstudy In Black daughter, has already surpassed his sire's show record with three Bests in Show, four Specialty Bests in Show and 26 Group firsts. Eleven of his offspring have

Ch. Aizbel Collector's Item

Ch. Aizbel The One and Only

169

Ch. Aizbel All About Angels

Ch. Aizbel Headstudy In Black

Ch. Aizbel The Heir Apparent

already finished their titles as of this writing. Heir Apparent's full younger brother, Ch. Aizbel The Dignitary, was the Top Winning Miniature Poodle in Canada in 1983 and 1984.

Recognizing that the strength of the Aizbel line rests mainly on its excellent producing males, Luis and Maria Aizcorbe have periodically acquired bitches to bring back to their studs, such as Can. Ch. Escapade's Mistress of Sigma Chi, already mentioned. Karadale Bonne Amie by Can. Ch. Highlane Bonhomme Richard out of Ch. Tophill Thunderbird has produced several champions when bred to One and Only. Ch. Aizbel Sunday Punch, sire of eight champions, is by Headstudy In Black out of Bonne Amie. More recently Alyndee Earth Angel, a Highlane bred bitch also linebred to Bonhomme Richard, became the Top Producing dam of four champions, two of them by Knockout. Ch Vanguard A Bit Okay (by Aristocrat ex Ch. Rochambeau's Midnight Genie) joined the Aizbel clan and has particularly distinguished herself as a producer of five champions to date, four of them sired by her half brother, Heir Apparent. Several others are presently pointed. Karadale Christie Love (Headstudy In Black ex a Bonhomme Richard daughter) has four finished offspring sired by three different Aizbel stud dogs.

Obviously using line-breeding to achieve consistency of type and temperament, the Aizbel line is proof of the success that can be attained by small breeders with limited resources through knowledge, proper planning and hard work.

Ch. Woodland Snow Storm shown going Best of Opposite Sex to his dam Ch. Woodland Snow Fall, C.D., going Best of Variety at 1961 Queensboro K.C. Show handled by Douglas and Nancy Adams.

Ch. Woodland Snow Storm

Ch. Woodland Fair Haired Boy

172

23

Woodland Kennels

WHEN Doug and Nancy Adams bought their first Miniature Poodle in 1955, they thought she was apricot and named her Woodland Golden Flurry. She grew up to be cream, fine boned, short coupled, with good feet. Trained in Obedience, Flurry earned her Companion Dog degree in only three shows. At one of those shows Doug and Nancy saw the white Miniature English import Am. Eng. Ch. Adastra Magic Fame being shown in the breed ring. Impressed with his beautiful head and glorious expression, his sound easy way of going and his many, many wins (53 Bests in Show) they eventually bred Flurry to him and in 1956 had their first litter at Woodland. It contained Ch. Woodland Snowfall, C.D., an adored companion all her long life and the foundation of Woodland Kennels, which has had a widespread influence in white Miniatures.

On reading that linebreeding to the best side of the family was the right course to take, they drove Snowfall to Ohio to be bred to Silhou-Jette's Magic Fame (also by Am. Eng. Ch. Adastra Magic Fame). This litter contained the smallish, short-coupled, beautiful headed Ch. Woodland Snow Storm, who finished owner-handled. Though seldom used at stud, Snow Storm sired seven champions.

Snow Storm's litter sister, Woodland Snow Flurry, was bred to Ch. Tedwin's Top Billing (63 Bests in Show) and produced Woodland Angel. Angel, bred back to her uncle Ch. Woodland Snow Storm, produced the magnificent headed Ch. Woodland Fair Haired Boy. He was the Top Producing sire of 14 champions. Snow Flurry was also bred to Ch. Summercourt Square Dancer of Fircot and produced Woodland Anitra. She, bred to Ch. Woodland Snow Storm, produced the Best in Show winner Ch. Woodland Cassandra. Cassandra bred back into the family to Ch. Ralann's Count Monti (ex Ch.

Woodland Angel Face by Ch. Round Table Cognac) produced Woodland Angelica. Angelica, bred back to Ch. Woodland Fair Haired Boy, produced Ch. Chinquapin's Almost An Angel. She, bred to Ch. Karelea's What's Happening (his sire's dam was Ch. Woodland Angel Face), produced the multiple Best in Show winner and Top Producer, Ch. JLC Critique. Critique won the Group at Westminster in 1979 and again in 1981.

When the original foundation bitch Ch. Woodland Snow Fall was bred to Ch. Summercourt Square Dancer of Fircot in 1963 she produced two of Woodland's best producing bitches, Ch. Woodland Lovely Light and Ch. Woodland Love Affair. Love Affair produced four champions—two sired by Ch. Woodland Fair Haired Boy and two sired by Ch. Ralann's Mr. Smart. One of the latter, Ch. Woodland Love Lady, went to the Melange Kennels of Maryann and Ed Howarth in New Jersey to become one of their foundation bitches.

Lovely Light was also bred to Fair Haired Boy. One of her non-champion daughters, Ralann's Woodland Beauty, became a Top Producer for the Ralann Kennels of the late Ann Nucelli, as the dam of four Ralann champions including Ch. Ralann's Good Time Charlie (now a Top Producer for the Meixners at the Merri-Sher Kennels in Pennsylvania) and Ch. Ralann's Mr. Smart (who became a Top Producing sire for Dennis McCoy). Mr. Smart is also behind many of the champions at the Manorhill Kennels of Gregory and Elaine Ross in Ohio.

Another Lovely Light daughter was the gorgeous cream bitch, Ch. Woodland Prize Possession, whelped December 20, 1967. Prize Possession was breeder-owner handled throughout her show career. She had many Group placements, four Group Firsts and a Specialty Best of Breed. In 1973 she became the first breeder-owner handled Miniature Poodle in the history of the breed to win Best of Variety at Westminster (from an entry of 21 champions) and the only amateur-handled Miniature to place in the Non-Sporting Group there.

Prize Possession represented everything Woodland had hoped to produce —a head of remarkable beauty, tight oval feet, fine bones and straight legs. She had an easy, floating, truly sound gait and an elegant ring presence, with a most affectionate disposition. Prize Possession became the focal point of all of Woodland's future breeding program. She had six champion children, three of whom became Top Producers.

Her son, Ch. Woodland That's More Like It, who tragically lived only four years, nevertheless sired 13 champions, the first and most notable of which is Karen and Philip Leabo's Ch. Karelea's Master Key of Alcala, also a Top Producer.

One of Prize Possession's daughters, Ch. Woodland Priceless, is the Top Producing dam of an all-champion litter of four by Ch. Wavir McBray. Another of Prize Possession's daughters, Ch. Woodland Impossible Dream, is the dam of five champions, one of which is Ch. Woodland This Is It, who was exported to

Sweden to become a Nordic (as well as an American) champion and the sire of several champions in Scandinavia.

Woodland has also had a great deal to do with the tremendous improvement which has taken place in apricot Miniatures through the impact made by their well-known apricot stud dog, Ch. Woodland Burning Bright. With 15 champion get, he was for many years the Top Producing apricot Poodle, all varieties, until his record was exceeded in 1984 by his grandson, Ch. Lyca Dime Store Novel, the top Miniature sire for 1983.

In thirty years of hard work, Woodland achieved their goals by linebreeding and culling, going out to breed to unrelated dogs only occasionally and then returning to linebreeding. The result has been nearly 40 Woodland champions, some of them Group and Best in Show winners. Four of their stud dogs have become Top Producers, siring a total of 50 champions among them, and six bitches are Top Producers with three to six champions each.

Ch. Woodland Prize Possession

Ch. Woodland That's More Like It

24

Miniature Kennels of the Past

ADASTRA—Mr. & Mrs. L. H. C. Coventon (Great Britain)
BEAUJEU—Marjorie Tranchin (*Also Toys*)
BLAKEEN—Hayes Blake Hoyt (*Also Standards, Toys*)
BRAEVAL—Phyllis Austin-Smith (Great Britain)
CARLICLAN—Dallas Carley
CAPPOQUIN—Mary Griffin (*Also Toys*)
CARTLANE—Miriam Hall (*Also Standards, Toys*)
CHALLENDON—Tom & Ann Stevenson (*Also Toys*)
CHRISCREST—Christobel Wakefield
CUTLER'S—Nancy Cutler (*Also Toys*)
DIABLOTIN—Mrs. I. Stowell Morse
DUNWALKE—Clarence Dillon
ESTID—Ernest E. Ferguson (*Also Standards*)
FIRCOT—Elsie Thomas (Great Britain)
FIREBRAVE—Alida Monro (Great Britain) *Also Toys*
FIRETHORNE—Cynthia Fontneau
GREGELLA—Pat Hancock
HIGHLAND SAND—Dorothy Thompson (*Also Toys*)
HOLLYCOURT—M. Ruelle Kelchner
MANNERHEAD—Mrs. M. Campbell Inglis (Great Britain)
MEISEN—Hilda Meisenzahl (*Also Toys*)
MIDCREST—Robert Middleton
MISTY ISLES—Alice Lang Rogers (*Also Standards*)
PERREVAN—Betty Van Sciver Atkinson
PIPERSCROFT—Grace E. L. Boyd (Great Britain) *Also Standards*
PLAZA TORO—Mrs. R. E. Dolan

POODANN—Anne Austin
SHERWOOD HALL—Lydia K. Hopkins *(Also Toys)*
TRANCHANT—Trudy Edge (Great Britain)
VENDAS—Audrey Tyndall (Great Britain)

Three famous breeders at the 1954 Richmond, England Championship Show: Mrs. A. D. Jenkins, owner of the Fontclair Kennels, handling her Eng. Ch. Rudolph of Piperscroft; Judge, Philippe Howard Price of Montfleuri Kennels and Phyllis Austin Smith handling her homebred Eng. Ch. Braeval Black Nylons.

25

Present Day
Miniature Kennels

THERE ARE more dedicated Miniature Poodle breeders now than at any point in the history of the breed. This despite the fact that individual Poodle registrations have been down in number for the past two years. This does not indicate a lack of interest or effort on the part of Miniature breeders. Actually the decline is a healthy sign indicating a slowing down in the number of people who were just breeding Miniature puppies as pets. There is nothing to be gained by breeding a poor Miniature bitch today. This shakeout occurred about 15 years ago in Standard Poodles. At about that time Standard breeders gave a great deal of thought before breeding a litter of Standard puppies, resulting in only the best bitches being bred, which in turn has resulted in a definite up-grading in the quality of Standards. Miniature breeders are now following suit to their benefit.

The following is a list of breeders who have made, and are currently making, noteworthy contributions to the Miniature variety:

AIZBEL—Luis & Marie Aizcorbe
ANDECHEZ—Blanche & Rebecca Tansil
APOGEE—Nancy Hafner
ARGOSY—Hilayne Cavanaugh
ASPEN—Sheila MacKenzie-Spencer (Great Britain) *Also Toys*
BAR-KING—Kathleen Poe
BELL-AIRE—Beverly Bellamy
BERITAS—Rita Gee (Great Britain)
BEVANTON—Barbara Furbush
BRIC A BRAC—Ruth B. Sayres

BRAEWYN—Jean Bray
BRIERS—Barbara Herrold
CHAROB—Charles Arnold
CHERWILENE—Irene Geurds
CINBREN—Beva L. Wahl
CLARION—Ann Helgeson (*Also Toys*)
COLLETTE—Dot & Neil Bates (*Also Toys*)
CORNLEACROFT—Dorris Anzalone
DAKTARI—Monroe McIntyre
DESHLER'S—Patricia Deshler
ELISSIAN—Esther Hurst
FONTELLA—Del Dahl, Josephine McCool
FREELANDS—Monique Devine, Mildred Imrie
GARDENCOURT—Lucille Hooper
GAY EL—Gale A. Rivers
GEMWOOD—Beatrice Muggli
HEATHERLY—Beverly Jean Nelson (*Also Toys*)
HERMSCREST—Frances Herms
HIGHLANE—Elaine Crawford
JANDIS—June Moon Spielberg
LANGCROFT—Harold & Marie Langseth
KARELEA—Karen Leabo
LEDAHOF—Joan Dalton
LOCHRANZA—Miss J. MacMillan & Mrs. Gillespie (Great Britain)
LOUBELLE—Louis Goldman, Dianne Flanagan
MANORHILL—Gregory & Elaine Ross
MARAIS—Mrs. Merle Marsh
MONTFLEURI—Nadia & the late Philippe Howard Price (Great Britain)
MONTMARTRE—Erna Conn (*Also Toys*)
PARADE—Nancy Kinowski
PENCHANT—Betsey Leedy
POODHALL—Andrena & Hans Brunotte (*Also Toys*)
PRAVER'S—Roy Prado
PUTTENCOVE—Katherine Putnam (*Also Standards*)
RAVENDUNE—Todd J. Patterson (*Also Standards*)
ROADCOACH—Mary Barrett (*Also Standards*)
ROUND TABLE—Caroline Keene
SURREY—Anne & James Edward Clark
TIOPEPI—Claire Coxall (Great Britain) *Also Toys, Standards*
TOPHILL—Betty Strawson (Great Britain) *Also Toys*
VALCOPY—Dana L. Plonkey (*Also Toys, Standards*)
WAVIR—Virginia & Walt Milroy
WILDWAYS—Dorothy Hageman (*Also Toys*)
WOODLAND—Douglas & Nancy Adams

Ch. Fairview's No Nonsence shown winning First in the Toy Group at the 1985 Westminster Kennel Club under Mrs. Glen Sommers, handled by Dennis McCoy, owned by Joan Hartsock. Nonsence has 12 All Breed and 12 Specialty Bests in Show to her credit. She was the top Poodle, all varieties and the top Toy all breeds for 1984.

The Toy Poodle

Portrait of a child with small white Poodle, German, circa 1620.

26

The Toy Poodle

EARLY HISTORY

The original small white Poodle is perhaps the oldest member of the three Poodle varieties—so old in fact, that his origins are somewhat of a mystery. There are little dogs which look like Poodles represented on monuments at the time of the Emperor Augustus about 30 A.D. Much later, we have evidence of a small white Poodle affectionately looking up at a child in a German painting, circa 1620.

In the early illustrations the small Poodles are captioned "Petit Bouffon" or "Barbet." The small Poodle was used as a "truffle dog" on the Continent and in England. Most were white or white with markings that made them easier to see at night, which was considered the proper time for hunting truffles (a small globular rootless and leafless fungus prized by gourmets). One line of truffle hunters in England is traceable back to its Spanish origins 300 years ago. From paintings these earlier dogs do not seem to have been very tiny, but rather about the size of the smaller Miniatures of today. Their heads were similar to the larger Poodles of their era with broad skulls, round eyes and ear leathers which were short and high set.

One theory on the origin of the very small Toy credits the French with having introduced the Maltese and a very tiny white Cuban dog called the Havanese in order to produce the very tiny size which was so highly desired. There are paintings in the Louvre in Paris showing tiny white Poodles as elegant drawing room pets in the early 1800's where they were great favorites at the French court. The Maltese characteristics are known to be among the most dominant and persistent in dogdom, and the Toy Poodle even today is plagued with the short legs, long bodies, round eyes with pink rims, short wide heads and soft silky coats which resulted from the initial cross. That these specimens were regarded as Toy Poodles at all was due more to the manner in which they were trimmed than their type. A pair of Continental whites, Jimmy von Monbijou and his sister Baby von Monbijou, were imported by the Piperscroft Kennels in England, and laid the foundation for the white Miniature and white Toy there. Small white Continental Poodles were also the foundations for the white Toy Poodle in America.

THE TOY POODLE IN AMERICA

Few realize that whereas almost all American Miniature and Standard Poodles that finished after 1928 were either imports or descended from stock imported after 1928, the original white Toy Poodles in this country had been established here as far back as 1896. Starting with the 1912 AKC Stud Book, Toy Poodle competition was listed separately. The first Toy Poodle champion was recorded in 1910. A year later the International Toy Poodle Club was organized in the Philadelphia area, where monthly meetings, specialty shows and bridge parties were held for many years. Its president was one Thomas W. C. Hartmann, who bred 48 Toy champions and finished 50. In fact, his early whites represent 42% of all the Toys that finished their championships before 1929. He often won the first three places in all classes! Mr. Hartmann died in December 1928. The International Toy Poodle Club went into a decline during the Depression, and as it faded from the scene the Toy Poodle Club of America was organized in 1942 with Mrs. Charles Clark of Muriclar Poodles of San Francisco as president and Daisy Miller of New York as Secretary-Treasurer, dividing its membership equally on each coast.

Writing of her introduction to the white Toy Poodle, Mrs. Clark said: "Memory and records take us as far back as 1917 and the personal acquaintance of two Toy Poodle breeders, now dead, who were breeding true Toys as far back as 1896. These breeders were Mrs. Sinclair of Orkney Kennels and Mrs. Kronholm, who used the prefix Kay's. Both lived in San Francisco. When we visited the Orkney Kennels in 1917, there were some twenty mature Toy Poodles. Several were very tiny, and under five pounds. Ch. Some Boy Boy, whom we saw, weighed three and a quarter pounds. Others, principally bitches, were larger, but none as recollected exceeded the present breed standard of ten inches at the shoulder. It should be remembered that the breed standard at that time only required that a Toy Poodle be under 12 pounds with no stipulation as to height at the shoulder. In the early 1930's we became acquainted with Mrs. Kronholm, who was then an elderly woman in her 80's. She reported that she had bred Toys for fifty years and had never owned a Miniature. The trophies that lined the walls of the homes of these women indicated their success in the show ring.

"Their bloodlines are still in existence today but way, way back in the pedigrees. As a comparison on type in Toy Poodles of the original lines mentioned, the Orkney and Kronholm lines were very tiny, and quite faulty according to modern judgment; the more recent Orsie and Peaster lines had much better conformation and better heads. The eyes on the old lines were much too round."

In the Toy Poodle standard (written by the International Poodle Club and approved by the American Kennel Club) which was published in the first edition of the AKC's official book of breed standards in 1929, qualification was by weight, not height. It specified that a Poodle must be "under 12 pounds" to be considered a Toy. Mrs. Clark, president of the new Toy Poodle Club of America, quickly realized that her small whites could not compete successfully with the larger colored Toys bred down from Miniatures (who were well within the liberal weight allowance), so in an apparent fit of pique she proposed a height limitation of ten inches or less, and it was accepted!

In 1929, Mrs. Lucy Kingsland finished a female named Sasin. Mrs. Bertha Peaster of the La Rex Doll Kennels in Philadelphia, Mrs. Winfield S. Pruden and Mrs. Minnie Lafferty were all early breeders in the East.

Ch. Happy Chappy

An important development in the history of the Toy Poodle was the birth on December 30, 1932 of Ch. Happy Chappy. Happy Chappy was bred by Florence Orsie of Burbank, California. Happy Chappy, who finished his title with a Group win, was a definite improvement on the Toys that had been bred up to that time, and early Toy breeders were quick to recognize and take advantage of his superior quality. Fortunately he proved to be a great sire, and almost all American-bred Toy Poodles trace back to him. Happy Chappy's son, Ch. Beau Beau of Muriclar (bred by Mrs. Charles Clark), carried his valuable lines to Eastern breeders, and he sired six champions.

To Happy Chappy also goes the honor of having sired the first colored Toy champions. Bred to a gray Miniature, Chee Chee of Carlsgate, he produced a litter whelped May 19, 1940 containing Orsie's Chan-Son and Tinker Tim of Carlsgate. Both were silver and both finished their titles. After Tinker Tom won a Group, a protest was sent to the American Kennel Club stating that he was not of pure ancestry since he was from the pure white Toy strain, which some thought did not spring from the same source as the Miniature strain. The registration papers were revoked by the AKC from this first Toy to Miniature breeding and other litters similarly bred.

After a great deal of research, data was presented to the AKC by Col. E. E. Ferguson, which influenced them to accept the colored Toy as purebred. In 1943, the AKC *Gazette* announced that henceforth Toy Poodles would be considered Poodles, and would be judged as a variety of the breed instead of as a separate breed. The breed standard for the first time was the same for all three varieties, the only difference being in size. Up to this time the Toy Poodles were judged mostly by Toy judges, who placed great emphasis on tiny size and compared the Toy Poodle with the other members of the Toy Group. With the new status and the new breed standard, the Toy enthusiasts set about trying to make the Toy Poodle more closely resemble his larger counterparts.

The Poodle breed standard states that the Poodle should be an *"elegant appearing dog, squarely built, well proportioned"* and *"10 inches or under at the withers."* These are the two biggest problems in producing show quality Toys. The quickest way of improving quality was to breed the white Toy males to colored Miniature females, hoping to attain the superior Poodle type and color from the Miniature while retaining the small Toy size. (Breeders felt that breeding a Miniature male to a smaller Toy female might well present a real whelping hazard for the Toy bitch, due to the increase in size coming from the Miniature and the small pelvis of the Toy bitch). From literally thousands of Toy-Miniature crosses, comparatively few small well-balanced Toys resulted. Actually the first generation crossed seemed amazingly successful because the Miniature head and eye and overall quality was dominant, but so were the short Toy legs. All too often it was necessary to grow huge coats on these short-legged Miniatures (who only qualified as Toys because they were under 10 inches due to their short legs) to make them look like balanced Poodles. Some even became big winners, but when the coat was pressed down at the shoulder or cut off, far too few had the overall balance that is so important to the essential elegance of the Poodle. In the second and subsequent generations there were even greater problems with size and color.

The consistent breeding of under-10-inch Toys is still a serious problem, and will probably be for some time to come. There were many Toys resulting from the first generation of the Toy-Miniature cross but the larger genes did not just disappear; they were just waiting for a chance to exert their influence and often represented a hazard to the breeder. When these crossbreds were bred to similar crossbreds (doubling up closely on the Miniature genes), the puppies were often too large for the Toy size dam to whelp normally, resulting in Caesarian sections, and sometimes in the death of the dam or puppies or both.

Several breeders who were greatly disappointed in oversized puppies set on a course of action that would solve the problem once and for all. The plan was very simple—why not breed several generations of all under-10-inch Poodles, discarding everything that went oversize? Surely these would be pure for their small genes and prepotent for their small size. Again Mother Nature asserted herself, for by the third and fourth generation many of the bitches were much too small to be bred at all. Toy breeders have also learned that in breeding Toys it is an almost invariable truth that the bigger the puppy in a litter, the better it is in quality. The larger puppies seem to revert to their Miniature ancestry in size and quality, while the smaller puppies tend to resemble their old-fashioned Toy ancestry. Also, if there is a testicle problem in a litter it seems more apt to affect the smaller males than the larger males.

These problems are recognized by the serious Toy breeders, and they are striving to overcome them. It has been found that the oversized Toy males, even with superior quality, rarely get the chance to exert their potential because many of the females to be bred already have a size problem, and their breeders are hoping to achieve the small size through the selection of a small male. However, the oversized Toy females have proven to be very valuable for breeding. Not only are they usually better in quality than their undersized sisters, and therefore possessing superior type to transmit, but they are also apt to produce larger numbers of puppies in a litter and thus give the breeder a larger choice of selection. The opportunity of selection is the keynote for breed improvement. If the small bitch has only one or two puppies, and faults are present (as they invariably are)—such as a size problem, a color problem, or a bite problem—then the entire litter may be a complete failure. Hopefully, if there are four or more puppies in the litter, there may be at least one or more that have show possibilities. This is where the Standard breeder with litters of ten or more has a far greater opportunity for improving his variety. Even the Miniature breeder with five or six has an easier time, for he can exert more control through selection from one generation to the next.

The Toy breeder has to make every puppy count, so he has to breed much more carefully to try to control the variables. In other Toy breeds, it was learned long ago that an oversized quality bitch that carried a small gene (usually through her sire) bred to a small male (with a Toy background) would produce a good proportion of within-size Toy get.

Color Breeding

Of equal importance to size in the breeding of Toy Poodles is the problem of color. When white Miniatures are bred to white Toys there are no color problems since all the puppies will be white, for white is a recessive. In the breeding of white Toys to colored Miniatures there were many problems for future generations. Usually in the first generation of the Toy-Miniature cross all of the puppies were solid, as the dominant Miniature colored genes succeeded in covering the white recessive genes. However, these hybrids presented special breeding problems. The white genes which were so easily covered in the first generation often reappeared in the second and subsequent generations in the form of white chest marks, white toes, and sometimes out-and-out particolors (basically a white dog with colored spots, sometimes called harlequins).

There are three forms of mismarkings in Poodles, and all are disqualifications: 1. the white spots, mentioned above, on what would otherwise be a solid dog; 2. particolors; and 3. the two-tone (sometimes called "phantoms" or "dobe" markings because the pattern is the same as that of the tan spots on the Doberman Pinscher). This pattern can be brown markings on a black, silver markings on a black, or any number of weird combinations and all wrong. Perhaps the most dangerous form of this is the two-tone silver which quite often will blend so that it is very hard to distinguish. The pattern on all is a simple recessive and is inheritable. The sure sign in a new-born puppy is the light triangle under the tail. As the puppy matures the lighter color develops on the feet and legs, a bar across the chest, and dots over the eyes.

The Toy Poodle has benefited enormously from the introduction of the Miniature bloodlines and type but in the 70's and 80's it became apparent that such crosses were no longer necessary. It was easier to produce lovely refined, short bodied, high on leg Toys by breeding Toys to Toys (or oversize Toys), keeping balance and refinement uppermost in planning matings. It is rare today to find a Toy Poodle champion with even one Miniature parent. The days of the long, low dwarfy Toys have almost disappeared. The lovely in-balance Toys of the 80's are a joy to see and a tribute to the concerted efforts on the part of conscientious Toy Poodle breeders.

Toy breeders have learned through experience that the fastest way is not always the most worthwhile, and they have learned that patience is a most important asset. There is no one line in Toy Poodles that has all of the virtues and none of the faults. If this were true, all the other lines would be discarded in favor of that one. Toy breeders have learned that the safest course to follow is to breed color to color, i.e., black to black or brown, apricot to apricot, silver to silver, and white to white. Certain lines have been established that can be counted on to reproduce their color with a good degree of consistency. These will be the lines to which to adhere. There is no purpose to be served in the further mixing of colors.

Show quality puppies do not appear in every litter. It isn't that easy. But the quality of Toy Poodles has improved through the years, and it is easier to breed good puppies now than it was twenty, or even ten years ago. There are a number of sires and dams which not only have won high honors in the show ring, but also have demonstrated their ability to reproduce quality in their offspring. Two Toy Poodles achieved the highest honors in this country by winning Best in Show at the Westminster Kennel Club. Ch. Wilber White Swan, who won in 1956, was the sire of 38 champion get. Ch. Cappoquin Little Sister, who took top honors in 1961, was the dam of four champions. All Toy Poodle breeders can look to their accomplishments with pride.

27

The "Happy Chappy" Line— Ch. Happy Chappy

DESPITE the hundreds and hundreds of old-fashioned pure white Toy Poodles that had been bred, it was not until the advent of Ch. Happy Chappy that the variety even remotely began to look like a Poodle. Until his presence began to make itself felt, the Toy Poodle seemed more closely akin to the Maltese.

Ch. Happy Chappy appears in the ancestry of virtually all winning Toy Poodles in this country. Bred and owned by Mrs. Florence Orsie of Burbank, California, Ch. Happy Chappy was whelped December 30, 1932.

At the time Toy Poodles were looked down on as little white fluff balls, and were not as popular as today. Ch. Happy Chappy as a show dog and sire helped to dispel this belief. He was a very sound little dog with a longer, leaner, and better head than the white Toys of his time, and he carried a profuse stiff coat of the correct texture. He had an outstanding personality, was a good sport in the ring and a born showman. Because Toy Poodles were comparatively rare then, he did not finish his title until he was five years old in 1937. That same year he also won the Toy Group at San Bernardino, California.

Ch. Happy Chappy made a further name for himself by appearing in several motion pictures, including "My Golden Calf" with Sue Carol and "Gigolo." He also worked with Billie Burke in the Ziegfeld Follies.

In 1943 the AKC announced that henceforth the Toy Poodle would be considered as Poodles and judged as a variety of the breed instead of as a separate breed. This announcement added great impetus to the smaller variety and a few clever breeders realized the advantages of adding Miniature blood for improving type in the Toy variety. Later this was to become the goal of many

CH. HAPPY CHAPPY

Whelped December 30, 1932   Died November 8, 1941

Bred and owned by
Mrs. Florence I. Orsie, Burbank, California

```
                              Prince Toy (wh)
                  Dandy Jim (wh)
                              Gloria Anne (wh)
          Fluffy-Man (wh)
                              Ch. Kibo (wh)
                  Fanny II (wh)
                              Fidget (wh)

CH. HAPPY CHAPPY—White

                              Ch. Madero's Tad Toy (wh)
                  Madero's Fou Fou (wh)
                              Madero's Girlie (wh)
          Nada (wh)
                              Dandy Jim (wh)
                  Madero's Tiddly Winks (wh)
                              Trixie May (wh)
```

breeders—the type and color of the Miniature while holding the size under the 10 inch limit. To Happy Chappy goes the honor of siring the first Toy/Miniature cross to finish, his silver daughter, Ch. Orsie's Chan-Son, who finished in August, 1943. Chan-Son's silver litter brother, Ch. Tinker Tim of Carlsgate, also finished and was the first colored Toy Poodle to win a Group.

Toy Chart 1

Ch. Beau Beau of Muriclar, a son of Ch. Happy Chappy, came to the East Coast, and was a popular sire. His son, Ch. Gremlin (ex a Miniature dam), was the first brown Toy champion and Gremlin's daughter, Ch. Cherin, was the first black Toy champion.

Beau Beau's son, Ch. Pruden's Little Skipper, bred to Beau Beau's daughter, Ch. Leicester's Fidele de Lafferty, produced the great Ch. Leicester's Bonbon on January 3, 1945. Bonbon was 8½ inches, and 4½ pounds of pure old fashioned white Toy breeding, but he represented an enormous stride forward in Toy Poodle history. Bonbon was the first Toy Poodle to win Best of Variety at the Poodle Club of America Show, in 1947, when Toys were first allowed to be shown there. He was never beaten except by his half brother Ch. Leicester's Peaches and Cream. All the more amazing is the fact that Bonbon was only three years old when he died and in his two years at stud produced the amazing total of 12 Toy champions and influenced the breed for all times.

Bonbon's most important son, Ch. Leicester's Bonbon's Swan Song, came from his breedings to Leicester's Alouette (a Miniature), a combination which produced five champions, including three Group winners. Swan Song, an 8⅝ inch, 5¼ pound blue, sired nine champions including Ch. Leicester's Silver Boots, Ch. Leicester's Angelo, and Am. Can. Ch. Wilber White Swan, who made breed history and focused national attention on the Toy Poodle by his Best in Show win at the 1956 Westminster Kennel Club show. White Swan was the sire of 38 champions including: Ch. Plath's White Wilber (sire of six champions), Ch. Wayne Valley Sir Galahad (sire of six champions), Ch. Pixdown Little Bit (sire of eight champions) and Ch. Wayne Valley Prince Valiant, who sired the non-title Top Producer Wayne Valley Skippy. A silver son of White Swan, Ch. Alltrin Adonis of Cartlane sired the Best in Show winner and Top Producer Ch. Shiran Citation (sire of six champions).

Bonbon's Swan Song also sired Ch. Leicester's Silver Boots. Silver Boots had a beautiful long lean head, long neck, well developed body, clear silver harsh coat and well muscled and angulated hindquarters. He was to found the greatest silver Toy family in the history of the variety.

Ch. Leicester's Silver Boots sired the Group winner and Top Producer, Ch. Nizet's Mr. Antoine D'Argent, who had a Best in Show winner and Top Producing son in Int. Ch. De Tetrault Bitzie's Beau. Silver Boots sired the Top Producer, Ch. Leicester's Golden Slippers. Slippers in turn produced the Best in Show winner, Int. Ch. Thornlea Silver Souvenir.

CH. LEICESTER'S BONBON

Whelped January 3, 1945   Died March 25, 1948

Bred and owned by Leicester Harrison

Ch. Happy Chappy (*wh*)
Ch. Beau Beau of Muriclar (*wh*)
Fluffy of Muriclar (*wh*)
Ch. Pruden's Little Skipper (*wh*)
Ch. Mitor of Muriclar (*wh*)
Justine de Muriclar (*wh*)
Dena of Muriclar (*wh*)

CH. LEICESTER'S BONBON—*White*

Ch. Happy Chappy (*wh*)
Ch. Beau Beau of Muriclar (*wh*)
Fluffy of Muriclar (*wh*)
Ch. Leicester's Fidele de Lafferty (*wh*)
Rowdy (*wh*)
Lafferty's Dimples (*wh*)
Lafferty's Dream Girl (*wh*)

AM. CAN. CH. WILBER WHITE SWAN

Whelped December 11, 1951   Died January 21, 1966

Bred and owned by Mrs. Bertha Smith

Ch. Pruden's Little Skipper (*wh*)
Ch. Leicester's Bonbon (*wh*)
Ch. Leicester's Fidele de Lafferty (*wh*)
Ch. Leicester's Bonbon's Swan Song (*blu*)
Ch. Robin Goodfellow (*blu*)
Leicester's Alouette (*blu*)
Minette (*blk*)

AM. CAN. CH. WILBER WHITE SWAN—*White*

Gamin Greenleaf (*si*)
Wil-Ber Valentin (*si*)
Dorem Gaminette (*gr*)
Wil-Ber Victoire (*si*)
Ch. Barrack Hill Bomber (*blk*)
Barrack Hill Truffle (*blk*)
Barrack Hill Mince Ruissaune (*blk*)

Ch. Pixdown Little Bit

Ch. Leicester's Golden Slippers

Ch. Wayne Valley Sir Galahad

Int. Ch. Stortuvans Silver Figaro

Ch. Evan's Lord Happiness Is

Ch. Nilsson of Silcresta

CH. HAPPY CHAPPY LINE

Ch. Beau Beau of Muriclar (*wh*)
   Ch. Pruden's Little Skipper (*wh*) 2
      Ch. Leicester's Bonbon (*wh*) 12
         Ch. Leicester's Bonbon's Swan Song (*blu*) 9
        Ch. Wilber White Swan (*wh*) 38
          Ch. Plath's White Wilber (*wh*) 6
          Ch. Wayne Valley Sir Galahad (*wh*) 6
          Ch. Wayne Valley Prince Valiant (*wh*) 2
            Wayne Valley Skippy (*wh*) 6
          Ch. Pixdown Little Bit (*wh*) 8
          Ch. Alltrin Adonis of Cartlane (*si*) 1
            Ch. Shiran Citation (*si*) 6
        Ch. Leicester's Silver Boots (*si*) 8
          Ch. Nizet's Mr. Antoine D'Argent (*si*) 5
            Ch. DeTetrault's Bitzie's Beau (*blu*) 5
          Ch. Leicester's Golden Slippers (*chpn-si*) 7
            Ch. Thornlea Silver Souvenir (*si*) 35
              Ch. High Heritage Heirloom (*si*) 6
              Jo-Field Silver Heirloom (*si*) 6
            Ch. Silver Sparkle of Sassafras (*si*) 84
              Ch. Silver Sunday of Sassafras (*si*) 9
                Ch. Evan's Lord Happiness Is (*si*) 40
                  Ch. Evan Simple Simon of Farobs (*si*) 5
                  Can. Ch. Evanz Sparkling Scimitar (*si*) 5
              Ch. Sea Spray of Sassafras (*si*) 5
              Ch. Sassafras Starfire (*si*) 5
              Ch. Sassafras The Snowball (*wh*)
                Ch. Snow Imp of Sassafras (*wh*) 6
                  Ch. Snow Crown of Sassafras (*wh*) 5
            Sw. Ch. Silver Selsendy of Sassafras (*si*)
              Sw. Nord. Ch. Stortuvans Silver Yankee Bomb (*si*)
                Int. Ch. Stortuvans Silver Royal Fling (*si*)
                Ch. Stortuvans Silver Future (*si*) 5
                Int. Ch. Stortuvans Silver Figaro (*si*) 9
                Ch. Nilsson of Silcresta (*si*) 7
      Ch. Gran-Ellen Kid Boots (*crm*)
        Ch. Highland Sand Boll Weavil (*wh*)
          DeManfor Cimbia (*wh*)
            Peeples Tamer Lane (*wh*)
              Peeples Constant Comment (*wh*)
              Kendor's Frostie Fiddler (*wh*) 2
                Ch. Hell's A Blazen Kinda Kostly (*wh*) 54
                  Ch. Stonewood's Fancy Piper (*wh*) 7
                  Ch. Hell's A Blazen Fagin's Pride (*wh*) 5
                    Hell's A Blazen Stormennorman (*crm*) 6
                Ch. Silhou-Jette's Snob Appeal (*wh*)
                  Ch. San-Gai's So Appealing of Lynns (*wh*) 6
                Ch. Arundel Some Like It Hot (*wh*) 6

AM. CAN. CH. THORNLEA SILVER SOUVENIR

Whelped April 2, 1956   Died August 4, 1970

Bred and owned by Mrs. George Dow

Ch. Leicester's Bonbon's Swan Song (*blu*)
Ch. Leicester's Silver Boots (*si*)
Leicester's Silver Shoon (*si*)
Ch. Leicester's Golden Slippers (*chpn-si*)
Ch. Leicester's Peaches and Cream (*crm*)
Leicester's Peach Melba (*crm*)
Lafferty's Ma Chere (*wh*)

AM. CAN. CH. THORNLEA SILVER SOUVENIR—*Silver*

Ch. Silver Dynamo de Gladville (*si*)
Sylvideo de Gladville (*si*)
Bonnie Marie de Gladville (*gr*)
Ch. Miss Sylvideo de Gladville (*si*)
Orsie's Son Sa Ses (*gr*)
Susie of Pickwick Manor (*gr*)
Belle of Pickwick Manor (*gr*)

CH. SILVER SPARKLE OF SASSAFRAS

Whelped September 5, 1957   Died August 27, 1970

Bred and owned by Pamela A. P. Ingram
Sassafras Kennels, Topanga, California

Ch. Leicester's Silver Boots (*si*)
Ch. Leicester's Golden Slippers (*chpn-si*)
Leicester's Peach Melba (*crm*)
Am. & Can. Ch. Thornlea Silver Souvenir (*si*)
Sylvideo de Gladville (*si*)
Ch. Miss Sylvideo de Gladville (*si*)
Susie of Pickwick Manor (*gr*)

CH. SILVER SPARKLE OF SASSAFRAS—*Silver*

Sylvideo de Gladville (*si*)
Ch. Bon Chance de Sassafras (*si*)
Sunny Sue de Gladville (*si*)
Ch. The Infanta of Sassafras (*si*)
Quietcorner Gille Gorm (*si*)
Quietcorner Susie Fry (*si*)
Quietcorner Brunette (*brn*)

Souvenir was a combination of the best of the East and West Coast lines and proved to be a very dominant sire. Souvenir had a beautiful head and was well up on his legs with beautiful balance and type. Because Souvenir was one of the first outstanding silver Toy males with an excellent silver bred, Toy bred background, he was widely used on bitches of varying sizes, types, and backgrounds. Even with these obstacles, his puppies were strikingly similar in type. He heads a large winning and producing family. His daughter Ch. Thornlea Silver Dollar was a Top Producer.

Souvenir sired the Best in Show winner, Ch. High Heritage Heirloom. Heirloom sired six champions and the non-titled Top Producer Jo-Field Silver Heirloom (ex a Souvenir daughter).

Souvenir's most famous offspring was Ch. Silver Sparkle of Sassafras, a Best in Show winner, and sire of 84 champions. Sparkle was short, high and refined, all qualities much needed in his day, and thankfully he was capable of passing on his virtues and those of his immediate ancestors. Being color safe was also a plus factor. Silver breeders had been waiting for a force and Souvenir and Sparkle were just what was needed. Sparkle was in even greater demand than his sire and the fact that his home kennel had numerous bitches just right for him was a tremendous help. If anything, breeders grew too complacent with Souvenir and Sparkle—it was so easy, too easy, just send them a good bitch and they did all the rest. In their time and with their help it was probably easier to breed a good silver than any other color. Unfortunately with their passing, although there have been good silvers from time to time, there has been nothing that could match their production abilities. Sparkle's son, Ch. Silver Sunday of Sassafras, produced nine champions including Ch. Evan's Lord Happiness Is, who sired 40 champions. An inbred son of Sparkle, Swedish Ch. Silver Selsendy of Sassafras, went to Sweden where he produced well. His great grandson, Int. Ch. Stortuvans Silver Figaro, returned to America for a short while where he became a Group winner and Top Producer. He then went to Donald Wickens' Silcresta Kennels where he gained his English title and sired more champions.

Ch. Leicester's Silver Boots had a third important son, Ch. Gran-Ellen Kid Boots, a cream. Kid Boots sired Ch. Highland Sand Boll Weavil, who in turn sired DeManfor Cimbia. Cimbia produced Peeples Tamer Lane, the sire of Peeples Constant Comment, the sire of Kendor's Frostie Fiddler. We have passed through a succession of non-champion males who did not gain their titles for one reason or another, but DeManfor, Peeples and Kendor were all show-oriented kennels and not just pet breeders. Fiddler, bred back to his English import granddam, Branslake Floris, produced a major stud force in Ch. Hell's A Blazen Kinda Kostly. Kinda Kostly, a Best in Show winner, heads a large and growing family. Already three of this sons and two of his grandsons are Top Producers.

Swan Song's son, the Best in Show winner Ch. Leicester's Angelo, bred to the cream Ch. Leicester's Little Eva (also by Swan Song) produced the silver

CH. HELL'S A BLAZEN KINDA KOSTLY

Whelped March 22, 1972   Died August 1982

Bred and owned by
Frances Rubinich, Hell's A Blazen Kennels

Peeples Tamer Lane (*wh*)
Peeples Constant Comment (*wh*)
DeManfor Fleur De Lis (*crm*)
Kendor's Frostie Fiddler (*wh*)
Ch. Silhou-Jette's Sugar Twist (*wh*)
Ch. Hell's A Blazen Carnival Joy (*wh*)
Branslake Floris (*wh*)

CH. HELL'S A BLAZEN KINDA KOSTLY—*White*

Eng. Ch. Sudbrook Sunday Best (*wh*)
Barsbrae Tino (*wh*)
Seahorses Baby Cham (*wh*)
Branslake Floris (*wh*) Eng.
Bbormot Billy Boy (*wh*)
Contessa Alicia (*wh*)
Prizette Glandore Marie Elena (*wh*)

Ch. San-Gai's So Appealing of Lynn's

Ch. Arundel Some Like It Hot

Ch. Stonewood's Fancy Piper

Ch. Hell's A Blazen Fagin's Pride

200

Group winner and Top Producer Ch. Renrew's Stardust. Stardust's full brother, Renrew's Fandango, was the sire of the black Ch. Tar Baby of Whitehall who won 45 Group Firsts and 11 Bests in Show.

Ch. Leicester's Bonbon also sired Leicester's Bonny Bit of Nibroc and Ch. Georgian Don. Bonny Bit sired the silver Nibroc The Imp, who in turn sired the blue Ch. Blakeen Candyman. Candyman's son Ch. Challendon Ivy League sired the top winning brown Toy with 85 Best in Shows, Ch. Loramar's I'm A Dandee. I'm A Dandee was the sire of six champions. Ch. Georgian Don sired Ch. Gregoire's David Dumpling who produced five champions.

Toy Chart 2

Ch. Beau Beau of Muriclar was a key dog in early pedigrees. His brown son, Ch. Gremlin (referred to earlier), was bred to Beau Beau's daughter, Ch. Leicester's Fidele de Lafferty (also mentioned earlier as the dam of Ch. Leicester's Bonbon) and produced Ch. Leicester's Peaches and Cream. Peaches sired Ch. Leicester's I'll Take Vanilla (sire of four champions) and the blue Ch. Leicester's Eudoron. Although Eudoron was a monorchid and finished when they could still be shown, his small size and color made him much in demand at stud. He produced nine champions and the Top Producer Fieldstreams Topflight (ex Ch. Fieldstreams French Toast, a Ch. Gremlin daughter). Eudoron and Topflight were effective size reducers.

Another Ch. Gremlin son, Barnell's Tres Joli, a gray, sired Voltaire II, also gray, who sired the black Baron de Gladville. Baron bred to the 10½ inch pure Miniature black, Puttencove Dot, produced two Best in Show winning sons, Ch. Blakeen King Cole and Ch. Blakeen King Doodles. Ch. Blakeen King Doodles was the winner of 50 Bests in Show. He was the sire of 13 champions including Ch. J. C. King Doodles and his full sister Ch. J. C. Doodle's Penny— both Top Producers. Ch. J. C. King Doodles was the sire of 38 champions. The two Doodles, father and son, represented one of the strongest influences in black Toy Poodles in the '50s and '60s.

Ch. J. C. King Doodles produced a Top Producing son in Specialty Best in Show winner Ch. J. C. Readi Teadi, but the male tail line descends through the handsome Ch. J. C. Darktown Strutter to his son Calvinelle Nightwatch. Nightwatch sired the black Ch. Most Happy Fella of Camelot, who sired six champions including the brown Ch. Amberly's Destiny of Camelot. Destiny bred to his blue granddam, Ro Mo Cinderella, produced the white Group winner Ch. Amberly's White Rock of Delnor.

White Rock was the sire of 27 champions including the leading white Toy sire, Ch. Syntifny's Piece of the Rock. Rocky, who was whelped in the spring of 1974, blazed like a comet across the Toy Poodle horizon before he was stolen at six years of age. In his brief five years at stud he sired 86 champions, making him the top Toy Poodle sire of all time. Sixteen of his get are Top Producers, 12 sons and four daughters, so the line is continuing with great strength.

Ch. Blakeen King Doodles

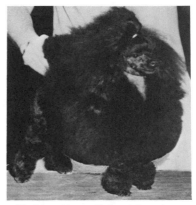

Ch. Most Happy Fella of Camelot

Ch. J. C. King Doodles

Ch. Rae Donas Tiny Teddi Terrific

Ch. J. C. Readi Teadi

Ch. Amberly's Destiny of Camelot

CH. HAPPY CHAPPY LINE

Ch. Beau Beau of Muriclar (*wh*) 6
  Ch. Gremlin (*brn*) 4
    Ch. Leicester's Peaches and Cream (*crm*) 4
      Ch. Leicester's Eudoron (*blu*) 9
        Fieldstreams Topflight (*blk*) 6
  Ski Mo (*gr*) 1
    Ch. Pulaski's Masterpiece (*si*) 5
      Pulaski's Master D.C. (*gr*)
        Ch. Frere Jacques of Crestwood (*si*)
          Betz' Beau Jacques Silverpiece (*si*)
            Betz' Chocolate Bon Bon (*brn*) 5
  Barnell's Tres Joli (*gr*)
    Voltaire II (*gr*)
      Baron de Gladville (*blk*) 2
        Ch. Blakeen King Doodles (*blk*) 13
          Ch. J.C. King Doodles (*blk*) 38
            Ch. J.C. Readi Teadi (*blk*) 5
            Ch. J.C. Darktown Strutter (*blk*)
              Calvinelle Nightwatch (*blk*)
                Ch. Most Happy Fella of Camelot (*blk*) 6
                  Ch. Wissfire Teddi Bear (*blk*)
                    Ch. Raedonas Tiny Teddi Terrific (*blk*) 5
                  Ch. Amberly's Destiny of Camelot (*brn*)
                    Ch. Amberly's White Rock of Delnor (*wh*) 27
                      Ch. Syntifny's Piece of the Rock (*wh*) 86
                        Ch. Syntifny On The Move (*wh*) 38
                          Ch. Darrette's Das Es All (*wh*) 20
                      Ch. Syntifny Snapshot (*wh*) 10
                      Ch. Camelot Rockford Files (*wh*) 12
                        Ch. Camelot Rocky Reflections (*wh*) 6
                      Ch. Bellview's Worth Chat 'N About (*wh*) 7
                      Ch. Jodan's Winter Storm (*wh*) 6
                      Ch. Kornel's Keeper of the Kastle (*wh*) 8
                      Ch. Regence Raised On Rock (*wh*) 5
                      Mari Storm Warning (*wh*) 8
                      Ch. Wilmar Howlene Stone Broke (*wh*) 7
                      Ch. Yerbrier Syntifny Shamu (*wh*) 6
                        Ch. Patrician With A Twist (*wh*) 8
                      Ch. Leecroft Coined Silver (*si*) 5
                    Can. Ch. Camelot Rock A Beatin' Boogie (*wh*) 5

Ch. Amberly's White Rock of Delnor

Ch. Syntifny On The Move

Ch. Camelot Rockford Files

Ch. Darrette's Das Es All

Ch. Camelot Rocky Reflections

Jap. Am. Ch. Kornel's Keeper of the Kastle

204

CH. SYNTIFNY'S PIECE OF THE ROCK

Whelped March 31, 1974   Missing

Bred and owned by
Jane A. Winne, Syntifny Kennels

Ch. Most Happy Fella of Camelot (*blk*)
Ch. Amberly's Destiny of Camelot (*brn*)
Amberly RoMo Sheer Fantasy (*blk*)
Ch. Amberly's White Rock of Delnor (*wh*)
Ch. RoMo Little Prince (*blk*)
RoMo Cinderella (*blu*)
RoMo Lady of the Night (*wh*)

CH. SYNTIFNY'S PIECE OF THE ROCK—*White*

Ch. Snow Crown of Sassafras (*wh*)
Shannon Valley's Frosty O (*wh*)
Dixon's Sassafras Ice Cricket (*wh*)
Ch. Adiona of Aurora (*wh*)
Nomar's Sauci Prinz (*blk*)
Lee's Lil Bit-O-Sno (*wh*)
Bon'lees Lil Bit-O-Licorice (*blk*)

Most Happy Fella also sired the black Ch. Wissfire Teddi Bear who in turn sired the short bodied, high on leg Ch. Raedonas Tiny Teddi Terrific. Teddi is the sire of five champions.

Toy Chart 3

On the West Coast, Ch. Happy Chappy sired Ch. Mitor of Muriclar, who sired Officieux de Muriclar (sire of four champions) and Ch. Petit Magistrate de Muriclar. Petit Magistrate produced two important sons, Homme du Monde de Muriclar who continued the white line, and Aether de Muriclar who heads an important colored branch of the family. Homme du Monde sired the tiny Ch. Le Monde Chic de Larson who produced the popular Andre Boy who sired 10 champions. Andre Boy's Top Producing son Ch. Barnes Edmund was the great grandsire of Ch. Meisen White Mite who produced five champions including Ch. Hilltop Dancing Boy of Faith and Ch. Faith's Fireball of Hilltop. Dancing Boy was the grandsire of Ch. Cutler's Kismet of Hilltop (six champion get) and he in turn was the grandsire of the multiple Best in Show winner Ch. Pamper's All Gusto of Arundel. All Gusto is the sire of 37 champions including two Top Producing sons, Ch. San-Gai's First Impression and Ch. Excalibur Bristol Cream. Ch. Faith's Fireball of Hilltop sired Ch. Durant's Thunderball who was the grandsire of the Top Producer Ch. Durant's Delphinus.

Ch. Petit Magistrate de Muriclar mentioned above was bred to the black Miniature Ch. Blakeen Nyx de Muriclar to produce the black Aether de Muriclar. This was in the early days of breeding colored Miniatures to Toys in the hopes of producing colored Toys. Using a champion Miniature bitch with a Toy sire was rather unusual in those days; not many Miniature bitches of championship quality were used in what was at that time regarded as something of an experiment. In this case the results were pleasing and it was decided to continue on those lines. Aether was bred to the black Mannerhead Belle de Muriclar, a daughter of Ch. Beau Beau of Muriclar out of the small black Miniature English import Highlight of Mannerhead, and this produced an important early day sire, Ch. Eurus de Muriclar, whelped in January 1947.

Eurus, one of the early colored champions, was a combination of the best existing Toy and Miniature lines of his day. He sired two highly influential sons, Ch. Orsie's Mi-Ra-Bi-Le and Orsie's Son Sa Ses. Mi-Ra-Bi-Le, a black, sired five champions. Bred to his own daughter, he sired the prepotent Orsie's Petit Drole, who sired eight champions—all of whom in turn produced champions. One son, Ch. Moissonner O'Millhurst, was the sire of five champions. A Moissonner son, Swanson's Tar Baby, bred to a Moissonner daughter gave Am. Can. Ch. Suchan's Little Black Sheikh. Little Black Sheikh, a Best in Show winner at All Breed and Specialty Shows with 61 Best of Varieties to his credit, was the sire of 15 champions. Sheikh's son, Suchan's Little Napoleon, sired six champions. Another son of Mi-Ra-Bi-Le, Bijoux X, sired two champions including the Best in Show winner Ch. Fieldstreams Bojangles.

CH. HAPPY CHAPPY LINE

Ch. Mitor of Muriclar (*wh*) 4
   Officieux de Muriclar (*wh*) 4
     Ch. Petit Magistrate de Muriclar (*wh*) 1
       Homme du Monde de Muriclar (*wh*) 1
         Int. Ch. Le Monde Chic de Larson (*wh*) 2
           Andre Boy (*wh*) 10
             Ch. Barnes Edmund (*wh*) 5
               Ding Ding de Terrytown (*wh*)
                 Tommy Tucker's Cricket (*wh*)
                   Ch. Meisen White Mite (*crm*) 5
                     Ch. Hilltop Dancing Boy of Faith (*wh*)
                     Hilltop Show See and Tell (*wh*)
                       Ch. Cutler's Kismet of Hilltop (*wh*) 6
                         Ch. Pamper's Happens to Alexa (*wh*)
                           Ch. Pamper's All Gusto of Arundel (*wh*) 37
                             Ch. San-Gai's First Impression (*wh*) 10
                             Ch. Excalibur Bristol Cream (*crm*) 8
                     Ch. Faith's Fireball of Hilltop (*wh*)
                       Ch. Durant's Thunderball (*wh*)
                         Ch. Durant's Bound For The Stars (*wh*)
                           Ch. Durant's Delphinus (*wh*) 6
   Aether de Muriclar (*blk*) 1
     Ch. Eurus de Muriclar (*blk*) 1
       Ch. Orsie's Mi-Ra-Bi-Le (*blk*) 5
         Orsie's Petit Drole (*blk*) 8
           Ch. Moissonner O'Millhurst *(blk)* 5
             Swanson's Tar Baby (*blk*) 1
               Ch. Suchan's Little Black Sheikh (*blk*) 15
               Suchan's Little Napoleon (*brn*) 6
         Bijou X (*blk*) 2
           Ch. Fieldstreams Bojangles (*blk*) 1
             Ch. Fieldstreams Valentine (*blk*) 13
             Ch. Carlima's J.D. (*blk*) 16
               Ch. Tropicstar In The Black (*blk*) 7
               Ch. Tropicstar Do It Up Brown (*brn*) 5
               Ch. Carnival Idle Chatter (*brn*) 4
             Ch. Starfire My Funny Valentine (*blk*) 7
             Ch. Jodan's Dark Star (*blk*) 14
     Orsie's Son Sa Ses (*See Toy Chart 4*)

Ch. Suchan's Little Black Sheikh   Ch. Pamper's All Gusto of Arundel

Ch. Mitor of Muriclar

Ch. Fieldstream's Valentine

Andre Boy

Ch. Carlima's J.D.

Ch. Barnes Edmund

Ch. Tropicstar Do It Up Brown

208

Bojangles bred to Ch. Chaman Grouse, a brown Toy English import, gave the beautiful Ch. Fieldstreams Valentine. Valentine sired 13 champions including the black litter brothers Ch. Carlima's J. D. and Ch. Starfire My Funny Valentine. J. D. had an impressive show career with 38 Group Firsts and 12 Bests in Show, and was the sire of 16 champions. His son Ch. Tropicstar In The Black sired seven champions. Valentine and J. D. were considered by many the best black males to appear on the scene up to that time, just as Ch. Cappoquin Little Sister was considered tops in black bitches.

Toy Chart 4

The small gray Orsie's Son Sa Ses was from Ch. Eurus de Muriclar's breeding to Orsie's Chere-Ami (by Ch. Marmaduke of Meisen ex Ch. Orsie's Chan-Son—two of the earliest colored Toy champions). Although Son Sa Ses was not a champion, he represented a blending of excellent Toy and Miniature lines and he exerted a wide range of influence. Orsie's Son Sa Ses sired the gray Lohn's Petit Fils D'Anatole (sire of five champions) and the black Ch. La Gai Happy Go Lucky. Lucky's son, Bric A Brac Bonney Lad, sired two champions including the group winning Top Producer, Ch. Valzac's Tiny Tim—sire of six champions. On the West Coast the line continued down through Ch. Arsenal Little Punk to his grandson Ch. Boarzell Briser De Coeur who sired six champions including Ch. Poodletown's Little John. Little John was of exceptional quality and his beauty was appreciated. He was a Group winner and was twice Best of Breed at Specialties. At a time when progressive retinal atrophy (P.R.A.) was becoming a concern among Toy breeders, Little John proved to be not a carrier and was much in demand at stud. He sired 18 champions including four Top Producing sons.

Orsie's Son Sa Ses, who was quite small and fine boned, was particularly successful bred to Miniature bitches. His son Ch. Medley's Silver Demon, ex a Miniature, was one of the first Toys to win Best in Show at both Specialty and All Breed shows and promoted a great deal of interest in breeding show quality Toys. Strangely enough, perhaps because of lack of opportunity of suitable bitches, Silver Demon produced only two champions, but his sons were much more successful. One, Ch. Poquito Perro LaNudo, sired six champions. Another son, the gray Panorama Hideho, sired seven champions including the Best in Show winner Triple Int. Ch. Mariman Silver Beau, who had 11 champion get. Silver Beau sired Ch. La Gai Beau's Bitzie Boy and he in turn produced Ch. La Petite Gai Dondi who sired five champions. His sons and grandsons have been dominant forces in silver Toys particularly on the West Coast. Gai Dondi sired the full but not litter brothers Ch. Consentino's Silver Dollar (five champions) and Ch. Consentino's Dandi Dondi—both Best in Show winners. Dandi Dondi produced two Top Producing sons, Ch. Consentino's Dandison and Ch. Consentino's Mario. Mario went to New Jersey where he helped to spread the Consentino silver line on the East Coast. Gai Dondi also

Ch. Suncrest Santana

Ch. Poodletown's Polaris

Ch. Mariman Silver Beau

Ch. Consentino's Dandi Dondi

Ch. Hilltop's Das Es Alles

Ch. Huber's White Sprite of El-Har

210

CH. HAPPY CHAPPY LINE
(Subdivision)

Orsie's Son Sa Ses (*gr*) 7
    Ch. La Gai Happy Go Lucky (*blk*)
        Bric A Brac Bonney Lad (*blk*) 2
            Ch. Valzac's Tiny Tim (*blk*) 6
                Ch. Arsenal Little Punk (*blk*)
                    Pepe Le Moko of Dragon's Lair (*blk*)
                        Ch. Boarzell Briser De Coeur (*blk*) 6
                            Ch. Poodletown's Little John (*blk*) 18
                                Ch. Bo-Car's Black Power (*blk*) 10
                                Ch. Richlawn's L'il Toot O'Manorhill (*blk*) 6
                                Can. Ch. Poodletown's Polaris (*brn*) 8
                                Can. Ch. Sivam's Peter Scott of High Wings (*blk*) 5
                                Ch. Suncrest Santana (*brn*) 4
    Lohn's Petit Fils D'Anatole (*gr*) 5
    Ch. Medley's Silver Demon (*si*) 2
        Ch. Poquito Perro La Nudo (*si*) 6
        Panorama Hideho (*gr*) 7
            Ch. Mariman Silver Beau (*si*) 11
                Ch. La Gai Beau's Bitzie Boy (*si*)
                    Ch. La Petite Gai Dondi (*si*) 5
                        Ch. Consentino's Silver Dollar (*si*) 5
                        Ch. Consentino's Dandi Dondi (*si*) 13
                            Ch. Consentino's Dandison (*si*) 8
                            Ch. Consentino's Mario (*si*) 6
                    Ch. Montoya's La Petite Rafael (*si*)
                      Ch. Montoya's Uncle Albert (*si*) 12
        Blackaboy of Sassafras (*blk*) 8
            Blackabit of Sassafras (*blk*) 16
                Ch. Black Scamp II of Sassafras (*blk*) 5
                    Blackabug of Sassafras (*blk*) 6
                      Ch. Black Baronet of Sassafras (*blk*) 7
                      Black Jockey of Sassafras (*blk*)
                        Ch. Sundown Sassafras Bootblack (*blk*) 46
                Ch. Black Bijou of Sassafras (*blk*)
                Sarsaparilla of Sassafras (*brn*) 8
    Medley Boy de Gladville (*blu*) 2
        Ch. Silver Dynamo de Gladville (*si*) 1
            Sylvideo de Gladville (*si*) 2
                Ch. Bon Chance de Sassafras (*si*) 10
                    Ch. Silver Fleece of Sassafras (*si*) 16
                      Ch. Silver Strike of Sassafras (*si*) 5
                        Can. Ch. Winne's Silver Manolito (*si*) 2
                        Ch. Syntifny Silverdrift (*si*) 9
                Ch. Silver Swank of Sassafras (*si*) 8
                    Ch. DiFrey's Silver Dart of Swank (*si*)
                      Ch. DiFrey's Dazzle of Sassafras (*si*)
                      Hilltop's Prince of Snows (*wh*)
                        Ch. Hilltop's Das Es Alles (*wh*) 5
                            Rosehayven's Tiny Tim (*wh*)
                              Ch. Faith's Gay Whisper of Clardon (*wh*) 5
                      Ch. Hilltop's Lucky Strike (*wh*)
                        El-Har's Majestic Prince (*wh*)
                          Ch. Huber's White Sprite of El-Har (*wh*) 5
                          Ch. Durant's Centaurus (*crm*) 7

211

sired Ch. Montoya's La Petite Rafael whose son Ch. Montoya's Uncle Albert is one of the leading living silver Toy sires.

The gray Panorama Hideho bred to a black bred, Toy bred bitch produced the 10½ inch Blackaboy of Sassafras who became an important stud at Sassafras. Blackaboy did not produce browns. He produced three sons of value: the handsome Blackabit of Sassafras (16 champions), Ch. Black Scamp II of Sassafras (five champions) and Ch. Black Bijou of Sassafras. Black Bijou produced the eight inch brown Sarsaparilla of Sassafras who sired eight champions. Black Scamp II, a Group winner, sired the 7½ inch, 3 pound Blackabug of Sassafras. Blackabug sired six champions including Ch. Black Baronet of Sassafras (seven champions) and the non-champion Black Jockey of Sassafras. Black Jockey sired the 1976 P.C.A. Regional Specialty winner, Ch. Sundown Sassafras Bootblack, who is the leading black Toy sire.

A full brother of Ch. Medley's Silver Demon, a blue Toy with 14 points, Medley Boy de Gladville, sired two champions including Ch. Silver Dynamo de Gladville. Dynamo was a pretty headed, short bodied, gay, heavily coated little silver. Dynamo represented the best of the early silver Toys from the West from a type and breeding standpoint, as did Ch. Leicester's Silver Boots in the East. The combination of these two dogs was to bring enormous improvement in silver Toy Poodles, perhaps best represented by Ch. Thornlea's Silver Souvenir and his descendants. Dynamo's son, Sylvideo de Gladville, sired Ch. Miss Sylvideo de Gladville (dam of Souvenir) and the Top Producer, Ch. Bon Chance de Sassafras, whose sons, Ch. Silver Swank of Sassafras and Ch. Silver Fleece of Sassafras, were both Top Producers. Bon Chance also sired Ch. The Infanta of Sassafras, the dam of Ch. Silver Sparkle of Sassafras (by Souvenir).

Silver Fleece, a Best in Show winner, sired 16 champions including Ch. Silver Strike of Sassafras. Silver Strike sired five champions including Can. Ch. Winne's Silver Manolito. Silver Manolito's son, Ch. Syntifny's Silverdrift, was the sire of nine champions.

Silver Fleece's litter brother, Ch. Silver Swank of Sassafras, sired eight champions including Ch. DiFrey's Silver Dart of Swank. Silver Dart's son Ch. DiFrey's Dazzle of Sassafras produced the white Hilltop's Prince of Snows. His son the Top Producer Ch. Hilltop's Das Es Alles is the sire and grandsire of Top Producing whites.

Another son of Orsie's Son Sa Ses, Roi de L'Argent, was an important sire at de Gladville. His best known son was the white Group winner Ch. Sir Lancelot de Gladville Kennels, who is generally conceded to have been years ahead of his time. Lancelot sired Silhou-Jette's Minute Man (ex Silhou-Jette's Pip Squeak, an 11 inch Miniature) and Minute Man bred back to his dam produced the outstanding litter brothers, Ch. Silhou-Jette's Snow Sprite and Ch. Silhou-Jette's Cream Topping—both Best in Show winners and Top Producers. Snow Sprite sired 11 champions. Ch. Silhou-Jette's Cream Topping sired 15 champions. Oddly enough the male line today comes down through an untitled full brother, Silhou-Jette's White Sprite. White Sprite sired the cream

CH. HAPPY CHAPPY LINE
(Subdivision)

Orsie's Son Sa Ses
   Roi de l'Argent (*si*) 5
     Ch. Sir Lancelot de Gladville (*wh*) 5
       Silhou-Jette's Minute Man (*wh*) 5
         Ch. Silhou-Jette's Snow Sprite (*wh*) 11
           Ch. Silhou-Jette's Cream Topping (*crm*) 15
          Silhou-Jette's White Sprite (*wh*)
            Ch. Silhou-Jette's Sugar Foot (*crm*) 7
             Silhou-Jette's Sugar Time (*wh*) 6
              Ch. Silhou-Jette's Sugar Twist (*wh*) 7
                Ch. Hell's A Blazen Carnival Fame (*wh*) 12
                  Ch. Chrisward A OK of Arlrich (*wh*) 5
                    Ch. Caralandra's Disco Boy (*wh*) 5

Ch. Chrisward A OK of Arlrich   Ch. Caralandra's Disco Boy

Ch. Silhou-Jette's Sugar Foot who had seven champion get. His son, Silhou-Jette's Sugar Time, produced six champions, including Ch. Silhou-Jette's Sugar Twist who produced seven champions. Sugar Twist sired the Best in Show winner Ch. Hell's A Blazen Carnival Fame who sired 12 champions including the Best in Show winner Ch. Chrisward A OK of Arlrich who is also a Top Producer. A OK is the sire of the Top Producer Ch. Caralandra's Disco Boy out of Ch. Peeple's Sahara. Carnival Fame's daughter, Ch. Fairview's No Nonsense, was the Top Poodle, All varieties, for 1984.

CH. POODLETOWN'S LITTLE JOHN

Whelped January 22, 1968   Died May 11, 1983

Bred and owned by
Ellen Michel, Poodletown Kennels

Ch. Arsenal Little Punk (*blk*)
Pepe Le Moko of Dragon's Lair (*blk*)
Velvet Frolic of Dragon's Lair (*blk*)
Ch. Boarzell Briser De Coeur (*blk*)
Palmares Lieux (*blk*)
Boarzell Tasse Du Cafe (*brn*)
Ch. Kendall's Tonette (*blk*)

CH. POODLETOWN'S LITTLE JOHN—*Black*

Brownie Bambino of Sunkist (*brn*)
Poodletown's Mr. Brown (*brn*)
Sunkist Baby Doll (*brn*)
Poodletown's Coffee (*brn*)
Brownie Bambino of Sunkist (*brn*)
Poodletown's Truffles (*brn*)
Bijou Creme D'Etoile (*wh*)

CH. SUNDOWN SASSAFRAS BOOTBLACK

Whelped October 17, 1974

Bred by Pamela Ingram, Sassafras Kennels
Owned by Mrs. James Goodson, Montec Kennels

Int. Ch. Black Scamp II of Sassafras (*blk*)
Blackabug of Sassafras (*blk*)
Great Imperial Grecian Iris (*blk*)
Black Jockey of Sassafras (*blk*)
Mort (*blk*)
Minette Koko (*blk*)
Mert (*blk*)

CH. SUNDOWN SASSAFRAS BOOTBLACK—*Black*

Ch. Black Bijou of Sassafras (*blk*)
Sarsaparilla of Sassafras (*brn*)
Coquette Fleur Noir (*blk*)
Brown Lulu of Sassafras (*brn*)
Pravers Mickey Finn of Fredina (*brn*)
Fredina's Lulu (*brn*)
Fredina's Angele D'Amour (*blk*)

CH. MONTOYA'S UNCLE ALBERT

Whelped July 7, 1972

Bred by D. K. Eberhardt
Owned by Arthur Montoya

Ch. La Gai Beau's Bitzy Boy (*si*)
Ch. La Petite Gai Dondi (*si*)
Petite Poupee d'Amour (*si*)
Ch. Montoya's La Petite Rafael (*si*)
Ch. La Petite Gai Dondi (*si*)
La Petite Dondi's Gai Tassha (*si*)
La Petite Gidget of Jan-Neal (*si*)

CH. MONTOYA'S UNCLE ALBERT—*Silver*

Ch. Consentino's Silver Dollar (*si*)
Consentino's Silver Torino (*si*)
Renie Antoinette (*si*)
Dawn's Silver Moi Cheri (*si*)
Cypress Jon d'Argent (*si*)
Drudee's Christina (*si*)
Dru Dee's Desiree (*blk*)

Am. Can. Ch. Silhou-Jette's Snow Sprite.
Bred and owned by Martha Jane Ablett.

Am. Can. Ch. Silhou-Jette's Cream Topping.
Owned by Challendon Kennels.

AM. CAN. CH. SILHOU-JETTE'S SNOW SPRITE
AM. CAN. CH. SILHOU-JETTE'S CREAM TOPPING

Whelped March 13, 1956   Both deceased

Bred by Martha Jane Ablett

Roi de l'Argent (*si*)
Ch. Sir Lancelot de Gladville (*wh*)
Barnes' Little Gay Fluffball (*wh*)
Silhou-Jette's Minute Man (*crm-wh*)
Bubbles of Piperscroft and Blakeen (*wh*)
Silhou-Jette's Pip Squeak (*wh*)
Ch. Blakeen Snow Flurry (*wh*)

AM. CAN. CH. SILHOU-JETTE'S SNOW SPRITE—*White*

AM. CAN. CH. SILHOU-JETTE'S CREAM TOPPING—*Cream*

Michel of Piperscroft (*wh*)
Bubbles of Piperscroft and Blakeen (*wh*)
Dimple of Piperscroft (*wh*)
Silhou-Jette's Pip Squeak (*wh*)
Ch. Snow Boy of Fircot (*wh*)
Ch. Blakeen Snow Flurry (*wh*)
Ch. Blakeen Flurry (*wh*)

GEORGIAN BLACK MAGIC

Whelped August 8, 1950   Died November 5, 1966

Bred and owned by Georgie Shepperd
Nibroc Kennels, Basking Ridge, N.J.

Zoulou-Labory (*blk*)
Pinochio-Labory (*blk*)
Bouboule-Nice-Labory (*blk*)
Vichnou-Labory of Blakeen and Nibroc (*blk*)
Zoulou-Labory (*blk*)
Cloe-Labory (*blk*)
Janyre-Labory (*blk*)

GEORGIAN BLACK MAGIC—*Black*

Ch. Pruden's Little Skipper (*wh*)
Ch. Leicester's Bonbon (*wh*)
Ch. Leicester's Fidele de Lafferty (*wh*)
Nibroc Silver Star (*si*)
Beau's Black Racquet (*blk*)
Mistinguette (*gr*)
Smilestone's Letty (*gr*)

218

28

The "Black Magic" Line—
Georgian Black Magic

ALTHOUGH the Georgian Black Magic sire line is considered smaller in influence than that of the Ch. Happy Chappy line, and more recent, dating from the early fifties, it is nevertheless an important one. Actually it is an offshoot of the other line since Black Magic's dam was a daughter of Ch. Leicester's Bonbon. The Happy Chappy line was of pure white origin and the colored Toys that came from it were developed through the introduction of colored Miniature bitches. The introduction of the Black Magic line offered breeders an opportunity to obtain a concentration of black bloodlines and small size—both of which were sorely needed.

The story of Georgian Black Magic begins with the importation of his sire, Vichnou-Labory of Blakeen and Nibroc, to this country. Mrs. Sherman Hoyt brought him from Switzerland and sold him to Mrs. C. K. Corbin of the Nibroc Toy Poodles. Vichnou was of all-black Continental Toy breeding. He was described as a very nice little jet-black dog, well under 10 inches, a real Toy. He had a beautiful, heavy thick coat and was short-bodied and stylish. He was Winners Dog at the 1950 Interstate Poodle Club Specialty Show, but his early death prevented finish of his championship. From his few breedings came Ch. Nibroc Adoreable, Ch. Smilestone's Mascot, and Ch. Smilestone's Fancy Fee. Fancy Fee, a Best in Show winner, was also Best of Variety at Westminster for four consecutive years—1952, 1953, 1954 and 1955.

Bred to Nibroc Silver Star, a daughter of Ch. Leicester's Bonbon, Vichnou sired Georgian Black Magic. Black Magic, whelped August 1950, was bred and owned through his long life by Mrs. Georgie Shepperd. Black Magic was about nine inches tall, with an outstandingly beautiful head, very heavy coat, good legs

Ch. Peapacton's Rackarock

Ch. High Heritage Hellzapoppin

Ch. Wee Wee Martini

Ch. High Heritage High Copy

Twinbrook Farfadet A Tout Petit

Ch. Douai Fantasy

GEORGIAN BLACK MAGIC

Ch. Nibroc Pixie (*blu*) 4
Ch. Ardlussa Gascon (*blk*) 3
Ch. Barcwyn Etienne (*blk*) 1
    Ch. Turner's New Adventure (*blu*) 3
        Douai Ulysses (*blk*) 2
            Ch. Douai Fantasy (*blk*) 9
                Ch. Douai Mixmaster (*blk*) 5
Ch. Escapade of Exton (*blk*) 5
    Ch. Escapades Echo of Exton (*gr*) 12
    Ch. Peapacton's Rackarock (*blk*) 1
    Ch. Wee Wee Martini (*blk*) 1
        Twinbark Farfadet A Tout Petit (*blk*) 1
            Ch. High Heritage Hellzapoppin (*blk*) 5
            High Heritage Hullabaloo (*blk*) 9
            Can. Ch. High Heritage Hellraiser (*blk*) 7
                Ch. High Heritage High Copy (*blk*) 7
            Renea's Raven Rook (*blk*) 5
                Ch. Dassin's David (*blk*) 2
                    Ch. Gregella Vanilla Vindictive (*wh*) 5
                Peeples Mahogany Mister (*brn*) 5
                    Ch. Raedona's Blackberry Brandy (*blk*) 6
              Jap. Ch. Arundel The L'il Heart Throb (*wh*)
              Ch. Arundel A Lovin Spoonful (*wh*) 34
                Ch. Yerbrier Lovem 'N' Leavem (*wh)* 27
                    Ch. Yerbrier Matchmaker (*wh*) 6
                    Ch. Yerbrier Masterpoint (*wh*) 5
              Ch. Meridian Momentum (*wh*) 21
                Ch. Chez Doral Jean Pierre (*wh*) 6
                Ch. Amberly Milestone of Arundel (*wh*) 5
                    Ch. Richburg's Snowman (*wh*) 10
                Int. Ch. Elenshar's Little Topper (*wh*)
                  Int. Ch. Evanz Anchor Man (*wh*) 7
                    Int. Ch. Evanz Evening Edition (*wh*) 18

Int. Ch. Evanz Evening Edition

Ch. Meridian Momentum

and hindquarters. His back could have been shorter but he was not long-bodied. Black Magic was shown only twice and won his class both times. Several handlers were interested in showing him but he did not care for the ring. He was, however, much in demand at stud. Black Magic was one of the first good black Toys and he founded a large family of winning and producing descendants. He was outstanding for producing beautiful heads, good coats, and sturdy, cobby puppies. He was a consistent size reducer and produced puppies that were extremely small and refined. Black Magic sired blacks for the most part, with occasional browns, silvers, and beautifully pigmented whites. He never sired a particolor.

Georgian Black Magic bred to his half sister, Ch. Nibroc Adoreable, produced Ch. Nibroc Comet II, Ch. Nibroc Marla and Nibroc White Shadow. White Shadow sired Ch. Nibroc Gary who was Best of Breed at the Poodle Club of America Specialty in 1956. Bred to another half sister through Vichnou, Black Magic sired the small blue Ch. Nibroc Pixie, who was the sire of four champions, and the foundation of the Renea Kennels. Black Magic was bred to Burlingame Mimi II (of English breeding) to produce the black Toy Ch. Barcwyn Etienne. Etienne in turn sired the 11¼ inch blue Miniature Group winner Ch. Turner's New Adventure. New Adventure sired three black champion Toy daughters: Ch. Avron's Cha Cha Cha, Can. Ch. Harlane Black Adventuress and Ch. Douai Unity. A litter brother of Ch. Douai Unity, Douai Ulysses, was the sire of the black Group winner Ch. Douai Fantasy (sire of nine champions). Fantasy, bred to Ch. Douai Atlanta, produced Ch. Douai Mixmaster who was Winners Dog at Westminster in 1963. Mixmaster, a Group winner from the classes, was the sire of five champions.

Another son of Georgian Black Magic, Ch. Ardlussa Gascon, was the sire of Ch. Applewood Cider and the famous Ch. Cappoquin Little Sister. Little Sister was Best in Show at Westminster 1961, and Best of Breed at the Poodle Club of America Specialty in 1960. After her sensational show career Little Sister was retired for maternal duties. She produced four champions: Ch. Tropicstar Do It Up Brown and Ch. Tropicstar In The Black (by Ch. Carlima's J.D.), Ch. Tropicstar Sister Sue (by Blackabit of Sassafras), and the Best in Show winner Ch. Tropicstar Tequila (by her son Do It Up Brown).

Another son of Georgian Black Magic was the black Group winner, Ch. Escapade of Exton. Escapade sired five champions including the gray Ch. Escapades Echo of Exton, who was the sire of 12 champions and founder of the Raines Ranch Kennels. Ch. Escapade of Exton also sired the small black Group winner, Ch. Peapacton's Rackarock. Rackarock sired one of the smallest Poodles to ever win its championship, the 6½ inch Ch. Wee Wee Martini. Martini sired the 7½ inch black Twinbark Farfadet A Tout Petit who had seven points including one major.

Tout Petit was the sire of the 8½ inch black Ch. High Heritage Hellzapoppin who was Best Toy Puppy and Best Junior Puppy, All Varieties at the William Penn Puppy Futurity. Hellzapoppin, a dynamo of a dog in such a small size, was the sire of five champions and three Top Producing black sons—High Heritage Hullabaloo (nine champions), Can. Ch. High Heritage Hellraiser and his litter brother Renea's Raven Rook. Hellraiser sired seven champions including the Best in Show winner Ch. High Heritage High Copy. High Copy sired seven champions including Ch. Denaire Alistad Ariel. Bred to Ch. Granly's Black Ben, Ariel produced the Top Producers Ch. Denaire Tomy of High Wings (14 champions) and Ch. Denaire Glory of High Wings (dam of six champions).

The Hellzapoppin line was strongly black bred, but interestingly he carried a white gene which was to prove useful in breeding whites. His untitled black son, Renea's Raven Rook, produced blacks, browns and whites. Rook sired the black Ch. Dassin's David, who had a sensational puppy career and finished with five majors by going Winners Dog at the Poodle Club of America Specialty in 1967 at just eight months of age. David sired the white Top Producer Ch. Gregella Vanilla Vindictive. Rook also sired the brown Top Producer Peeples Mahogany Mister. Mister sired the black Top Producer Ch. Raedona's Blackberry Brandy.

Renea's Raven Rook's most famous offspring was the lovely white Ch. Peeples Sahara whose show career was impressive. She was the Number One Poodle for 1975. She won the Best of Variety three years in a row at Westminster in 1974, 1975 and 1976. She had 9 Specialty Bests in Show, 11 All Breed Bests in Show and 65 Group Firsts, one of those at Westminster. She retired with her second Best of Breed at the Poodle Club of America Parent Club Specialty in 1976. And then, well past the debutante stage, she had a litter (by Ch. Chrisward A OK of Arlich) which contained the multiple Group winner and Top Producer Ch. Caralandra's Disco Boy and Ch. Caralandra's Farah, a champion producer.

Rook also sired the highly influential Jap. Ch. Arundel The L'il Heart-throb, who went to Japan after siring Ch. Arundel A Lovin' Spoonful, sire of 34 champions worldwide. Spoonful sired Ch. Meridian Momentum (sire of 21 champions) and Ch. Yerbrier Lovem 'N' Leavem (sire of 27 champions). Lovem 'N' Leavem has been a highly successful stud force, especially through his two Top Producing sons Ch. Yerbrier Matchmaker and Ch. Yerbrier Masterpoint at Betty Yerington's Yerbrier Kennels, as well as through his daughters. At Marilyn Pauley's Evanz Kennels a Momentum son, Int. Ch. Elenshar's Little Topper, his son Int. Ch. Evanz Anchor Man (seven champions) and his Top Producing son, Int. Ch. Evanz Evening Edition, have continued the white influence.

The Georgian Black Magic line, especially through Renea's Raven Rook and his descendants, has offered another source of whites to combine with the highly successful Syntifny and Hell's A Blazen families.

RENEA'S RAVEN ROOK

Whelped: May 12, 1965   Died: 1977

Bred by High Heritage Kennels
Owned by Byron Elder, Renea Toy Poodles
Last owned by Joyce Peeples

Ch. Wee Wee Martini *(blk)*
Twinbark Farfadet A Tout Petit *(blk)*
Twinbark Joyeuse *(blk)*
Ch. High Heritage Helizapoppin *(blk)* 8½"
Eng. Ch. Tophill Toyboy *(blk)*
Tophill Dancing Shoes *(blk)* ET
Penelope of Tobruk *(blk)*

RENEA'S RAVEN ROOK—*Black*

Douai Ulysses *(blk)*
Can. Ch. Douai Inspiration *(blk)*
Douai Anticipator *(blk)*
High Heritage Forever Amber *(brn)*
Montmartre What-A-Boy *(blk)* Min.
High Heritage Tiny Thimble *(brn)* Sm. Min.
Dunwalke Ruffina *(blk)* Min.

CH. YERBRIER LOVEM 'N' LEAVEM

Whelped: June 25, 1972   Died: 1985

Bred and owned by Betty J. Yerington, Yerbrier Kennels

Renea's Raven Rook (*blk*)
Jap. Ch. Arundel The L'il Heart Throb (*crm*)
Arundel L'il Black Bonnett (*blk*)
Ch. Arundel A Lovin' Spoonful (*wh*)
Renea's Ring Tiger (*wh*)
Int. Ch. Pamper's Arundel Pixilation (*wh*)
Int. Ch. Pamper's Spring Sunshine (*wh*)

CH. YERBRIER LOVEM 'N' LEAVEM—*White*

Jap. Ch. Arundel The L'il Heart Throb (*crm*)
Can. Ch. Arundel Rollickin Romeo (*wh*)
Hilltop's Miss Honey For Fun (*crm*)
Yerbrier Rippling Rhythm (*wh*)
Ch. Jarshay's Bis Baloo (*wh*)
Yerbrier Bianca (*wh*)
Yerbrier Channan Glow (*wh*)

Ch. Cappoquin Little Sister

Can. Ch. Yerbrier Fun 'N' Fancy

Cygnet's Red Fox, C.D.

Evanz Puffenz Pooed D'Naer

29

Leading Toy Dams

THE number of Top Producing Bitches (those that have been the dam of three or more champions) in Toys is considerably less than in either Miniatures or Standards, which is understandable in view of the comparatively few puppies a Toy bitch is capable of producing during her lifetime.

The problem of size adds a further difficulty to making a production record. The Toy is less established as a variety than either the Miniature or Standard due to the influx of Miniature breeding, which—although improving type—has presented a continuing size problem. Only recently have certain lines and families been created that can be depended upon to produce Toy quality in generation after generation. Another problem is the fact that by the time many show quality Toy bitches have completed their ring careers their best years for whelping and raising litters has passed. Despite this there are a few notable exceptions such as Ch. Cappoquin Little Sister and Ch. Mari A Spring Storm who retired from the ring and became Top Producers.

The top honors as dam of American Toy Poodle champions is held by Can. Ch. Yerbrier Fun 'N' Fancy (Ch. Yerbrier Lovem 'N' Leavem ex Merry's Sparkle of Hilltop) with 11 champions to her credit. All of her champions were sired by Ch. Syntifny Piece of the Rock or his son Can. Ch. Syntifny Snapshot. Fancy was co-owned by Jane Winne of Syntifny Kennels and Patricia McMullen's Michanda Kennels.

The leading silver dam of 11 Toy champions was Evanz Puffenz Pooed D'Naer (Can. Ch. Evanz Slingapore Swing ex Evan's Short Story Por Renee). Puffenz was owned and bred by Marilyn Pauley's Evanz Kennels.

The leading black dam of eight champions was Mademoiselle Mimi II (Ch. Emsie's Black Knight ex Westwood's Lady Pamela). Mimi II was owned by Mrs. Frank Dean's Whitehall Kennels.

Ch Leicester's Bonbon shown going Best of Variety at the Poodle Club of America Specialty 1947, handled by his breeder-owner Mrs. Leicester Harrison.

The leading apricot Toy dam was Cygnet's Red Fox (Peeples Red Rooster ex Barbru Tia Maria) with five champion get for Nancy Swan's Cygnet Kennels.

Special salute should be paid to Ch. Cappoquin Little Sister, who did not begin her maternal duties until after her outstanding show career. In her first litter, at almost five years of age, this Westminster Best in Show winner produced Ch. Tropicstar Sister Sue (by Blackabit of Sassafras). In Little Sister's second and third litters (both by Ch. Carlima's J. D.) were Ch. Tropicstar Do It Up Brown and Ch. Tropicstar In The Black. Little Sister was then bred to her son, Do It Up Brown, to produce the Best in Show winner, Ch. Tropicstar Tequila. Both Do It Up Brown and In The Black are sires of champions.

Of the 169 bitches that have produced three or more Toy champions to qualify as Top Producers, 56 have been champions themselves—truly an amazing accomplishment considering their delay in the whelping box and the small number of puppies produced by Toy bitches.

30

Leicester's Kennels

LEICESTER HARRISON owned her first Toy Poodle in 1916, but it wasn't until 1942 that she started the Leicester's Toy Poodles line that has played such a large role in the development of the Toy Poodle as we know it today. Mrs. Harrison began with the pure old-fashioned white Toy, and it is a tribute to her ability as a breeder that this line has come so far in such a comparatively short period of time. As Toy Poodles were scarce in 1942, Mrs. Harrison searched for some time before locating a six-weeks-old puppy bitch, Leicester's Fidele de Lafferty, who was to found the Leicester's line. Fidele was sired by Ch. Beau Beau of Muriclar (from the West Coast) ex Lafferty's Dimples. Prior to finishing her championship Fidele was bred to her half brother Ch. Pruden's Little Skipper (also by Beau Beau) to produce the famous little Ch. Leicester's Bonbon.

Bonbon, whelped January 3, 1945, was 8½ inches tall and weighed 4½ pounds. He represented a great stride forward in Toy development as he did not possess many of the faults that were then prevalent in Toy Poodles. Bonbon's outstanding features were his squareness of body, lovely almond eyes with flat cheeks, jet-black pigmentation, high tail set and correct rear quarters. His merry disposition and outstanding showmanship attracted attention not only to himself but to the Toy variety as well. When the Poodle Club of America first admitted the Toy variety as a participant at its annual specialty show in 1947, Bonbon was awarded Best of Variety. He had a successful show career and was never beaten except by his half brother Ch. Leicester's Peaches and Cream. Peaches and Cream was by the brown Ch. Gremlin (also by Beau Beau) and also out of Fidele. Bonbon died when he was only three years old but he sired 12 champions and left a legacy of winning and producing descendants.

Mrs. Harrison was one of the first Toy breeders to realize the value of breeding small Miniature bitches to Toy sires to improve the quality in Toys. She insisted that the Miniature bitches be of excellent quality with good

Ch. Leicester's Bonbon's Swan Song

Ch. Leicester's
Peaches and Cream

Ch. Leicester's Fidele de Lafferty

Ch. Leicester's Silver Boots

230

backgrounds. Bonbon was bred several times to the small blue Miniatures, Leicester's Alouette (by Ch. Robin Goodfellow), to produce five Toy champions: Ch. Leicester's Bonbon's Swan Song, Ch. Leicester's Bon Ami, Ch. Leicester's Ouida, Ch. Leicester's Frolic and Ch. Leicester's Valentine Nibroc. Three of these were Group winners. Frolic was bred to Peaches and Cream to produce Ch. Leicester's Eudoron. Valentine Nibroc was bred to Leicester's Bonny Bit of Nibroc (a son of Bonbon) to produce the silver Nibroc The Imp (sire of four champions). Bonbon sired Nibroc Silver Star whose son Georgian Black Magic founded another sire line. Bonbon's daughter Ch. Cartlane Once (ex a white Miniature) attracted much attention to the variety. She was Best of Variety at the parent specialty in 1949, 1950 and was Best of Breed there in 1951. She also won three Bests of Variety at Westminster and won the Toy Group there in 1950 and 1951.

Bonbon's most important son was the blue Ch. Leicester's Bonbon's Swan Song (ex Leicester's Alouette). Swan Song was the sire of eight champions including Am. Can. Ch. Wilber White Swan, Ch. Leicester's Silver Boots (silver), Ch. Leicester's Swan Song's Legacy (black), Ch. Leicester's Angelo (white) and Ch. Leicester's Little Eva (cream). Ch. Wilber White Swan was a great winner with 16 Bests in Show including Westminster 1956. White Swan exerted a tremendous influence on white Toys of his day and sired 38 champions. Ch. Leicester's Silver Boots was one of the foundation sires in silver Toys. Silver Boots, with limited opportunity, sired eight champions. His son, Ch. Leicester's Golden Slippers, was the sire of Ch. Thornlea Silver Souvenir. Another son of Silver Boots, the Group winner Ch. Nizet's Mr. Antoine D'Argent, was the sire of five champions. Ch. Leicester's Swan Song's Legacy was the sire of three champions. Ch. Leicester's Little Eva was the dam of Ch. Renrew's Yvette by Ch. Leicester's Angelo and of Ch. Renrew's Risque and Ch. Renrew's Apricot Brandy by Ch. Wilber White Swan. Risque was bred to Ch. Leicester's Angelo (a Best in Show winner) to produce the Group-winning silver Ch. Renrew's Star Dust (sire of eight champions).

Ch. Leicester's Peaches and Cream was the sire of four champions. Bred to the blue Ch. Leicester's Frolic (Bonbon ex Alouette) he produced Fieldstreams Kennels' blue Ch. Leicester's Eudoron. Eudoron sired nine champions including the beige Ch. Blakeen Penny Wise (dam of four champions at Lime Crest) and the white Ch. Pixdown Loabelo Blanchette (dam of four champions and founder of the Pixdown Kennels). Eudoron was also the sire of the black Fieldstreams Topflight (sire of five champions). Peaches and Cream was bred to Lafferty's Ma Chere to produce Ch. Leicester's I'll Take Vanilla (sire of four champions), and the Top Producing sisters Leicester's Saint Barbara and Leicester's Peach Melba. Saint Barbara was bred to Ch. Leicester's Bonbon's Swan Song to produce Ch. Leicester's Angelo, Ch. Leicester's Flirt In Silver and Can. Ch. Leicester's Raven Beauty. Peach Melba bred to her sire, Peaches and Cream, produced Ch. Leicester's Peach Charlotte and Leicester's Peach Parfait. Peach Parfait was the sire of the black Ch. Hollyday Cuddles. Peach Melba bred

Ch. Silver Sparkle of Sassafras

to Bonbon's Swan Song produced the black Ch. Leicester's Soprano Solo. Peach Melba was bred to Ch. Leicester's Silver Boots to give her third champion Ch. Leicester's Golden Slippers (sire of seven champions).

There were over 25 Leicester champions, in all colors. Many of these were handled by their owner. The Leicester's influence, starting in the East, spread over the entire country for the betterment of Toy Poodles. The only two Toy Poodles to go Best in Show at Westminster, Ch. Wilber White Swan and Ch. Cappoquin Little Sister, are both descended from this line.

Leicester Harrison died on June 10, 1980 in California at the age of 86. It was the end of a long and interesting life. Unknown to many of her friends was Leicester's earlier career as the first nationally broadcast astrologer, regularly appearing on radio from 1928 through 1931 as part of "The Million Dollar Program" with both the Paul Whiteman and Guy Lombardo orchestras from Chicago. Her segment was called "Helping To Happiness." She traveled all over the world, lived lavishly and spoke several languages fluently. She commented that in her later life her dogs were all she needed, as she had been fortunate in "going everywhere and doing everything when younger." Leicester was a tiny woman but one of the true giants of the breed, brilliant, opinionated and sometimes difficult, but she always held firm in her conviction that the Toy Poodle was first and foremost a Poodle and not a second-rate version of its larger cousins.

232

31

Sassafras Kennels

T HE SASSAFRAS KENNELS of Pamela Ingram was located on a hillside in Topanga, California. Mrs. Ingram first saw a gray Toy Poodle at a dog show in 1952 and became determined to breed silver Toys herself. She leased a bitch from the de Gladville Kennels, and in the resultant litter was a silver Toy male who founded the world famous Sassafras silver Toy line. This male, Ch. Bon Chance de Sassafras, became a Top Producer with 10 champions to his credit, including Ch. Silver Fleece of Sassafras (Best in Show winner, sire of 16 champions), Ch. Silver Swank of Sassafras (sire of eight champions) and Ch. The Infanta of Sassafras (dam of three champions). Fleece's multiple Best in Show winning son, Ch. Silver Strike of Sassafras, was the sire of six champions. The Infanta, a lovely headed little bitch, was bred to Ch. Thornlea Silver Souvenir to produce the littermates Ch. Silver Spark of Sassafras and Ch. Silver Sparkle of Sassafras.

Silver Sparkle, a Best in Show winner, was a refined, high-on-leg, short-bodied type. He remains the Top Producing silver Toy sire with 82 champions to his credit. There are several reasons for Sparkle's great success at stud. Mrs. Ingram states that he never sired a two-tone or particolor. Since many Toy bitches were low on leg and long in body, Sparkle was especially useful in breeding to them to shorten bodies and add length of leg. He was also an excellent size reducer. There were a great number of daughters of Bon Chance, Swank and Fleece in Sparkle's home area and he was bred to these with outstanding success.

Sparkle had three Top Producing silver sons: Ch. Silver Sunday of Sassafras (nine champions), Ch. Seaspray of Sassafras (seven champions) and the Best in Show winner Ch. Sassafras Starfire (five champions). An inbred Sparkle son went to Sweden where, as Swedish Ch. Silver Selsendy of Sassafras,

Ch. Blacklight of Sassafras

Ch. Bon Chance de Sassafras

he as well as his son and grandsons at Stortuvan Kennels had an influence in Scandinavia, in England, and eventually back in America. In addition to silvers, Sparkle also produced silver-beiges, blues, grays, creams and whites. Most of the Sassafras whites and creams were based on Sparkle's ability to produce those colors. Sparkle's son, Ch. Sassafras The Snowball, sired the Top Producer Ch. Snow Imp of Sassafras (six champions). Snow Imp sired the Top Producer Ch. Snow Crown of Sassafras.

Mrs. Ingram developed a winning family of blacks around the Top Producer Blackaboy of Sassafras (eight champions). An untitled son of Blackaboy, Blackabit of Sassafras, had the start of a promising career with a Best of Variety win over Best in Show specials, but because of a broken front leg which did not mend properly was unable to finish his championship. Blackabit was much admired for his beautiful type and sired 16 champions. Blackaboy also sired Ch. Black Bijou of Sassafras and he in turn sired the eight inch brown Top Producer Sarsaparilla of Sassafras. Sarsaparilla sired eight champions but his most important contribution was through his daughters. Blackaboy also sired the handsome, sound Ch. Black Scamp II of Sassafras (five champions). Black Scamp II sired the tiny and aptly named Blackabug of Sassafras (six champions). Blackabug sired the Top Producer Ch. Black Baronet of Sassafras (seven champions) and Black Jockey of Sassafras. Black Jockey bred to Brown Lulu of Sassafras (by Sarsaparilla) produced the top living black Toy sire Ch. Sundown Sassafras Bootblack at Susan Goodson's Montec Kennels. Bootblack was linebred to Blackaboy in the fourth generation on both sides of his pedigree.

234

Ch. Silver Fleece of Sassafras

In 1966 Mrs. Ingram acquired the beautiful headed, heavy coated Group winner, Ch. Tophill Tops of High Heritage. Tops, an English import, was by Eng. Ch. Tophill Toyboy, a vital stud force in England. Tops sired three champions including the magnificent headed Ch. Blacklight of Sassafras who finished his title with a Group win. Blacklight was out of Sassafras The Fandancer, an eight inch daughter of Sarsaparilla of Sassafras (mentioned previously). Blacklight sired Meridian First Fiddle (nine champions), Ch. Woodbrae Desire of Sassafras (sire of six champions) and Ch. Brownstar of Sassafras. Brownstar, a multiple All-Breed and Specialty Best in Show winner, was the Top Toy All Breeds for 1969. Brownstar sired four champions including Ch. Granly's Black Ben, one of the current leading black Toy sires.

Mrs. Ingram was a very clever breeder with an almost uncanny ability to predict the results of any mating. She had a real flair for selecting breeding mates. Mrs. Ingram was generous in sharing her knowledge and breeding stock with other breeders. Sassafras, which was disbanded in 1975, was one of the largest and most successful kennels in the history of the breed with more than 200 champions worldwide.

Little Sir Echo of Meisen

Ch. Meisen Golden Gaiete (Miniature)

Ch. Meisen Bit O'Gold

Meisen Bit O'Golden Glow

32

Meisen Kennels

HOW many Poodle breeders have started out to breed one color, and have ended up becoming more famous for another? Certainly, the Meisen Kennels of Hilda Meisenzahl must be one of the best known, for it is world famous for its apricots. Miss Meisenzahl's original plan was to breed black Toys, but nature in the form of recessive apricot genes asserted itself, and Miss Meisenzahl was wise enough to utilize her good fortune.

The start was in 1941 with the cross of the white Toy Ch. Orsie's Kumsi to the gray Miniature Maree Ang. A year later, an accidental mating from two of this litter produced the black Toy Ch. Marmaduke of Meisen. As there were no color-bred Toy lines then available, and as Miss Meisenzahl did not wish to introduce more white Toy breeding for fear of mismarking and poor type, she imported a small black Miniature male, Giovanni of Toytown, from one of England's smallest Miniature lines. She was not aware at the time that Giovanni's dam, Etroite of Toytown, was an 8½ inch apricot. Since apricot is recessive and needs an apricot gene from each parent to make its appearance, Giovanni did not sire any apricots himself (none of the bitches he was bred to carried an apricot gene). However in subsequent generations, when linebreeding to Giovanni occurred, beautiful golden apricot puppies appeared from time to time. Apricots were very rare in those days and these were not only good in color, but also good in type. While she was carefully establishing her black Toy line, Miss Meisenzahl was at the same time creating a good background for her apricots. In line with her plan for breeding blacks she bred Giovanni to Meisen's Meri-Tot (by Ch. Marmaduke of Meisen) to produce the black Meisen's Bright Knight. More small black breeding was added with the purchase of the 12-inch black Ch. Sherwood Petite Poupee. Petite Poupee was by the 10½ inch black Ch. Sherwood Pocket Edition, who finished undefeated as a Miniature. Pocket

Edition sired two black Toy champions at Sherwood Hall. Petite Poupee was bred to Bright Knight to give Meisen's Little Bit O'Black, C.D. Little Bit O'Black was bred to the black Susan's Mademoiselle GiGi (by Giovanni of Toytown) to produce the 10½-inch black Little Sir Echo of Meisen. Although himself black, Little Sir Echo (from a grandson to daughter of Giovanni) fortunately inherited the ability to produce apricots.

Little Sir Echo has played a key role at Meisen. He was the sire of black champions and apricot champions, Toy champions and Miniature champions. Little Sir Echo was bred to Peg O' My Heart of Meisen to produce three champions: Mex. Ch. Meisen Marcella (black Toy), Ch. Meisen Mademoiselle Zsa Zsa (apricot Miniature) and Ch. Meisen Golden Gaiete (apricot Miniature). Golden Gaiete has been an exceptional sire and has produced six apricot champions. Gaiete is the sire of the Group winner, Ch. Meisen Golden Gamin.

Gamin was the sire of four champions including the beautiful Miniature, Ch. Pixiecroft Sunbeam. Sunbeam finished her championship with a Group win as a puppy. Sunbeam has been the greatest winning apricot in the history of the breed in this country. Winner of 19 Best in Shows. She won the Non-Sporting Group at Westminster in 1965. Sunbeam was the dam of three champions.

Little Sir Echo also sired two black Toy champions, Ch. Sequoia's Iron Duke and Ch. Meisen Robert Rascal. Robert Rascal finished his championship by going Winners Dog at the Westminster Show in 1960. He had a lovely head, and was short in body and high on leg. Many Toy breeders felt he had a great deal to offer to the Toy variety. Miss Meisenzahl seemed close to her goal in black Toys but unfortunately Rascal died too early to leave his mark as a stud dog.

Little Sir Echo of Meisen also sired the cream Toy, Meisen Ecru Elf. Elf was bred to the Group-winning white Ch. Meisen Paper Doll (by the Best in Show winning Miniature, Ch. Paper Boy of Toytown, who had an apricot gene) to produce the beautiful tiny Ch. Meisen Bit O'Gold. Bit O'Gold was bred to a dark apricot daughter of Ch. Meisen Golden Gaiete to produce Ch. Meisen Flaming Fella and Meisen Bit O'Golden Glow. Golden Glow has proven to be an exceptional sire with nine apricot Toy champions to his credit. Of these, four are Group winners.

Miss Meisenzahl's apricots have furnished the background for many of the apricot Miniatures and Toys in this country. Her accomplishments have made the breeding of apricots easier for those who have followed her lead.

33

Syntifny Kennels

THE SYNTIFNY KENNELS of Jane Winne in Michigan, famous for its whites, was first interested in breeding silver Toys and met with some success. A small, pretty bitch, Can. Ch. Winne's What Not of Sassafras, a granddaughter of Ch. Silver Sparkle of Sassafras, was bred March 1973 to Can. Ch. Winne's Silver Manolito and produced Am. Can. Ch. Syntifny Silverdrift, a Top Producer who sired nine champions.

On March 31, 1974 Syntifny whelped its first litter of white Toys. These were out of Am. Can. Ch. Adiona of Aurora and sired by the Top Producer Ch. Amberly's White Rock of Delnor. This litter contained one of those history making males every breeder aspires to produce, in Ch. Syntifny Piece of the Rock. "Rocky," a special puppy from the beginning, was to become the leading Toy sire of all time. Todd Patterson has been an integral part of the Rocky story, showing him to his title and finishing many of his descendants.

This is how Jane Winne describes Rocky:

"He was first and foremost a happy dog. His temperament was so marvelous, it is difficult to put into words. Whatever you wanted or asked of him, is exactly what he wanted to do. He sparkled with delight over any kind of attention, and was equally generous with his love and affection for everyone, although he always let me know that I was his 'special' person.

"Rocky was a very proud and masculine dog, with a beautifully expressive face, good length of foreface with a clean backskull, although his was not an extreme type head. Perhaps his most outstanding features were his tremendously thick coat and his marvelous big body. His front was near perfection with great rib spring and depth of chest, correct shoulder layback, good tight elbows, and very straight front legs. He was extremely short backed and his rear was strong and well angulated. He had a lovely length of neck and beautiful carriage. His outline was one of elegance and total balance. He also had bigger feet than I really like and a very gay tail, which he transmitted to most of his offspring. But, after all, the Rocky temperament goes along with that gay tail!

"Rocky was the product of an outcross breeding, but was a very dominant sire for producing puppies similar to his own type, with heavy coats, big bodies, short backs and super show temperament. Almost all of his champion children are the result of outcross breedings. However, he was bred back to a few of his granddaughters with fabulous results. We also had excellent success with half brother-sister breedings. One of his most outstanding daughters has been the very beautiful Ch. Mari A Spring Storm, the Top Winning Toy Poodle for 1978, multiple Best in Show winner, and Best in Show twice at the Poodle Club of America Specialties.

"Rocky's production is still a source of wonder to me. In all the books I've read on breeding and genetics, every author advocates linebreeding and inbreeding as an absolute must, in order to stamp a line for dominant traits. Rocky was the result of a total outcross breeding. Why then was he such a dominant sire? His look was stamped on almost every puppy he sired, and that has continued on to the third and fourth generations that I'm seeing now. It is a constant joy for me to see and admire dogs in the ring, and later learn that they are his grandchildren and great grandchildren. It makes me so proud for him."

Mrs. Winne has worked closely with a number of breeders in sharing the Rocky legacy. His Top Producing sons are: Ch. Syntifny On The Move, Ch. Kornel's Keeper Of The Castle, Can. Ch. Syntifny Snapshot, Ch. Yerbrier Syntifny Shamu, Mari Storm Warning, Can. Ch. Camelot Rock A Beatin' Boogie, Ch. Camelot Rockford Files, Ch. Wilmar Howlene Stone Broke, Ch. Jodans Winter Storm, Ch. Leecroft Coined Silver, Ch. Bellview's Worth Chat'n About and Ch. Regence Raised On Rock. Rocky's Top Producing daughters are Syntifny Beloved Memory, Ch. Mari A Spring Storm, Ch. Syntifny Swing Into Spring and Ch. Syntifny Patty Pizazz.

Just three days short of his sixth birthday on March 28, 1980, Rocky and his small Top Producing son Ch. Yerbrier Syntifny Shamu were stolen from their kennel. Despite intensive efforts, they have never been located. This has been one of the great tragedies in the breed. In only five years at stud Rocky became the leading Toy sire of all time with 86 champion get. One can only wonder what record might have been achieved with a few more producing years.

Fortunately Mrs. Winne had a number of Rocky children with which to continue and they have made impressive records. His son Can. Ch. Syntifny Snapshot, co-owned with Pat McMullen, is a Top Producer. Mrs. Winne also co-owns with Pat McMullen Can. Ch. Yerbrier Fun 'N' Fancy, who is the all time Top Producing Toy dam. She has produced an amazing 11 champions with either Rocky or his son Snapshot. Mrs. Winne also owns Syntifny Sweettalk who produced six champions when bred to Rocky.

Syntifny has bred 51 American titleholders, 13 who have finished in Canada or abroad, and in addition Mrs. Winne has finished another 14 champions who were not homebred. This has never been a large kennel, so the record is even more impressive, making Syntifny one of America's top Toy Poodle kennels.

Am. Can. Ch. Adiona of Aurora

Ch. Syntifny Piece of the Rock

Can. Ch. Syntifny Snapshot

Ch. Syntifny Silverdrift

241

Branslake Floris

Ch. Hell's A Blazen Carnival Fancy

Ch. Hell's A Blazen Kinda Kostly

Ch. Hell's A Blazen Carnival Fame

242

34

Hell's A Blazen Kennels

T HE HELL'S A BLAZEN KENNELS of Frances Rubinich now located in Maryland started first with Standard Poodles and bred eight Standard champions.

As is often true, the story of the Hell's A Blazen Kennels is in reality the story of their foundation bitch.

While visiting with Jenny Beech in England, professional handler Wendell Sammet saw a lovely little bitch with a captivating personality named Branslake Floris. After much persuasion Mrs. Beech agreed to part with her. Floris was strongly linebred on England's premier white Toy line—Sudbrook, which was noted for lovely heads and eyes and overall quality.

Mrs. Rubinich described her foundation bitch:

"Floris was everything I wanted. She was very typey and way ahead of her time. She had a pretty head and eye, straight front legs and a neck carried high and proudly. She weighed 4½ pounds. She was ten inches tall but looked smaller as she was so short backed and beautifully proportioned. We could not show her because there was nothing in the ring then that looked like her. She was so charming and winsome that when anyone came to look at a puppy or consult about a stud service I would bring out Floris and she would immediately charm them. We are extremely fortunate that Floris was able to pass on not only her superb quality but also her wonderful disposition generation after generation."

Floris' first litter, whelped October 12, 1969, was by the Top Producer Ch. Silhou-Jette's Sugar Twist and all three in that litter became champions: Ch. Hell's A Blazen Carnival Fame (12 champion get), Ch. Hell's A Blazen Carnival Joy, and Ch. Hell's A Blazen Carnival Fancy (5 champion get), thus making her a Top Producer with her very first litter.

Floris' next litter consisted of one pretty bitch puppy who was too small for showing or breeding.

Floris' third and unfortunately last litter was by Kendor's Frostie Fiddler. He was selected because he had a beautiful balance, size of bone, and head type. He was heavily English bred, and he was her grandson. The two resulting puppies were Ch. Hell's A Blazen Kinda Kostly and the multiple All Breed and Specialty Best in Show winner Ch. Hell's A Blazen Kiss A Me.

Floris' sum total as a producer is little short of incredible: three litters—a total of six puppies, five of whom were champions and three of these Best in Show winners.

Kinda Kostly and Kiss A Me were startlingly uniform, although Kinda Kostly ("Kenny") was very different in type from Floris' previous offspring. He was not as ultra short backed but more square with a longer neck. He had great dignity and moved with reach and drive. Kenny won an All Breed Best in Show on the way to his title.

Kenny's abilities as a sire were apparent with his first litters. His get were easily recognizable in the show ring by their heads, overall type, hindquarters, feet, coat and temperament. Close breeding within the family has been very successful as have outcrosses. Kenny produced a total of 54 champions and was the leading Toy sire for 1984.

Kenny bred to his granddaughter, Hell's A Blazen Cherry Cool, produced seven champions. Bred to his half sister, Ch. Hell's A Blazen Carnival Fancy, he produced another five champions. Bred to Carnival Fancy's blue daughter, Hell's A Blazen Yes Yes (by Ch. Fifi's Sunny Lee) Kenny produced seven champions, including the multiple Best in Show winner and Top Producer Ch. Hell's A Blazen Fagin's Pride.

Hell's A Blazen has produced a total of 53 Toy Poodle champions and they are all descended from the one foundation bitch, Branslake Floris.

35

British Toy Line— Wychwood Gatesgarth Monarch

ONE of the first great Toys to appear in England was the black Wychwood Gatesgarth Monarch, a direct descendant of the Miniature Eng. Ch. The Monarch in male tail line. In those days Toy Poodles were shown in the Miniature competition in specially provided classes. Wychwood Gatesgarth Monarch won many "Under 11 inch" classes and was an extremely useful sire for those interested in reducing size.

Monarch's sire, Jervis of Rosvic, was a grandson of Ch. Toomai of Montfleuri and Ch. Toy Boy of Toytown—both small 13 inch Miniatures. Wychwood Gatesgarth Monarch was whelped October 5, 1953 and was a real "stallion type" even in his reduced size. He was very handsome with an exaggeration of Poodle quality. He was a good black with long, lean head, small eye, low-set ears, well developed body, good tailset and extreme angulation. Monarch was used extensively to reduce size and improve quality. He consistently reduced size to under 11 inches even when bred to full sized Miniatures. Monarch sired a total of eight champions. His lovely daughter, Ch. Merrymorn Lita, was the first English bred Toy Poodle to go Best in Show in the United States. Monarch's influence was so great that at every Crufts Show from 1959 through 1967 (with one exception, 1964) a direct descendant of Monarch was either Best of Breed or Best of Opposite Sex. Monarch's son, Eng. Ch. Tammy of Manapouri, was Best of Breed there in 1966. Monarch's son, Eng. Ch. Keitrix Tiny Tim, was Best of Breed at Crufts in 1959. Monarch's daughter, Emmrill Mona Lisa, came to the United States where she played an important

Wychwood Gatesgarth Monarch

Meridian First Fiddle

Eng. Ch. Tophill Toyboy

Aspen Antibody

Eng. Ch. Wemrose Newboy

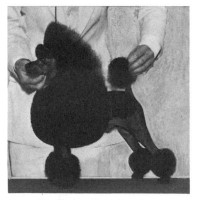

Ch. Trebor Toastmaster

WYCHWOOD GATESGARTH MONARCH (British Line)

Eng. Ch. Tophill Trotabout (*blk*) 1
Eng. Ch. Tammy of Manapouri (*blk*) 1
   Eng. Ch. Rafael of Manapouri (*blk*)
Eng. Ch. Tophill Toyboy (*blk*) 11
   Eng. Ch. Wemrose Newsboy (*blk*) 10
   Swedish Ch. Tophill Perky (*blk*) 9
   Aspen Angry Young Man (*blk*)
      Aspen Antibody (*blk*) 6
         Ch. Trebor Toastmaster (*blk*) 11
   Ch. Tophill Tops of High Heritage (*blk*) 3
   Ch. Blacklight of Sassafras (*blk*) 29
      Meridian First Fiddle (*blk*) 9
      Ch. Blackwatch of Sassafras (*blk*)
         Suncrest Vaquero (*blk*) 6
      Ch. Woodbrae Desire of Sassafras (*blk*) 6
         Ch. Woodbrae Mission Impossible (*blk*) 6
      Ch. Brownstar of Sassafras (*brn*) 4
         Ch. Granly's Black Ben (*blk*) 27
            Ch. Denaire Tomy of High Wings (*blk*) 14
Wychwood Tom Tit (*blk*)
   Montmartre Minimax (*blk*)
      Eng. Ch. Montmartre Madcap (*blk*) 2
         Eng. Ch. Tallasee Snuff Box (*brn*)
      Montmartre Million Dollar (*blk*) 2
         Eng. Ch. Tuttlebees Donalyn Discussion (*blk*)
         Maribrens Monty (*blk*)
            Eng. Ch. Maribrens Marty (*blk*)
            Tuttlebees Rather Royal (*blk*) 6
               Eng. Ch. Malibu The Love Bug (*blk*) 4
                  Eng. Ch. Suraliam Boogy Woogy from Velveteen (*blk*) 5
Tophill Cupidon (*blk*)
   Tenaver Montravia Little Riot (*blk*)
      Eng. Ch. Capilon Toy Minstrel (*blk*)
      Eng. Ch. Capilon Toy Pedlar (*blk*)
         Eng. Ch. Capilon Graywood Pedlar's Chick (*blk*)
         Capilon Toy Gambler (*blk*)
            Eng. Ch. Ranji's C'est La Vie (*blk*)

Ch. Brownstar of Sassafras

Ch. Denaire Tomy of High Wings

role in the development of the Douai and Baliwick Toys through her daughters, Ch. Douai Atlanta and Ch. Douai Overture. Monarch's son, Wychwood King Cole, sired Eng. Ch. Marysmeadow I Am Sarah (B.O.B.—Crufts 1960). Tammy's full brother, Wychwood Tich of Manapouri, sired Eng. Ch. Sharnette LeSave Her Glory and LeSave Black Soloist. Soloist's son, Pixiecroft Bellboy, sired Pixiecroft President. President in turn sired Eng. Ch. Pixiecroft Plutocrat and Eng. Ch. Pixiecroft Lisa.

Monarch's black son, Eng. Ch. Tophill Toyboy, was whelped January 1, 1957, the same year that the British Kennel Club recognized the Toy Poodle as a separate variety. Toyboy was a handsome little dog, small enough to have won in the United States. He had a beautiful head, short body, was high on leg and with a good rear end. Toyboy exerted a strong influence on the Toy in England and abroad. His son, Swedish Ch. Tophill Perky, was the sire of nine champions.

From the breeding of Eng. Ch. Tophill Toyboy to Eng. Ch. Aspen Black Affronted came Aspen Angry Young Man. Young Man bred to Aspen Black Ashamed (a Toyboy daughter) gave Aspen Antibody, who came to the Clarion Kennels in California where he sired six champions including the Top Producer Ch. Trebor Toastmaster. Toastmaster is a leading black Toy stud force on the West Coast.

Toyboy's daughter, Eng. Ch. Sibon As Toy Like It, was the dam of two champions; and another daughter, Sibon Ooh La La of Jalahalli, was the dam of three champions. Toyboy's son, Eng. Ch. Wemrose Newsboy, sired one of England's top winning bitches, Eng. Ch. Barsbrae Branslake Harriet, who won 11 C.C.'s. Harriet was the dam of Eng. Ch. Barsbrae Fleur. Newsboy's daughter, Snippet of Petitbrun, was the dam of Eng. Chs. Tea Tray and Tea Cup of Petitbrun.

Toyboy's black son, Am. Ch. Tophill Tops of High Heritage, was a Group winner and sire of three champions. His son, Ch. Blacklight of Sassafras, also a Group winner, was a Top Producer at Sassafras where he had a strong influence. Blacklight's son, Ch. Brownstar of Sassafras, who was the top winning Toy of all breeds in America for 1969, sired four champions including Ch. Granly's Black Ben, who is one of the leading black Toy sires. Black Ben's son, Ch. Denaire Tomy of High Wings, was the sire of 14 champions.

Another branch of the Monarch family is through his son Wychwood Tom Tit. Tom Tit's son, Montmartre Minimax, was the sire of Eng. Ch. Montmartre Madcap. Madcap was the sire of Eng. Ch. Tallasee Snuff Box, Ch. Karronbrae Black Mystic and Montmartre Million Dollar. Million Dollar was the sire of Eng. Ch. Great Westwood Montmartre Marcia and Eng. Ch. Tuttlebees Donalyn Discussion. Discussion was the sire of Maribrens Monty (out of Eng. Ch. Maribrens Miss Delightful). Monty bred to his half sister, Maribrens Victoria (also out of Eng. Ch. Maribrens Miss Delightful) gave Eng. Ch. Maribrens Marty. Marty was the sire of Eng. Ch. Vallencia Short 'N' Sweet and Tuttlebees Rather Royal (out of different dams) and they, bred together,

248

Eng. Ch. Grayco Hazelnut, brown Toy bitch, England's top winning Toy Poodle of the early 1980s with 34 Challenge Certificates, 12 Bests in Show at Poodle Club Ch. shows, and 7 Bests in Show at all-breed Ch. shows including Cruft's in 1982 and Ladies Kennel Assn. over a record entry in 1980. Bred, owned and handled by Mrs. Lesley Howard.

produced Eng. Ch. Vallencia Mr. Wonderful. Rather Royal produced six champions including Eng. Ch. Malibu The Love Bug. The Love Bug is the sire of four champions including Eng. Ch. Suraliam Boogy Woogy from Velveteen. Boogy Woogy's daughter, Eng. Ch. Velveteen Boogylicious, is the winner of 26 C.C.'s. She won 13 C.C.'s in 1982 and was the Top Toy Poodle that year. Boogy Woogy has attained Top Producers status.

A full brother of Eng. Ch. Tophill Toyboy, Tophill Cupidon, was the sire of Tenaver Montravia Little Riot. Little Riot's son, Eng. Ch. Capilon Toy Minstrel, sired Eng. Ch. Capilon Toy Pedlar. Pedlar in turn sired the lovely headed Eng. Ch. Capilon Graywood Pedlar's Chick. Pedlar's Chick sired Capilon Toy Gambler and he sired Eng. Ch. Ranji's C'est La Vie. C'est La Vie, a black, was bred to the brown Eng. Ch. Bartat Burnt Almond of Grayco, to produce England's most famous Poodle of recent years, Eng. Ch. Grayco Hazelnut, who was born July 23, 1978. Hazelnut's most exciting win was Best in Show at the 1982 Crufts Dog Show in London over 9,884 entries.

Hazelnut began her illustrious career as a finalist for Puppy of the Year in 1979, as Supreme Champions Stakes Winner in 1980, and was that year voted *Our Dogs'* "Top Dog" and *Dog World's* "Dog of the Year." She has 34 Challenge Certificates, 29 of those with Best of Breed awards, including Cruft's 1980, 1981 and 1982. She has 11 Utility Group wins at Championship Shows and seven All Breed Championship Shows Best in Show, including the Ladies Kennel Association 1980 over a world record entry of 11,964 dogs.

The Wychwood Gatesgarth Monarch Toy line is predominantly black with a few browns. A study of the chart will indicate its influence both in England, America and other countries.

CH. BLACKLIGHT OF SASSAFRAS

Whelped: March 6, 1966   Died: 1978

Bred by Shirley Logan
Owned by Pamela Ingram, Sassafras
Last owned by Dr. C. Evan Sawyer

Wychwood Gatesgarth Monarch (*blk*)
Eng. Ch. Tophill Toyboy (*blk*)
Tophill Tuppence (*blk*)
Ch. Tophill Tops of High Heritage (*blk*)
Tophill D'Arcy (*blk*)
Penelope of Tobruk (*blk*)
Twinkletoes of Merriworth (*blk*)

CH. BLACKLIGHT OF SASSAFRAS—*Black*

Ch. Black Bijou of Sassafras (*blk*)
Sarsaparilla of Sassafras (*brn*)
Coquette Fleur Noire (*blk*)
Sassafras The Fan Dancer (*blk*)
Ch. Foster's Little Bit O'Luck (*blk*)
La Nez (*blk*)
Petite Josette (*champagne*)

CH. GRANLY'S BLACK BEN

Whelped January 25, 1973

Bred by Lucy Onsager, Granly Poodles
Owned by Janice Brady, Charade Kennels

Ch. Tophill Tops of High Heritage (*blk*)
Ch. Blacklight of Sassafras (*blk*)
Sassafras The Fan Dancer (*blk*)
Ch. Brownstar of Sassafras (*brn*)
Int. Ch. Silver Sunday of Sassafras (*si*)
Sassafras Something Spicey (*si-be*)
Pocahontas of Sassafras (*brn*)

CH. GRANLY'S BLACK BEN—*Black*

Branslake Diablo (*blk*)
Eng. Ch. Trespetite Jansteen Black Wings (*blk*)
Jansteen Sunnitoun Sweet Sherry (*brn*)
Trespetite Morita (*blk*)
Eng. Ch. Ardynas Gay Scandal (*blk*)
Teresian Sophistication (*blk*)
Black Symphony of Selborne (*blk*)

36

British Toy Line
Adam of Evesgarden

THE Adam of Evesgarden line goes back through his sire, Braebeck Tino of Montfleuri, to Tino's sire, Am. Eng. Ch. Braebeck Toni of Montfleuri. Toni was a Top Producing Miniature and a Best in Show winner in England and the U.S. Braebeck Toni goes back in male tail line directly to Eng. Ch. The Monarch. Braebeck Tino, who was on the small side for a Miniature, was advertised as siring "Toy sized and near Toy sized offspring." Tino was a dominant black, siring no other color. Adam of Evesgarden, a black (whelped September 12, 1952), was the sire of Ch. Chaman Grouse and Hydegate Noel.

Grouse, a lovely little brown, came to the U.S. where she became the dam of the great Ch. Fieldstreams Valentine, a Best in Show winner and sire of 12 champions. In the early days of the English Toy Poodle, Mrs. M. Campbell Inglis in awarding Best in Show at the 1958 British Toy Poodle Club Open Show to Hydegate Noel described him as ". . . very sound, good black coat, good mouth, nice feet and good ear leathers, quite fearless." No less an authority than Philippe Howard Price commented about Noel, "Every breeder's dream of a Toy Poodle, with an excellent head, the darkest of eyes, very short back, and is a perfect mover and absolutely abounding in Poodle type." Because of his small size, Noel was much sought after at stud. In one litter he produced Am. Ch. St. Aubrey Emmrill Nose Gay and Am. Ch. St. Aubrey Emmrill Nick Nack. Prior to leaving England, Nick Nack sired the brown Eng. Ch. Tzigane Zants. In America he produced another four champions to make him a Top Producer.

Hydegate Noel's son, Braebeck Gogi, sired Ch. Crescentina Easter Bunny of Catalpa. Easter Bunny's son, Barsbrae Bunny's Boy, produced Eng. Ch.

Barsbrae Baboo. Baboo sired Barsbrae Mr. Solo, who became a champion in South Africa. Mr. Solo is the sire of three important sons: Australian Ch. Barsbrae Outward Bound (13 Bests in Show, sire of five champions) and the full brothers Eng. Ch. Barsbrae Branslake Darty (sire of six champions) and Branslake Diablo.

Eng. Ch. Barsbrae Branslake Darty was the sire of six champions including Eng. Ch. Conersk Campari and Eng. Ch. Leander Lawrance. Campari sired Am. Ch. Vernlil Arden Fogle who has produced six champions in California. Lawrance was a big winner with 12 C.C.'s. He sired 12 champions including Eng. Ch. Leander Spring Fever who first went to California and then on to Japan. Spring Fever is the sire of 15 champions.

Darty's brother Branslake Diablo was top show quality but oversize at 11½ inches tall. He possessed a beautiful long lean head with a tiny dark eye, a long neck, short loin and deep chest. He was all these and yet refined—a real stallion of a dog. Breeders recognized his quality and his potential at stud. He sired 17 champions, 11 of them English, including the under 10 inch Eng. Ch. Aesthete Branslake Black Magic (winner of 10 C.C.'s) and Eng. Ch. Trespetite Jansteen Black Wings, who won the dog C.C. at Crufts in 1971, 1972 and 1973. Black Wings was the sire of eight champions including Eng. Ch. Trespetite Classic and several who finished in the States.

Another highly influential son of Hydegate Noel was the small black Braebeck Achievement (by a son out of a granddaughter of Adam of Evesgarden). Achievement was a beautiful headed, sound, honest dog with a thick heavy coat. Time proved that Achievement was well named, as his get and grandget have extended his sphere of influence. Achievement sired six champions, but that is only the beginning of his story. Achievement had the ability to reduce size well under the 11 inch English limit and two of his get finished in the U.S.—the short bodied, high stationed Ch. Trespetite Kapitan (Top Producer of six champions) and Ch. Trespetite Carnival Caper. Achievement's son, Braebeck Arturo, sired Montravia Capilon Circus Boy. Circus Boy sired three champions, including Eng. Ch. Sibon Circus Dancer. Achievement bred to his own daughter gave Eng. Ch. Trespetite Gorgeous, and Gorgeous bred to Eng. Ch. Trespetite Jansteen Black Wings gave the aptly named Am. Ch. Trespetite Gorgeous Gal, who finished in the U.S. as a puppy.

The Ardynas Kennels, then in England, used Achievement when he was still quite young. For them he sired Ardynas Crackerjack, who produced the 9½ inch brown Top Producer Ardynas Sorrel. Sorrel sired five champions including Can. Mex. Ch. Ardynas Nicodemus of Molynews, who went to Canada. Nicodemus sired seven champions and Jeanie's Black Dina-Mite who is a top black sire with 19 champions to his credit. Crackerjack also sired the handsome Eng. Ch. Ardynas Gay Whisper who in turn sired eight champions. Gay Whisper produced Eng. Ch. Ardynas Gay Scandal who sired five champions. Gay Scandal's under 10 inch black son Ardynas Gay Gossip went to Canada where he became an Am. Bda. Mex. Int. (FCI) champion. Gay

Adam of Evesgarden

Eng. Ch. Leander Lawrance

Eng. Ch. Barsbrae Branslake Darty

Branslake Diablo

Eng. Ch. Leander Spring Fever

Int. Ch. Ardynas Gay Gossip

ADAM OF EVESGARDEN (British Line)

Hydegate Noel (*blk*) 2
   Ch. St. Aubrey Emmrill Nick Nack (*blk*) 5
      Ch. Tzigane Zants (*brn*)
    Braebeck Gogi (*blk*)
       Ch. Crescentina Easter Bunny of Catalpa (*blk*)
         Barsbrae Bunny's Boy (*blk*)
           Eng. Ch. Barsbrae Baboo (*blk*)
             So. Afr. Ch. Barsbrae Mr. Solo (*blk*) 2
               Aus. Ch. Barsbrae Outward Bound (*blk*) 5
               Eng. Ch. Barsbrae Branslake Darty (*blk*) 6
                  Eng. Ch. Conersk Campari (*blk*)
                    Ch. Vernlil Arden Fogle (*blk*) 6
                  Aesthete Secret Edition (*blk*) 3
                  Eng. Ch. Leander Lawrance (*blk*) 12
                    Eng. Ch. Leander Spring Fever (*blk*) 15
                Branslake Diablo (*blk*) 17
                  Eng. Ch. Trespetite Jansteen Black Wings (*blk*) 8
                    Eng. Ch. Trespetite Classic (*blk*)
                      Lotsmoor Talk About Grayco (*blk*)
                        Grayco Talk About Lotsmoor (*blk*)
                          Eng. Ch. Lotsmoor Honky Tonk (*brn*)
Braebeck Achievement (*blk*) 6
  Ch. Trespetite Kapitan (*blk*) 6
  Ardynas Crackerjack (*blk*)
    Eng. Ch. Ardynas Gay Whisper (*blk*) 8
      Eng. Ch. Ardynas Gay Scandal (*blk*) 5
      Int. Ch. Ardynas Gay Gossip (*blk*) 8
      Ardynas Sergei *(blk)* 7
         Ch. Ardynas Sir Jasper (*blk*) 9
         Ch. Ardynas Gay Houdini (*blk*) 6
    Ardynas Sorrel (*brn*) 5
      Can. Mex. Ch. Ardynas Nicodemus of Molynews (*blk*) 7
      Jeanie's Black Dina-Mite (*blk*) 19
        Ch. Ravendune Ken D'Lee Typesetter (*blk*) 7
        Ch. Hobnob Halston (*blk*) 5
Braebeck Dimanche of Meadstone (*blk*)
  Solo of Greatcoats (*blk*)
    Kingpin of Greatcoats (*blu*) 9½"
      Midas of Greatcoats (*apr*) 10"
        Greatcoats Orange Pip (*apr*)
          DeRegis Golden Realm (*apr*) 11
            Beaujolais Burnt Sienna (*apr*) 14
            Ch. Cygnet's Gold Rush (*apr*) 5
            Ch. Secota's Entre Nous Hi Voltage (*apr*) 9
            Peeples Red Rooster (*apr*) 2
              Ch. Secota's Red Dragon (*apr*) 5
         Greatcoats Lochmanor Sunny (*apr*)
          Ch. Lochmanor's Sunrise (*apr*)
            Ounce O'Bounce Lochmanor's Red (*apr*) 3
              Ch. Ounce O'Bounce Summer Wine (*apr*) 5
              Ch. Ounce O'Bounce Red Buttons (*apr*) 5
                Ch. Ounce O'Bounce Danny Boy (*apr*) 15
                  Ch. Spinnerin's High On Burgundy (*apr*) 7
                Ch. Ounce O'Bounce T.N.T. (*apr*) 5

CH. ARDYNAS SIR JASPER

Whelped: July 3, 1973

Bred by Jean and George Wright, Ardynas
Owned by Doris Cozart and Polly Allen

                         Eng. Ch. Ardynas Gay Scandal (*blk*)
             Int. Ch. Ardynas Gay Gossip (*blk*)
                         Sharnette Sheer Bliss (*blk*)
       Ardynas Sergei (*blk*)
                         Eng. Ch. Ardynas Gay Scandal (*blk*)
             Ardynas Whispered Words (*blk*)
                         Ardynas Whispering Grass (*blk*)

CH. ARDYNAS SIR JASPER—*Black*

                         Eng. Ch. Ardynas Gay Scandal (*blk*)
             Ardynas Lisbeck Jonathan (*blk*)
                         Ardynas Rebecca of Lisbeck (*blk*)
       Ardynas Jemima (*blk*)
                         Eng. Ch. Ardynas Gay Scandal (*blk*)
             Ardynas Charleston (*blk*)
                         Nina of the Black Girl (*blk*)

JEANIE'S BLACK DINA-MITE

Whelped September 19, 1970   Died December 19, 1983

Bred and owned by Jeanie T. Mazza, Wayne, New Jersey

Ardynas Crackerjack (*blk*)
Ardynas Sorrel (*brn*)
Ardynas Trespetite Delilah (*blk*)
Int. Ch. Ardynas Nicodemus of Molynews (*blk*)
Eng. Ch. Ardynas Gay Whisper (*blk*)
Molynews Mistinguette (*blk*)
Nicole Black Chiffon (*blk*)

JEANIE'S BLACK DINA-MITE—*Black*

Eng. Ch. Tophill Toyboy (*blk*)
Aspen Angry Young Man (*blk*)
Aspen Black Affronted (*blk*)
Aspen Black Diamond (*blk*)
Aspen Effervescence (*blk*)
Aspen Anita (*blk*)
Lady Jane of Cringlette (*blk*)

DeRegis Golden Realm

Ch. Secota's Red Dragon

Beaujolais Burnt Sienna

Ch. Spinnerin's High On Burgundy

Ch. Secota's Entre Nous Hi Voltage

Ch. Ounce O'Bounce T.N.T.

258

CH. OUNCE O'BOUNCE DANNY BOY

Whelped November 24, 1973   Died March 1985

Bred by Dorothy Gooch, Ounce O'Bounce Kennels
Owned by Bob Fry, Ounce O'Bounce Kennels

Ch. Lochmanor's Sunrise (*apr*)
Ounce O'Bounce Lochmanor's Red (*apr*)
Lochmanor's Red Twig (*apr*)
Am. Can. Ch. Ounce O'Bounce Red Buttons (*apr*)
Platina Petite Brandy Twist (*apr*)
Jonelle Marie (*apr*)
Lee Mac's Amber Erin (*apr*)

CH. OUNCE O'BOUNCE DANNY BOY—*Apricot*

Ch. Lochmanor's Sunrise (*apr*)
Ounce O'Bounce Lochmanor's Red (*apr*)
Lochmanor's Red Twig (*apr*)
Ounce O'Bounce Robin (*apr*)
Laura's Copper Sun of Luckys (*apr*)
Ounce O'Bounce Red Heather (*apr*)
Luckys Bronze Yvette (*apr*)

Gossip sired eight champions. Before leaving England he had produced an under 10 inch son, Ardynas Sergei. Sergei moved to the U.S. with his breeder-owners the George Wrights. In the U.S. he became a Top Producer with seven champions including the Top Producing sons Ch. Ardynas Sir Jasper and Ch. Ardynas Gay Houdini. This infusion of English breeding is blending well with American Toy lines.

Apricots

Up to this point the Adam of Evesgarden line has been predominantly black with a few browns. The late Kay Edwards in seeking both small size and quality in creating her apricot Greatcoats line in England used the black Braebeck Dimanche of Meadstone to produce her black Solo of Greatcoats who carried the apricot gene. Once she had the recessive color and quality, she proceeded to create her successful apricot Toy family. Solo's blue son, Kingpin of Greatcoats, was the great grandsire of DeRegis Golden Realm who came to the United States where he sired 11 champions. Three of Realm's sons are Top Producers: Beaujolais Burnt Sienna (14 champions), Ch. Secota's Entre Nous Hi Voltage (nine champions) and Ch. Cygnet's Gold Rush (five champions). Gold Rush's son Ch. Cygnet's Golden Glow Worm went to the Jodan Kennels in Texas where he produced the Best in Show winner, Ch. Jodan's Red Pepper. He is a multiple champion producer. Red Pepper, with his outstanding type and dark red color, is the best red Toy yet seen. Golden Realm's half brother Greatcoats Lochmanor Sunny (both by Greatcoats Orange Pip) sired Ch. Lochmanor's Sunrise. Sunrise's son, Ounce O'Bounce Lochmanor Red, went to the Ounce O'Bounce Kennels in Oregon where he established a family of winning and producing apricot Toys. Lochmanor's Red sired two Top Producers in Ch. Ounce O'Bounce Summer Wine (five champions) and Ch. Ounce O'Bounce Red Buttons. Red Buttons sired the leading apricot Toy sire, Ch. Ounce O'Bounce Danny Boy (15 champions), who in turn produced Ch. Spinnerin's High on Burgundy who has seven champions to his credit.

Many of England's leading kennels used the Adam of Evesgarden line to advantage. These include Barsbrae, Branslake, Emmrill, Trespetite, Bartat, Capilon and Ardynas. It has come to America particularly through the Ardynas line to further spread its influence in blacks and browns, and through the Greatcoats apricots to greatly improve our apricot Toys.

37

British Toy Line—
Sudbrook Sunday Knight

WHENEVER one thinks of white Toy Poodles in England, the Sudbrooks come immediately to mind. Sudbrook has had a major impact there and throughout the world. Mrs. Harold Cox has spent generations developing her Toy line and her success is no accident, starting with Sudbrook White Christmas, a daughter of Am. Ch. Wychwood White Winter, who was bred to Berinshill Briansky of Roningbrook to produce the beautiful headed Sudbrook Sunday Morning, who won the first Challenge Certificate awarded to a Toy Poodle bitch. Sunday Morning won two reserve C.C.'s but did not gain her title. Sunday Morning was all Miniature breeding, but she was under 11 inches in size. She was bred to the Toy, The Cherub of Braxted, who was intensely linebred to the small Seahorses Snow Marquess, foundation sire of the small white Seahorses Toy strain. This breeding produced Sudbrook Sunday Knight who heads his own white Toy line. Sunday Knight won eight Best of Varieties.

Sunday Knight was bred to his full sister, Sudbrook Sunday Eve, to produce Eng. Ch. Sudbrook Sunday Suit. Sunday Suit was the first Toy Poodle in England to win a Group First. Sunday Suit was also the first Toy Poodle to gain the coveted Junior Warrant award, based on the number of wins as a puppy. Sunday Suit bred to his half sister, Sudbrook Evening Star of Munchkin (also by Sunday Knight) produced Eng. Ch. Sudbrook Sunday Xpress. Xpress was the sire of Eng. Ch. Glandore Pandarus, Eng. Ch. Bbormot Bit O'Bother and Eng. Ch. Westwood Bbormot Blossom. Sunday Suit was bred to his great granddam, Sudbrook White Christmas, to produce Eng. Ch. Sudbrook Sunday Best who was a Best in Show winner. Mrs. Cox considers Sunday Best the finest Toy she ever bred.

Sunday Best was a successful sire with six champions to his credit. His most famous son was the 9½ inch Best in Show winner, Eng. Ch. Sudbrook Sunday Special. Sunday Special won a total of 9 C.C.'s and sired 14 champions. Sunday

Eng. Ch. Sudbrook Sunday Suit

Ch. Sudbrook Sunday Paperboy

Eng. Ch. Sudbrook Sunday Best

Ch. Collier's Paperboy Cupid

Eng. Ch. Sudbrook Sunday Special

Bragabout Sharpshooter

SUDBROOK SUNDAY KNIGHT

Eng. Ch. Sudbrook Sunday Suit (*wh*) 5
    Eng. Ch. Sudbrook Sunday Xpress (*wh*) 3
    Eng. Ch. Sudbrook Sunday Best (*wh*) 6
        Eng. Ch. Sudbrook Sunday Special (*wh*) 14
            Sudbrook Sunday Surprise (*wh*)
                Eng. Ch. Sudbrook Sunday Billing (*wh*)
                    Eng. Ch. Sudbrook Spring Sunday (*wh*)
                        Eng. Ch. Sudbrook Sunday Gladrags (*wh*)
            Am. Ch. Sudbrook Sunday Go T'Meeting (*wh*) 2
            Am. Ch. Bi-Je's Mr. Something Special (*wh*)
                Can. Ch. Hayfield's Sanway Dibo Caper (*wh*) 5
        Panavon Little Perry (*wh*) 2
            Am. Ch. Panavon Little Panton (*wh*)
            Bragabout Sharpshooter (*wh*) 5
                Am. Ch. Poco A Poco Sun of a Gun (*wh*) 6
      Am. Ch. Sudbrook Sunday Paperboy (*wh*) 7
      Am. Ch. Collier's Paperboy Cupid (*wh*) 5
      Am. Ch. Collier's Pretty Pretty Boy (*wh*) 2
        Am. Ch. Lotus Savory Salt (*wh*) 3
            Am. Ch. Lotus Jigger of Jen (*wh*) 5
                Am. Ch. Jobre Commander Jerry (*wh*) 5
    Braebeck Tino (*wh*)

Special's son, Sudbrook Sunday Surprise, sired Eng. Ch. Sudbrook Sunday Billing. Sunday Billing was the sire of Eng. Ch. Sudbrook Sunday Gladrags. From Sunday Knight to Sunday Gladrags represents eight generations of Sudbrook white Toy males in direct male line. Sunday Suit won the dog C.C. at Crufts in 1960. Twenty-three years later, in 1983, Sunday Gladrags' daughter, Eng. Ch. Ridingleaze Dainty Toes of Valetta, won the bitch C.C. and Best of Breed at Crufts at seven years of age and after having three litters. This was her 15th C.C. She had also won the C.C. and Best of Breed at Crufts in 1979. Sunday Special's son, Int. and Nordic Ch. Sudbrook Sunday Hymn, was the

Ch. Jobre Commander Jerry

Ch. Lotus Jigger of Jen

"Outstanding Dog of the Year" in Sweden for the year 1965. Four of Sunday Special's get have crossed the seas to become American champions: Ch. Sudbrook Sunday Go T'Meeting, Ch. Piccoli Little Peppermint, Ch. Panavon Poppet's Pauline and Ch. Alendore's Peter Pan.

Another son of Sunday Best, Panavon Little Perry, sired the import Am. Ch. Panavon Little Panton. Panton's son Bragabout Sharpshooter, and Sharpshooter's son Ch. Poco A Poco Son of a Gun, are both Top Producers.

Mrs. Cox exported another Sunday Best son, Am. Ch. Sudbrook Sunday Paperboy, to Texas where he sired seven champions including the Top Producer Ch. Collier's Paperboy Cupid and Ch. Collier's Pretty Pretty Boy. Pretty Boy sired the multiple champion producer, Ch. Lotus Savory Salt. Savory Salt's son, Ch. Lotus Jigger of Jen and Jigger's son, Ch. Jobre' Commander Jerry, are both Top Producers.

Yet another son of Sunday Best was to make important contributions especially in the U.S. This was Braebeck Tino. Tino was bred to Contessa Alicia, who was a granddaughter of Sunday Special and Sunday Xpress, to produce Branslake Floris. Floris came to the U.S. where she founded Hell's A Blazen Kennels. Floris whelped only six puppies—five became champions; three were Best in Show winners: Ch. Hell's A Blazen Carnival Fame, Ch. Hell's A Blazen Kiss A Me and Ch. Hell's A Blazen Kinda Kostly, and three were Top Producers—Carnival Fame, Kinda Kostly and Ch. Hell's A Blazen Carnival Fancy (dam of five champions). Carnival Fame sired Ch. Fairview's No Nonsense, the Top Winning Poodle, All Varieties for 1984. Kinda Kostly was the leading Toy Poodle sire for 1984.

The Sudbrooks, named after a small hamlet in Surrey, have gone all over the world to bring fame and glory to their name. There are more than 40 champions worldwide sired by the Sudbrook stud dogs.

At Sudbrook, Sheila Cox has placed emphasis on quality, balance and correct Poodle type. She feels that true type and soundness are the most difficult features to retain when size is reduced. The Sudbrooks are also noted for their beautiful Miniature type heads.

American white Toy breeders have had to practice continual selection away from the old fashioned, apple headed, pop-eyed American Toy. Toy breeders here are fortunate in having the benefit of so many years of careful breeding from Sudbrook to combine with their own efforts to produce the beautiful white Toys currently in the show ring.

Ch. Cartlane Once, the first Toy Poodle to win Best in Show at the Poodle Club of America Specialty 1951. Once is shown with Ruth Burnette Sayres, Handler; Mrs. Saunders Meade, presenting trophy and Kathleen Staples, Judge. Owned by Mrs. Charles Fleishman.

38

Toy Kennels of the Past

BERMYTH—Bertha Smith
DE GLADVILLE—Gladys Herbel
FIELDSTREAMS—Audrey W. Kelch
GREGOIRE—Mary Edith Gregory
J.C.—Mr. & Mrs. J. Stokes Smith
KORNEL—Nel Korbijn
LEICESTER'S—Leicester Harrison
LIME CREST—Robert & Doris Levy
LITTLE WONDERFUL—Thomas Hartmann
MEISEN—Hilda Meisenzahl *(Also Miniatures)*
PEEBLES—Joyce Peebles
POOD-I-MAN—Marion Spires *(Also Miniatures, Standards)*
RAINES—Mrs. Paul Raines
RENEA—Byron W. Elder
SASSAFRAS—Pamela A. P. Ingram
SEAHORSES—Lady Stanier (Great Britain)
SILHOU-JETTE—Martha Jane Ablett *(Also Miniatures)*
SUCHAN—Richard Suchan
THORNLEA—Adele (Sandy) Dow *(Also Miniatures)*

39

Present Day Toy Kennels

TOY POODLE breeders have every right to be proud of the tremendous improvement in type accomplished in the last thirty years—the greatest overall improvement in type in any of the three varieties. However, in all fairness the Toy Poodle had the greatest need for improvement. Although there are more correctly balanced Toys being shown than ever before Toy breeders recognize the need for constant vigilance to avoid slipping backwards into the longer, lower specimens. The opposite type of too short bodied and too high on leg which can result in a "chicken boned," too fine, spidery type must also be avoided. The ideal of the "squarely built appearance" as called for in the breed standard must always be sought.

Toy Poodles have a large number of breeders who are constantly seeking to maintain and improve this challenging size. The following is a list of breeders who have made and are currently making noteworthy contributions to the Toy variety:

AMBERLY'S—Judy Ambler
ARDEN—Jeannie T. Mazza
ARDYNAS—Mr. & Mrs. George Wright (Also Standards)
ARUNDEL—Judy Feinberg
BAYOU BREEZE—Henry Cohn (Also Miniatures)
BEAUJOLAIS—Beverly Valerio
BRAGABOUT—Charline Averill
CAMELOT—Marvin, Nancy and Mary Ellen Fishler
CAMELOT—Paula S. Smith
CHARADE—Janice Brady
CLARDON—June Suttie

CLARION—Ann Helgeson *(Also Miniatures)*
CONSENTINO—Jane Cosentino
COTIAN—Doris Cozart
DARRETTE—Annette & Darrell Andersen
DELHI—Marilyn Horn
DURANT—Jean Durant
EVANZ—Marilyn Pauley
FOGLE—Besse Fogle
HELL'S A BLAZEN—Frances Rubinich
HIGH HERITAGE—Mackey J. Irick, Jr.
HIGH-WINGS—Dorothy Briggs
HILLTOP—Darlene Harder
HUBER—Mirble & Gordon Huber
JODAN—Betty Jo & Dan Gallas
LANGCROFT—Marie & Harold Langseth *(Also Miniatures, Standards)*
LITTLE BIT—Domenick Nappi
MERIDIAN—Ruth Winston *(Also Miniatures)*
MICHANDA—Patricia McMullen
MONTEC—Susan Goodson
MONTMARTRE—Erna Conn (Great Britain) *Also Miniatures*
OUNCE O'BOUNCE—Dorothy Gooch, Bob Fry
PAMPER'S—Brenda Feik
PLATH'S—Beryl Plath
POODLETOWN—Ellen Michel
PRICE-PATRICK—Marjorie & Bill Dolan *(Also Miniatures)*
REGENCE—V. Jean Craft
SAN-GAI—Nancy Peerenboom
SUDBROOK—Sheila Cox (Great Britain)
SYNTIFNY—Jane A. Winne
YERBRIER—Betty Yerington
VALCOPY—Dana L. Plonkey *(Also Miniatures, Standards)*
WISSFIRE—Joan Scott

Group of Salmagundi white Standards. Dog on left
is Int. Ch. Prinz Alexander von Rodelheim.

The Standard Poodle

CH. BLAKEEN CYRANO

Whelped July 28, 1934   Deceased

Bred by Blakeen Kennels
Owned by Lowmont Kennels

Windsfield Joyful Joe (*brn*)
Nunsoe Aurelius (*brn*)
Nunsoe Hazel (*brn*)
Ch. Nunsoe David Darling of Blakeen (*brn*)
Eng. Ch. Tom (*blk*)
Nunsoe Mary Ann (*brn*)
Nunsoe Hazel (*brn*)

CH. BLAKEEN CYRANO—*Brown*

Eng. Ch. Whippendell Carillon (*blk*)
Ch. Nymphaea Jason (*brn*)
Eng. Ch. Nymphaea Juliette (*brn*)
Blakeen Vigee le Brun (*brn*)
Maupassant (*blk*)
Sophie (*blk*)
Madam Bella (*blk*)

270

40

Foreword to
Standard Male Lines

THERE ARE ONLY TWO important male lines in the Standard variety in the United States today: the "Prinz Alexander" line and the "Anderl" line. There were once four important male lines in Standards: the predominantly white "Prinz Alexander" line and the three colored lines: the "Anderl" line, the Eng. Ch. Whippendell Carillon line and the Ch. Blakeen Cyrano line. In the spring of 1949 a male puppy was born in Connecticut who was to change the direction of black and brown Standard Poodles. This puppy, Ch. Annsown Sir Gay (from the Anderl line), and his sons and their sons exerted such a profound influence that they eventually overwhelmed the other two colored male lines.

Eng. Ch. Whippendell Carillon was whelped in 1923 and his line was on the small side, no doubt due to a Chieveley Miniature grandsire, but it offered refinement and elegance needed by the heavier Continental lines. The American-bred brown Ch. Blakeen Cyrano (whelped 1934) was acclaimed as one of the truly great specimens of the breed. Cyrano was an outstanding winner and a successful sire, but not through the tail male line. This line was particularly rich in the strength of the bitches it produced (rather than producing males) which makes it appear less widespread than the others, but it is no less important in its impact on the variety. In fact, Ch. Annsown Sir Gay is descended from both Carillon and Cyrano, so they played a part in his creation, but it was through Anderl that he is descended in the male line. And it was through Sir Gay and his sons that the family has fanned out all over the world to great acclaim.

The Standard lines from the previous edition have been consolidated in

Int. Ch. Prinz Alexander von Rodelheim

this edition and greatly lengthened to bring them up-to-date. From 1970 through the end of 1984 there have been 2,203 new champion Standards recorded by the AKC. The charts have been compiled to simplify the relationships within a line. It should be noted that the ability to become a Top Producer seems to pass from father to son rarely skipping more than a generation or two at a time. This once again proves the value of keeping close to the best when selecting a sire for a litter. The charts note the male line of descent from father to son including those dogs which have sired 10 or more champions, plus some younger sires of particular promise and a few influential English sires. These figures include foreign champions, where known, and not just American champions. Each indentation denotes a new generation. A commentary relating the outstanding accomplishments of each line as winners and producers precedes the charts. These charts also give the colors, and the numbers in parentheses at the end of each name indicate the number of champions produced by each dog.

41

The "Prinz Alexander" Line— Ch. Prinz Alexander von Rodelheim

T HE OUTSTANDING Prinz Alexander family of white Standards had their beginnings in the snow capped mountains of Switzerland. The founder of this dynasty was Continental Ch. Prinz Alexander von Rodelheim, whelped June 30, 1925, a consistent winner in Europe. This family wore their royal titles of Prinz, Princess and the Duc with regal bearing and have handed down their beauty and brains for almost 60 years, not only as outstanding winners but also producers of note. Mme. Lucienne Reichenbach of the world famous Labory Kennels in Switzerland also developed the other great Standard male line, the black family of Ch. Anderl von Hugelberg. Mme. Reichenbach combined Prinz Alexander with La Terrace and the German Schneeflocke and Rodelheim lines with great success and the results were sent out all over the world to great acclaim.

These large and handsome dogs were originally of German origin. They were, as the records show quite clearly, far superior in size, type and showiness to the English white Standards exhibited in England before their arrival. The English dogs were, in many cases, small and snipey, inclined to weakness of hindquarters, or, if of another type, with coarse heads, wide skulls and with loose and wide fronts.

The white Labory Poodles were noted for their combination of size without coarseness, extreme elegance of type and pride of carriage, combined with good bone, black eyes and exquisite refinement and beauty of expression. Their skin was silver, not pink, and they carried immense snowy white coats of

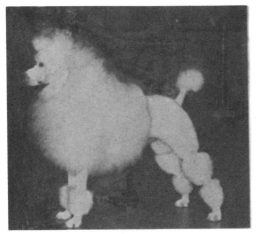

Ch. Pillicoc Barrister

Ch. Alekai Oli of Stonebridge

Ch. Paloma's Bon Vivant

Ch. Alekai Ouzo

Ch. Alekai Luau

Ch. Puttencove Presentation

INT. CH. PRINZ ALEXANDER VON RODELHEIM

Int. Ch. Prinz Alexander Von Rodelheim (*wh*) 5
  Int. Ch. Nunsoe Duc de la Terrace of Blakeen (*wh*) 10
    Marechal of Piperscroft (*wh*) 1
      Ch. Rettats Slick (*wh*) 3
        Ch. Pillicoc Pegasus (*wh*) 5
          Southland Swagger (*wh*) 1
            Ch. Sultan de San Souci (*wh*) 12
        Retatts Spinner (*wh*)
          Berkham Hansel of Rettats (*blu*) 1
            Spitfire of the Chain (*si*) 5
            Mist of Piperscroft (*blu*) 2
              Eng. Ch. Frenches Blue Peter (*blu*) 14
                Eng. Ch. Frenches Rockefella (*blu*)
                  Eng. Ch. Frenches Rockaven (*blk*) 6
                Eng. Am. Ch. Frenches Blue Marvel (*blu*) 12
    Piperscroft Pippo de la Terrace (*wh*) 2
      Ch. Scallawag of Piperscroft of Blakeen (*wh*) 1
        Ch. Torchlight St. Pierre Eglise (*blk*) 6
His Excellency of Salmagundi (*wh*) 6
Ch. Salmagundi's Choice (*wh*) 2
  Ch. White Cocade of Salmagundi (*wh*) 13
    Ch. Cartlane Laurent (*wh*) 1
      Ch. Tour D'Argent Christopher (*wh*) 8
    Ch. Carillon Jester U.D. (*blk*) 1
      Petitcote Baron Chico C.D. (*crm*)
        Int. Ch. Petitcote Domino C.D. (*blk*) 9
          Wencair's Frere Jacques (*blk*) 6
  Ch. Lucite of Salmagundi (*wh*) 2
    Ch. Ensarr Glace (*wh*) 8
      Ch. Hillandale C'Est Vrais (*wh*) 11
    Pillicoc Courier (*wh*) 1
      Ch. Pillicoc Barrister (*wh*) 6
        Ch. Blakeen Sorcerer's Apprentice (*wh*) 6
          Ch. Paloma's Bon Vivant (*wh*) 26
            Ch. Hallmark Harmony O'Windridge (*wh*) 8
        Ch. Blakeen Bali Ha'i (*wh*) 3
          Ch. Loabelo Jonny (*wh*) 2
            Ch. Puttencove Promise (*wh*) 28
              Can. Ch. Calvados de la Fontaine (*wh*) 5
                Ch. Merryleg's Cetin de la Fontaine (*wh*) 7
              Chantilly Lover Boy (*wh*) 5
              Ch. Alekai Nohea (*wh*) 13
              Ch. Ivardon Sheraton (*wh*)
                Ivardon Kenilworth of Ensarr (*wh*) 1
                  Ch. Alekai Kila (*wh*) 8
                    Ch. Alekai Ahi (*wh*) 21
                      Ch. Alekai Luau (*wh*) 15
                        Ch. Puttencove Presentation (*wh*) 9
                      Ch. Alekai Oli of Stonebridge (*wh*) 17
                      Ch. Alekai Ouzo (*wh*) 10

SWISS, FRENCH, ENGLISH AND AMERICAN
CHAMPION NUNSOE DUC DE LA TERRACE OF BLAKEEN

Whelped: September 1, 1928   Died: October 26, 1940

Breeder: Mme. Emile Warney, Switzerland
Owners: Mr. and Mrs. Sherman Hoyt, Blakeen Kennels

Bodo v. Furstenberg (*wh*)
Int. Ch. Prinz v. Oberesslingen (*wh*)
Priska-Reinblut (*wh*)
Int. Ch. Prinz Alexander v. Rodelheim (*wh*)
Prinz Troll v. Konigstuhl (*wh*)
Carmen v. Lennep (*wh*)
Sieger Cora v. Lennep (*wh*)

INT. CH. NUNSOE DUC DE LA TERRACE OF BLAKEEN—*White*

Prinz v. Park (*wh*)
Prinz v. d. Kornerweise (*wh*)
Boppi v. Elisenburg (*wh*)
Leonore v. d. Seestadt (*wh*)
German Ch. Rigo v. Konigstuhl (*wh*)
Sussi v. d. Hirschholde (*wh*)
Trude v. Lennep (*wh*)

perfect texture. Many had heads that were truly superb and were flawless in construction, putting to shame even the best heads among the blacks.

The faults, and alas, even the best families have them, were shortness of ear leather and wide fronts, which are characteristics descended from the German Schneeflocke line. These shortcomings have been largely overcome in the hands of our cleverest breeders, to whom we owe so much for their rare manipulation and interweaving of the white bloodlines obtained from Mme. Reichenbach, and for their own pluck and perseverance. America has reason to be proud of her white Standard Poodle fanciers and their really great achievements. Keeping a large white Standard clean and presentable requires a great deal of work but the results can be spectacular and the white devotees are firm in their dedication. This great winning and producing white Standard line has steadily held a top place among show dogs, generation after generation. This can, I believe, be accounted for by the fact that the foundation dogs were all of exceptional quality—famous on both sides of the water, and winners in all the Continental countries as well as their native Germany and their adopted Switzerland. Nor were the bitches any less excellent than the dogs, as the records prove. Therefore there is every reason for the continued success of this bloodline. Perhaps no other strain has had a more splendid beginning and present day breeders are wisely preserving this valuable heritage.

Prior to leaving Switzerland for America, Prinz Alexander produced two noted daughters, Ch. Edelweis du Labory of Salmagundi and Ch. Princess du Labory of Salmagundi, and two influential sons, Piperscroft Pippo de la Terrace and Int. Ch. Nunsoe Duc de la Terrace of Blakeen. Prinz Alexander came to Mr. and Mrs. Justin Greiss' Salmagundi Kennels in Massachusetts at ten years of age, after his show and stud career in Switzerland. In the United States, he was used at stud only at his home kennel and there he produced His Excellency of Salmagundi and Int. Ch. Salmagundi's Choice.

Prinz Alexander's most famous son was Int. Ch. Nunsoe Duc de la Terrace of Blakeen, bred by Mme. Emile Warney of the La Terrace Kennels in Switzerland. The Duc was selected as choice of litter in lieu of the stud fee by Mme. Lucienne Reichenbach.

The Duc was a magnificent specimen of the breed. His beauty, soundness, and confident stylish showmanship were to bring him international honors. After winning his Swiss and French championships he was sold by Mme. Reichenbach to Miss Jane Lane of Nunsoe fame in England, in 1932. Prior to the Duc's arrival, most British Standard Poodles were in the 19 to 23 inch size range. Even though he was taller and heavier boned than the English Poodles, he was not coarse. His beautiful proportions and elegant appearance changed the British breeders' opinions on size and substance. He had an outstanding show career in the fiercest competition. Shown for the first time in England in 1932, he won six Challenge Certificates and a Best in Show. British breeders wisely used him and he permanently improved the white Standard there.

In 1934 the Duc was purchased as a magnificent gift by Mrs. Whitney

CH. ENSARR GLACE

Whelped: October 30, 1946   Died: March 1, 1959

Bred by Henry Stoecker
Owned by Mrs. W. French Githens, Ensarr Poodles

Int. Ch. Prinz Alexander v. Rodelheim (*wh*)

Ch. Salmagundi's Choice (*wh*)

Ch. Edelweis du Labory of Salmagundi (*wh*)

Ch. Lucite of Salmagundi (*wh*)

Int. Ch. Prinz Alexander v. Rodelheim (*wh*)

Ch. Princess du Labory of Salmagundi (*wh*)

Alba de la Terrace (*wh*)

CH. ENSARR GLACE—*White*

Marechal of Piperscroft (*wh*)

Ch. Rettats Slick (*wh*)

Phidgity Swallow (*wh*)

Ch. Pillicoc Pearl (*wh*)

Pillicoc Avenir (*blk*)

Pillicoc Alabaster (*wh*)

Blakeen Spindrift (*wh*)

Blake for her daughter, Mrs. Sherman Hoyt. Shown only 18 times in this country he won 18 Bests of Breed, 16 Group Firsts including Westminster 1934, 1935 and 1936. He won 9 Bests in Show including Westminster 1935, handled by Mrs. Hoyt. The Duc was the first Poodle to win Best in Show at Westminster. At that time, whites were considered inferior to blacks and browns in England and America and the Duc was the first white to successfully defeat those colors in the ring. Mrs. Byron Rogers credits this win and the Duc in aiding the revival of the Poodle in America and making the general public Poodle minded.

Mrs. Hoyt described the Duc as being 26 inches at the shoulder and weighing between 65 and 70 pounds. He was considered too large at that time, but his power, strength and above all his beauty was the overriding impression.

Fortunately for the breed, the Duc proved to be a great sire. His two most famous children were Ch. Blakeen Jung Frau and Int. Ch. Blakeen Eiger. Jung Frau won 40 Groups and 19 Bests in Show, including the 1940 Morris and Essex show. Eiger won 57 Groups and 17 Bests in Show and gained his title in Canada by winning three straight Groups. Jung Frau and Eiger were an unforgettable brace. Other notable get of the Duc's were: Ch. Knight of Piperscroft and Blakeen, who won numerous Groups and Bests in Show; Ch. Blakeen the Ghost, winner of three Bests in Show; and Ch. Blakeen Cafe Parfait, winner of two Bests in Show. Can. Champions Blakeen Monch and Schatzy were also Best in Show winners. Ch. Nunsoe Con Amore of Salmagundi and Ch. Blakeen Schneeflocke complete the list of the Duc's titleholders. Of his 9 champion children 7 were Best in Show winners, truly an amazing record for a sire.

Interestingly, it is through an untitled son of the Duc, sired in England, that the Duc tail male line comes down today in England. This son, Marechal of Piperscroft, sired the brothers Ch. Rettat's Slick and Rettat's Spinner.

In the United States, Slick was bred to Pillicoc Alabaster (a granddaughter of the Duc and Ch. Pillicoc Rumpelstilskin) to produce Ch. Pillicoc Pegasus and Ch. Pillicoc Pearl. Pearl was the dam of Ch. Ensarr Glace. Ch. Pillicoc Pegasus sired five champions including the silver Ch. Astron Silver Star. An untitled Pegasus son, Southland Swagger, produced Ch. Sultan de San Souci (sire of 12 champions).

In England, Rettat's Spinner sired the blue Berkham Hansel of Rettats, who was definite show quality but never gained his title due to World War II and the cessation of shows for the duration of the war. Hansel sired the silver, Spitfire of the Chain (sire of five champions) and the blue Mist of Piperscroft. Mist sired Eng. Ch. Frenches Blue Peter. Blue Peter was a sound, short-backed dog with a refined head and an immense, clear-colored blue coat. Blue Peter was one of England's greatest Standard sires with 14 English champions to his credit, including Eng. Ch. Frenches Rockefella. Rockefella was the sire of one of England's top Standard winners, Eng. Ch. Frenches Rockaven, winner of 24 Challenge Certificates. Blue Peter was bred to White Lady of Burgois (dam of

Eng. Am. Ch. Frenches
Blue Marvel

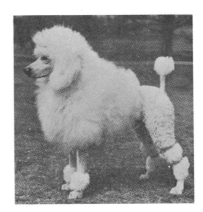

Ch. White Cocade
of Salmagundi

five champions) who was also a granddaughter of Berkham Hansel of Rettats, to produce Eng. and Am. Ch. Frenches Blue Marvel.

Blue Marvel completed his English title undefeated in three consecutive shows. He was then imported by the Clarion Kennels. He made his American debut at the Poodle Club of America Specialty in 1952 where he went straight through to Best of Breed. Blue Marvel sired 12 champions including the Best in Show winning cream Ch. Algonquin of Champaign. Algonquin is the sire of Ch. Kickapoo of Champaign who has five titled get. Blue Marvel, whelped in 1949, was the last English or Continental Standard import to have an important effect on the breed here.

A full brother of the great Duc, Piperscroft Pippo de la Terrace, went to England where he sired Ch. Scallawag of Piperscroft of Blakeen. Scallawag, imported to America, was bred to the black Ch. Torchlight Dunkerque to produce the black Ch. Torchlight St. Pierre Eglise (sire of six champions).

Prinz Alexander's lovely daughter, Ch. Edelweis du Labory of Salmagundi was a beautiful Poodle and a charming one. Mrs. Greiss bought her as a puppy in 1933 from Mme. Reichenbach and she was her constant companion from then on in Massachusetts. Her American owner was so fond of the beautiful bitch that it was very reluctantly that she consented to her show career, which proved so brilliant with 35 Group firsts and eight Bests in Show. Edelweis' dam was German Ch. Nelly von der Schneeflocke of Blakeen whom Mrs. Sherman Hoyt also brought to America.

As an old dog Prinz Alexander joined his famous daughters at Salmagundi where his greatness was properly appreciated, and he lived to a ripe old age. Prinz Alexander was bred to Edelweis to produce her best two children, Int. Ch.

Salmagundi's Choice (who, after completing his American title, was sent to England, where he promptly gained an English championship) and His Excellency of Salmagundi. Prinz Alexander, previously bred in Switzerland to his daughter Alba de la Terrace (litter sister of the famous Duc), produced Am. Ch. Princess du Labory of Salmagundi, whom Mrs. Greiss also imported. Princess bred to her three-quarter brother, His Excellency, gave six champions: Ch. Salmagundi Perhaps So Wise, Ch. Knight Errant, Ch. His Highness, Ch. Happy Choice, Ch. Dame Choice and Ch. Chosen Dame—all of Salmagundi. Princess was also bred to Ch. Salmagundi's Choice (His Excellency's full brother) to produce Ch. White Cocade of Salmagundi and Ch. Lucite of Salmagundi.

White Cocade, a Best in Show winner, went to Miriam Hall's Cartlane Kennels where he was greatly loved and retained his regal bearing to the end of his long life. White Cocade sired 13 champions, including Ch. Cartlane Laurent. Laurent was the sire of Ch. Tour d'Argent Christopher, who sired eight champions. White Cocade was bred to the black Ch. Carillon Colline to produce the great Obedience winner, Ch. Carillon Jester, U.D.T., who was black like his dam. Jester sired the cream Petitcote Baron Chico, C.D., who was the sire of Am. and Can. Ch. Petitcote Domino (sire of nine champions).

Marechal of Piperscroft

Ch. Blakeen Bali Ha'i

AM. CAN. CH. PUTTENCOVE PROMISE

Whelped January 20, 1955   Died: 1965

Bred and owned by Puttencove Kennels

Ch. Pillicoc Barrister (*wh*)
Ch. Blakeen Bali Ha'i (*wh*)
Blakeen Morning Star (*wh*)
Ch. Loabelo Jonny (*wh*)
Nunsoe The Duke (*wh*)
Vulcan Champagne Carmen of Blakeen (*wh*)
Vulcan Champagne Capella (*wh*)

AM. CAN. CH. PUTTENCOVE PROMISE—*White*

Pillicoc Courier (*wh*)
Ch. Pillicoc Barrister (*wh*)
Blakeen Surrey Romance (*wh*)
Astron Lily of Puttencove (*wh*)
Ch. Pillicoc Pegasus (*wh*)
Ch. Astron Silver Star (*si*)
Von's Jezebel (*blk*)

282

Domino sired Wencair's Frere Jacque (sire of six champions) as well as the greatest producing bitch in the history of the breed, Am. and Can. Ch. Wycliffe Jacqueline, U.D. (dam of 21 champions). It is through Jacqueline's black son, Ch. Wycliffe Thomas, that this famous white line lays claim to Ch. Acadia Command Performance, as a direct descendant but not in the tail male line.

Now to return to Cocade's litter brother, Ch. Lucite of Salmagundi. Lucite was bred to Ch. Pillicoc Pearl to produce the magnificent headed Ch. Ensarr Glace. Glace was an outstanding winner with two Bests in Show to his credit. He sired eight champions including Davdon Kennels' Best in Show winner Ch. Hillandale C'Est Vrais (ex Ch. Cartlane Hillandale Cadenza, a daughter of Ch. White Cocade of Salmagundi). C'Est Vrais bred to his Best in Show daughter, Ch. Davdon Miss Demeanor, produced Ch. Davdon Captivation (dam of four Alekai champions). C'Est Vrais' son, Ch. Valeway Temptation of Davdon, sired three champions including Ch. Davdon Summa Cum Laude (dam of six Alekai champions).

An unshown brother of Glace, Pillicoc Courier, was bred to Blakeen Surrey Romance to produce Ch. Pillicoc Barrister. Courier and Romance were both out of Ch. Pillicoc Pearl (three crosses to the Duc). Courier's sire, Ch. Lucite of Salmagundi, was by Ch. Salmagundi's Choice ex Ch. Princess du Labory of Salmagundi. Both were sired by Prinz Alexander ex daughters of Prinz Alexander. Surrey Romance was sired by Ch. Knight Errant of Salmagundi. Both of Knight Errant's parents, His Excellency of Salmagundi and Ch. Princess du Labory of Salmagundi, were by Prinz Alexander ex daughters of Prinz Alexander.

Barrister therefore represents strong intensification of these lines. A close study of his pedigree reveals a dozen crosses to the originator of the line, Ch. Prinz Alexander von Rodelheim. There are few bloodlines that can be put to such a close test of breeding and come through with flying colors, but Barrister's ancestors had been carefully selected for generation after generation. Barrister is the grandsire of two of the greatest members which this family has produced, Ch. Puttencove Promise and Ch. Paloma's Bon Vivant.

But to return to Barrister, he sired six champions including two important sons, Ch. Blakeen Bali Ha'i and Ch. Blakeen Sorcerer's Apprentice. Sorcerer's Apprentice went to the Forzando Kennels in California, where he sired six champions, including the small but handsome Ch. Paloma's Bon Vivant. Bon Vivant, a Best in Show winner, sired 26 champions including the Best in Show winner Ch. Hallmark Harmony O'Windridge (sire of eight champions) and Ch. Forzando Bergamasque (sire of five champions).

Ch. Pillicoc Barrister's other important son, Ch. Blakeen Bali Ha'i, a Best in Show winner, went to Puttencove Kennels. Bali Ha'i's son, Ch. Loabelo Jonny, sired one of the breed's greatest winners and producers, the magnificent Ch. Puttencove Promise (ex a Barrister daughter).

Promise, with his great tail-wagging showmanship, was a favorite with the ringsiders and with the judges too. He was acclaimed as "a nearly perfect dog" by the late, great judge Alva Rosenberg. Promise was Best of Breed at the 1957 Poodle Club of America Specialty, and climaxed his great career with his Best in Show win at Westminster in 1958. Promise sired a total of 28 champions, including Ch. Puttencove Moonshine (sire of four champions), Can. Ch. Calvados de la Fontaine (sire of five champions) and Ch. Alekai Nohea (sire of 13 champions).

Before going to California, Nohea sired Ch. Alekai Pokoi, winner of 22 Bests in Show at All Breed and Specialty shows. Of Pokoi's 16 children, 10 became champions. A Promise son, Ch. Ivardon Sheraton, produced Ivardon Kenilworth of Ensarr who went to Alekai Kennels. Alekai continued the process of family breeding as had been practiced earlier with such great success. Kenilworth (a Promise grandson) was bred to Ch. Puttencove Kaui (a Promise daughter) to produce Ch. Alekai Kila. Kila, winner of four Group firsts, stood 26 inches tall. He was the first homebred male that Alekai kept for showing and offered at public stud. Kila sired the legendary Ch. Alekai Marlaine, winner of 10 All Breed and Specialty Best in Shows. Kila's son, the beautiful headed Ch. Alekai Ahi, was 27½ inches tall and an even greater sire than his father. Ahi produced 21 champions in limited use. Ahi sired the top winning Ch. Alekai Luau, who scored 25 All Breed and Specialty Bests in Show. Luau sired 15 champions including the Top Producer and Best in Show winner Ch. Puttencove Presentation and his sister, Ch. Puttencove Perdita. Perdita was the dam of five champions, three of them Best in Show winners, including Ch. Valhalla's In Command by Ch. Acadia Command Performance (Anderl line). In Command is one of the leading white Standard sires. Ahi bred to his Best in Show daughter, Ch. Tamara of Stonebridge, produced Ch. Alekai Oli of Stonebridge. Oli was the sire of 17 champions including Ch. Alekai Ouzo. Ouzo, a Best in Show winner, went to Canada where he produced 10 champions prior to his early death.

The Ch. Prinz Alexander von Rodelheim line is without a doubt one of the greatest winning and producing strains in the history of dogdom. It also represents one of the closest bred families in the history of the breed. We have reduced the many complicated relationships to their simplest terms so that the sire line could be more easily followed.

The only three Standard Poodles ever to win Best in Show at Westminster, and incidentally all were whites, were descendants of this family. Int. Ch. Nunsoe Duc de la Terrace of Blakeen took top honors in 1935. Twenty three years later, in 1958, Ch. Puttencove Promise won Best in Show there. In 1973 Ch. Acadia Command Performance went to the top at the nation's most prestigious show. Although Command Performance was not in direct tail male line, as were the Duc and Promise, he was a descendant, as recounted earlier, through his White Cocade-Jester-Wycliffe connection. The Prinz Alexander line continues today producing outstanding winners and producers primarily through the Alekai family and its branches.

42

Alekai Kennels

THE ALEKAI KENNELS of white Standard Poodles was established originally in Honolulu, Hawaii by Mrs. Henry J. Kaiser. Alekai is a combination of her first name, Alyce, and Kaiser. Mrs. Kaiser wisely decided to found her kennel on the best white Standards then obtainable. From Puttencove Kennels she acquired Ch. Puttencove Kaui (by Ch. Puttencove Promise ex Ch. Puttencove Moonglow). From Ivardon Kennels came Ch. Ivardon Winter (granddaughter of Ch. Blakeen Bali Ha'i) and Ivardon Kenilworth of Ensarr (grandson of Ch. Puttencove Promise and Ch. Ensarr Glace). From the de la Fontaine Kennels in Canada came Ch. Tambarine de la Fontaine (by Ch. Puttencove Promise ex Can. Ch. Cillette de la Fontaine). From the Davdon Kennels came Ch. Davdon Captivation (by the Best in Show winner, Ch. Hillandale C'Est Vrais ex his Best in Show daughter Ch. Davdon Miss Demeanor) and Ch. Davdon Summa Cum Laude (a C'Est Vrais granddaughter). Several of these were selected prior to their show careers and finished their titles under the Alekai banner.

Mrs. Kaiser built a beautiful kennel, acclaimed as one of the finest in the world, with a spectacular view overlooking Maunalua Bay. Beginning with the first champions bred in 1961, Alekai has compiled an impressive list of winners and producers. Ch. Davdon Summa Cum Laude was bred to Ch. Puttencove Promise to produce a litter of five champions: Ch. Alekai Pikake (Best in Show winner), Ch. Alekai Hololaka (Best in Show winner), Ch. Alekai Mai Kai (Best of Winners at the 1962 Poodle Club of America Specialty), Ch. Alekai Kona and the Group winner, Ch. Alekai Nohea (sire of 13 champions). Ch. Tambarine de la Fontaine (a Best in Show winner) was the dam of Ch. Alekai Maunalua and Ch. Alekai Romance by Alekai Roma, and of Ch. Alekai Kalania by Ch. Alekai Kila. Kalania went to England where she finished in just six shows. Ch. Puttencove Kaui was the dam of three champions by Ivardon Kenilworth of Ensarr: Ch. Alekai Lawa, Ch. Alekai White Luan and Ch. Alekai Kila (sire of eight champions). Ch. Ivardon Winter was the dam of two Best in Show winners by Ch. Alekai Nohea)—Ch. Alekai Pokoi (16 Bests in Show) and Ch. Alekai Kuipo. Pokoi bred to Ch. Alekai Ahi produced Ch. Alekai Bali who finished his title with a Group win from the puppy classes and Ch. Alekai Luau. Luau, a Best in Show winner, sired 15 champions. Pokoi produced a total of 16 puppies; 10 became champions. Ch. Davdon Captivation was bred to Ch. Paloma's Bon Vivant to produce the Best in Show winner, Ch. Alekai Koe. Captivation was bred to Ch. Alekai Kila to produce one of Alekai's most important litters as it contained Ch. Alekai Marlin plus the beautiful Best in Show winner Ch. Alekai Marlaine and Ch. Alekai Ahi (Best of Winners at 1965 P.C.A. Specialty). Ahi was a great stud influence on Alekai white Standards. He sired 21 champions including Ch. Alekai Luau (15 champions), Ch. Alekai Oli of Stonebridge (17 champions) and Ch. Tamara of Stonebridge (ex Ch. Alekai Maunalua).

In the late 1960's Mr. Kaiser became ill and it became necessary for Mrs. Kaiser to devote most of her time to him. The kennel in Hawaii was closed and most of the dogs were sold or given away. Alekai retained a select few as a nucleus for the future. These were sent to Massachusetts to Alekai's agent and handler, Wendell J. Sammet. Alekai had shared its best results with others and now these friends helped the Alekai line to continue and prosper with the advice of Wendell Sammet.

Ch. Davdon Captivation

Ch. Alekai Kila

Ch. Alekai Pokoi

Ch. Alekai Nohea

Ch. Alekai Luau (Ahi ex Pokoi) and Ch. Alekai Bali were acquired by the Mayfair Kennels of Anne Seranne and Barbara Wolferman, famous for their Yorkshire Terriers. Luau compiled an impressive record with 17 Bests in Show All Breed, eight Specialty Bests in Show and 61 Group Firsts. He was Best of Breed at the 1969 P.C.A. Specialty. Up until this time, Alekai had specialed only bitches. Luau was the first Alekai male to be heavily campaigned but was used at stud only a few times. He became a Top Producer with 15 champion get.

Mayfair became so interested in white Standards that they wanted to breed a litter, so Mrs. Kaiser consented to lease Ch. Alekai Pokoi to Mayfair. Pokoi was bred to Ch. Merrylegs Cetin de la Fontaine, a grandson of Ch. Puttencove Promise. This litter holds the record for the most Poodle champions in one litter—seven: Chs. Alekai Bikini, Hauli, Kiele, Nahoa, Tiki, Umi and Kuke—all of Mayfair. Kuke was Best of Winners and Best Puppy in Show at the 1968 P.C.A. Specialty. Kuke was bred to Ch. Alekai Ahi and produced Chs. Alekai Karate, Ukele and Flowers—all of Mayfair. Flowers went to Mr. and Mrs. Terrence Levy's Aldeblou Kennels where she became a Best in Show winner at All Breed and Specialty shows. Flowers is the dam of the Best in Show winner Ch. Aldeblou's Morgana (by Ch. Alekai Rumble of Stonebridge) and Ch. Aldeblou's Mirabai (by Ch. Puttencove Presentation).

The Stonebridge Kennels of Dorothy Baranowsky acquired Ch. Alekai Maunalua (ex Ch. Tambarine de la Fontaine by Alekai Roma). She was bred to

CH. ALEKAI AHI

Whelped February 13, 1962   Deceased

Bred and owned by Alekai Kennels

                                Ch. Ivardon Sheraton (*wh*)

                  Ivardon Kenilworth of Ensarr (*wh*)

                                  Ivardon Meringue of Ensarr (*wh*)

Ch. Alekai Kila (*wh*)

                                Ch. Puttencove Promise (*wh*)

                  Ch. Puttencove Kaui (*wh*)

                                Ch. Puttencove Moonglow (*wh*)

CH. ALEKAI AHI—*White*

                                Ch. Ensarr Glace (*wh*)

                  Ch. Hillandale's C'Est Vrais (*wh*)

                                Ch. Cartlane Hillandale Cadenza (*wh*)

Ch. Davdon Captivation (*wh*)

                                Ch. Hillandale C'Est Vrais (*wh*)

                  Ch. Davdon Miss Demeanor (*wh*)

                                Davdon Rapport (*blk*)

Ch. Alekai Ahi to produce the multiple Best in Show winner, Ch. Tamara of Stonebridge. Tamara, bred back to her sire, Ahi, produced the littermates Ch. Alekai Oli of Stonebridge and Ch. Alekai Cocon't of Stonebridge. Oli sired 17 champions including the Best in Show winner Ch. Alekai Ouzo. Ouzo sired eight champions including three Group winners and the Best in Show winner Ch. Alekai Argus. Cocon't was the dam of the Best in Show winner, Ch. Alekai Aphrodite (by Ch. Alekai Zeus, a son of Ch. Alekai Luau). Aphrodite shown by the Terrency Levys won four All Breed and eight Specialty Bests in Show. She was Best of Variety at the 1977 P.C.A. Specialty.

Ch. Alekai Ahi's glamorous litter sister, Ch. Alekai Marlaine, was to establish her own worth. No one who ever saw her can speak of white Standards without thinking of her. Marlaine was the epitome of style and elegance. She won 10 Bests in Show All Breed, six Specialty Bests in Show and 51 Group Firsts. Her spectacular career was crowned with her Group win at the 1967 Westminster Show. Her combination of soundness and beauty was stunning. Marlaine was bred only once, at five years of age. Her litter by Ch. Alekai Luau gave two beautiful bitches, Ch. Alekai Maui and Ch. Alekai Hula. Maui started off with Best of Winners at the 1970 P.C.A. Specialty and finished two shows later with three five-point majors. Hula was purchased by Mr. and Mrs. James Lester of Longleat Poodles. She was outcrossed to the black Ch. Prince Philip of Belle Glen (by Ch. Wycliffe Thomas) and produced Ch. Longleat Hulagan, the top winning Standard for 1974. Hulagan was Best of Variety at Westminster 1974. Her career totaled eight Bests in Show at All Breed and Specialties. Hulagan produced three champions.

The Hula-Prince Philip breeding was repeated and from this Alekai acquired a white bitch, Longleat White Witch. Witch was bred to Ch. Alekai Luau and produced the Group winner Ch. Alekai Zeus, and Ch. Alekai Zoe. Zoe was the dam of five champions. Bred to Longleat Tar and Feathers (a black brother of Ch. Longleat Hulagan) she gave Ch. Alekai Tyrannus who finished as a puppy and went to Brazil where he became a Best in Show winner. Zoe's son, Ch. Alekai Ouzo (by Ch. Alekai Oli of Stonebridge), is also a Best in Show winner and Top Producer. Zoe bred to Aldeblou Kennel's Ch. Puttencove Presentation (Ch. Alekai Luau out of a daughter of Ch. Alekai Ahi) produced the ice white Ch. Alekai Brilliance, owned by Anna LeBlanc.

After Brilliance was finished she was leased back to Alekai for breeding. Bred to the Best in Show winner Ch. Alekai Argus she produced the beautiful Ch. Alekai All Together. All Together was Best of Winners at the 1980 P.C.A. Specialty over 139 class entries and finished easily. All Together represents the culmination of the various lines which Alekai brought together in the beginning.

Alekai's adventure into blacks started with the purchase of Montec Lady Hamilton (Ch. Haus Brau Clarion ex Montec Lady Mizo). Lady Hamilton was first bred to Ch. Alekai Oli of Stonebridge, an inbred white. This litter produced the Top Producing black bitch, Ch. Alekai Psyche, owned and shown

Ch. Alekai Marlaine (by Ch. Alekai Kila ex Ch. Davdon Captivation), Standard, shown going First in the Non-Sporting Group at 1967 Westminster Kennel Club show under Melbourne Downing, handled by Wendell J. Sammet. Owned by Alekai Kennels.

Ch. Alekai Aphrodite

Ch. Alekai Psyche

by Mr. and Mrs. Royal E. Peterson II of Deryabar. Psyche in turn produced a black Best in Show Specialty and multiple Group winner, Ch. Deryabar Pirate, as well as Ch. Shafto's Tiger Lily, a white bitch, in her first litter by Ch. D'Kamron Daemon. Bred to Ch. Alekai In Style, a black, Psyche's second litter produced the multiple Best in Show all breed and Group winner Ch. Deryabar Trumpet, a black-bred white. Trumpet is the sire of the Group winner, Ch. Alekai All The Rage, out of Ch. Alekai All Together, owned and shown by Wilhelmine Wielich. He is also the sire of a black bitch out of Ch. Alekai Absolute, Ch. Alekai Airy, owned and shown by Tatiana Nagro.

Montec Lady Hamilton was then bred to Ch. Alekai Ouzo. The results of this mating were two Top Producing bitches, Ch. Alekai Phaedra, owned and shown by Dorothe Matzner of D'Kamron, and Ch. Alekai Zephyr. Zephyr's only litter produced four champions sired by Ch. Puttencove Presentation, a Ch. Alekai Luau son. These were a black bitch, Ch. Alekai Absolute, and three whites, Ch. Alekai Ala La Mode, Ch. Alekai Antares, and Ch. Alekai Aim To Please.

There has been a total of 61 homebred Alekai Standard champions, 53 of them white, eight blacks. In addition, there have been ten Alekai champions at Mayfair and five at Stonebridge.

Mrs. Kaiser now lives in retirement in the Virgin Islands. In 1984, in recognition of his invaluable contributions, Mrs. Kaiser awarded all of the Alekai dogs and bitches to Wendell Sammet. Together they have kept white Standards in the limelight for almost a quarter of a century.

Eng. Ch. Whippendell Carillon

Ch. Whippendell Poli of Carillon, black English import, first Poodle
to win Group at Westminster (1933).

43

Black and Brown
Standards

THE American Poodles popular at the end of the nineteenth
century were undersized Standards of French origin. The French called them
"Caniche," which still remains the French designation for the breed we call the
Poodle. This term is presumed to have been derived from an early employment
of the Poodle in the hunting of ducks and the retrieving of game from water, just
as our current word Poodle, of German derivation, describes a "puddle dog."
The nomenclature removes any doubts that Poodles were originally a sporting
breed.

These Caniche were nondescript in type, too small for our present
concepts of a Standard and much too big for a Miniature, thick and short in
head, not too well made in the other parts of their anatomies, and deficient in
length of coat. They were frequently barbered in an elaborate manner with the
owner's monogram or even his coat of arms embossed on their flanks. But they
have melted into the distance, these Caniche, gone the way of the Victorian era
of which they were a part.

With the renaissance of the popularity of the Poodle in America in the
early 1930's or thereabouts came a revision of the concept of Poodle type and
structure. Along with increase of stature in the Standard Poodle, we came to
demand more gorgeous and spectacular coats, longer and leaner heads, longer
and better set ears, better structured shoulders and hindquarters, shorter
bodies, adequate feet, and refinements all around. Other breeds had bettered
through the years; and without some overhauling of our Poodle ideals, a
renewal of public interest in the long abandoned variety could never have been
brought about.

Int. Ch. Anderl von Hugelberg

Eric Labory of Misty Isles

294

Continental Int. Ch. Mousse Labory

44

The "Anderl" Line—
Ch. Anderl von Hugelberg

A CHANCE ENCOUNTER at a railway station in the mid 1920's resulted in the foundation of this great Standard male line. A young German girl living with the family of Madame Lucienne Reichenbach in Switzerland saw an unusual looking, medium sized hairy black dog and made casual inquiries. The railway station master advised that the dog was a Poodle, a first prize winner, and due to his wife's illness, the dog was for sale. The Reichenbach family acquired Anderl von Hugelberg, who was born July 22, 1923. He was their first Poodle. They showed him to his championship and he became the foundation of their great black and brown Labory line. He also fostered their interest in Poodles which later extended to white Standards and eventually to black Toys. Madame Reichenbach remains one of the truly great breeders not only for her ability to recognize quality itself but also for the ability to select the proper mates to perpetuate and improve the superior qualities once found.

The Anderl line is purely German in origin. Anderl became an International Champion on the continent. Interestingly, he sired only four litters and all of his important producing records come through the same Labory Kennels which later became famous for its white Standards. However, the white and black Laborys were not related. The Reichenbachs bred Anderl to Bella v. Zwisse which produced his, and their, first litter. The choice of this litter was Swiss and French Ch. Mira Labory who became the dam of five champions. Mira bred back to her sire, Anderl, produced European Ch. Nunsoe Chevalier Labory who went to England. Anderl bred to Int. Ch. Lidia von Feuerbachtal produced three important brothers: Eric Labory of Misty Isles (sire of 12 champions in

295

Ch. Griseley Labory of Piperscroft

Ch. Rimskittle Right On

Ch. Bel Tor Darkin Collaboration

Ch. Rimskittle Roue La Russe

Ch. Juel Destiny's Show Off

Ch. Longleat Alimar Raisin Cane

INT. CH. ANDERL VON HUGELBERG

Int. Ch. Anderl Von Hugelberg (*blk*)
    Eric Labory of Misty Isles (*blk*) 12
        Ch. Aucassin of Pommel Rock (*blk*)
            Ch. Cartlane Causeur (*brn*) 2
            Cartlane Alcindor (*blk*) 5
    Petit Poucet Labory (*blk*)
        Ch. Griseley Labory of Piperscroft (*gr*) 14
            Ch. Pillicoc Aplomb (*blk*) 4
            Ch. Kaffir of Piperscroft (*blk*) 4
                Ch. Puttencove Impetuous (*blk*) 11
                    Ch. Torchlight Piperheidsieck (*apr*) 1
                        Ch. Torchlight Jackanapes (*blk*)
                        Bel Tor Salad Days (*blk*) 25
                  Ch. Carillon Colin of Puttencove (*blk*) 21
                    Ch. Puttencove Halla's Hugo (*blk*) 6
                      Ch. Rimskittle Black Pirate (*blk*) 8
                  Fanfaron Impressario (*wh*) 5
                  Ch. Annsown Sir Gay (*blk*) 25
                    Ch. Carillon Dilemma U.D. (*blk*) 39
                      Ch. Monfret Merlin (*blk*)
                        Ch. Monfret Figaro (*blk*) 13
                          Ch. Nesral Dark Brilliance C.D. (*blk*) 6
                Ch. Bel Tor Gigadibs (*blk*) 28
                Ch. Bel Tor Morceau Choisi (*blk*) 18
                  Ch. Bel Tor Vintage Wine (*brn*) 7
                Ch. Bel Tor McCreery *(brn)* 38
                  Ch. Rondylo Here's Damon (*blk*) 7
                  Ch. Bel Tor St. Ay Better Mousetrap (*brn*) 20
                    Ch. Bel Tor Chance Of A Lifetime (*blk*) 6
                    Ch. Bel Tor Where The Action Is (*blk*) 13
                  Ch. Bel Tor Away We Go (*blk*) 10
                    Ch. Bel Tor Darkin Collaboration (*blk*) 11
                      Ch. Bel Tor All The Trimmings (*blk*) 11
                      Ch. Bibelot's Smart Cut (*blk*) 5
                Ch. Bel Tor Andrew of Rondylo (*brn*)
                  Ch. Bel Tor Bringing Home The Bacon (*brn*) 6
                    Int. Ch. Bel Tor Big Picture (*blk*) 52
                    Ch. Rimskittle Right On (*blk*) 22
                    Rimskittle Mugshot (*blk*) 4
                    Ch. Rimskittle Punchline (*blk*) 7
                    Ch. Rimskittle Roue La Rouse (*blk*) 14
                      Ch. Longleat Alimar Raisin Cane (*blk)* 12
                      Ch. Rimskittle Roughneck (*blk*) 5
                  Ch. Torbec A Touch of Class (*blk*) 11
                  Ch. Juel Destiny's Show Off (*blk*) 11
            Ch. Annsown Gay Knight of Arhill (*blk*) 14
            Ch. Wycliffe Timothy (*See Next Chart*)
            Ch. Wycliffe Thomas (*See Standard Chart 4*)

the U.S.), Cont. Int. Ch. Mousse Labory (the sire of Ilka Mignonne Labory, dam of three U.S. champions, and her sister Ch. Pierette Labory of Carillon, foundation bitch of Carillon Kennels), and Petit Poucet Labory. Poucet bred to his half sister, Ch. Mira Labory, produced Eng. Ch. Amour Labory of Piperscroft, Am. Ch. Manon Labory of Blakeen (dam of 3 Ensarr champions), and the famous gray, Ch. Griseley Labory of Piperscroft, C.D. All of these Poodles, except Griseley, were black.

Griseley went first to the Piperscroft Kennels in England, where he sired the black Ch. Kaffir of Piperscroft, and then to the Blakeen Kennels in the U.S., where he sired 14 champions. Mrs. Hayes Hoyt believed Griseley to be the first gray Standard in America. She observed that certain qualities displayed by these Labory Poodles and inherited by their descendants were marvelous feet, long ear leather, exuberant spirit, and high intelligence. When bred to blacks, Griseley produced only blacks, but when bred to his daughters, he produced some grays. Griseley was a handsome, wiry coated, well balanced Poodle. He was Winners Dog at Westminster in 1936. All of this detail is set forth here to establish that the Anderl-Griseley family represented the best of what was then available anywhere in the world and that it further withstood the crucial test of inbreeding.

Griseley's English-bred son, the black Ch. Kaffir of Piperscroft, was imported by the Carillon Kennels. Kaffir in turn sired Ch. Puttencove Impetuous, who sired 11 champions including the apricot Ch. Torchlight Piperheidsieck and the great Ch. Carillon Colin of Puttencove. Piperheidsieck's son, Ch. Torchlight Jackanapes, produced Bel Tor Salad Days, sire of 25 champions.

Mrs. George Putnam wrote of Ch. Carillon Colin of Puttencove: "Every so often a Poodle grows up that seems to embody qualities a serious breeder is striving to produce. To many, Colin had the elegance coupled with strength they had been searching for, as well as faultless disposition, beautiful clean-cut head and sound body, and that very masculine something so desirable in a sire." Colin won six Bests in Show, and sired 21 champions, and left a permanent influence on the breed. Colin sired Ch. Puttencove Halla's Hugo (sire of six champions), who in turn sired the Best in Show winner, Ch. Rimskittle Black Pirate (sire of eight champions).

Colin's most important son was Ch. Annsown Sir Gay, whelped March 14, 1949. Sir Gay made his ring debut at the 1950 P.C.A. Specialty where he went Winners Dog for five points. He had numerous Group first wins and was Best American-Bred in Show at Cape Cod, Massachusetts under Percy Roberts. Sir Gay's name suited him well as he was happy and eager to please, and yet a perfect gentleman. He was a good black, sound bodied and moved well. He was prepotent in passing on his expressive and intelligent head, a regal neck, a strong sound body, good legs and feet and his delightful disposition. Although he only sired 21 litters, he produced 22 champions and became one of the most impor-

298

CH. CARILLON COLIN OF PUTTENCOVE

Whelped August 21, 1943   Died 1957

Bred by Mrs. Whitehouse Walker and Miss Blanche Saunders
Owned by Puttencove Kennels

Ch. Griseley Labory of Piperscroft, C.D. (*gr*)
Ch. Kaffir of Piperscroft (*blk*)
Ch. Quality of Piperscroft (*blk*)
Ch. Puttencove Impetuous (*blk*)
Ch. Blakeen Cyrano (*brn*)
Puttencove Candida (*brn*)
Blakeen Solange (*brn*)

CH. CARILLON COLIN OF PUTTENCOVE—*Black*

Ch. Stillington Claus O'Carillon (*blk*)
Ch. Carillon Courage, C.D.X. (*blk*)
Carillon Tragedie (*blk*)
Ch. Carillon Colline (*blk*)
Ch. Nymphaea Jason (*brn*)
Ch. Carillon Celeste (*blk*)
Carillon Pivoine (*blk*)

Ch. Bel Tor Bringing Home The Bacon   Ch. Bel Tor St. Ay Better Mousetrap

tant sires in the history of the breed. He and his sons were to dominate the future of the variety, particularly in blacks and browns. Perhaps it was not immediately apparent what was happening, but with the passage of time and the success of this family, the other male lines could not compete and gradually faded into the background and were absorbed. Sir Gay produced four important sons: Ch. Carillon Dilemma, U.D., Ch. Bel Tor Gigadibs, Ch. Bel Tor Morceau Choisi and Ch. Annsown Gay Knight of Arhill. Ch. Carillon Dilemma sired 39 champions including Ch. Monfret Merlin. Merlin sired Ch. Monfret Figaro who was the sire of 13 champions.

Interestingly, the over-exaggerated Ch. Bel Tor Gigadibs sired 28 champions but all of his get who became Top Producers were daughters. Ch. Bel Tor Morceau Choisi was described as hard to fault, with a lovely head. It is through Morceau Choisi that the Bel Tor line wends its thread, and it is through Choisi and his two Top Producing brown sons that a strong brown tendency exerts itself. They are the first browns to appear on the chart as set forth here. Undoubtedly Rebecca Mason's great admiration for the brown Ch. Blakeen Cyrano and his multiple appearances in her pedigrees helped to strengthen the brown factor. Choisi sired the brown Ch. Bel Tor McCreery (38 champions), who sired two important producing brown sons, Ch. Bel Tor St. Ay Better Mousetrap (sire of 20 champions including three Top Producing sons) and Ch. Bel Tor Andrew of Rondylo. Andrew, in turn, sired Ch. Bel Tor Bringing Home the Bacon (six champions), who produced one of Bel Tor's greatest studs, the black Int. Ch. Bel Tor Big Picture (52 champions). Big Picture was big and strong with a long neck, excellent legs and feet and a beautiful expression. He sired four important producing sons: Ch. Rimskittle Right On (22 champions), Rimskittle Mugshot, Ch. Torbec A Touch of Class and Ch. Juel Destiny's Show Off. Big Picture's family continues strongly through the Rimskittles and the Juels, as well as through Torbec in Canada.

300

CH. ANNSOWN SIR GAY

Whelped March 14, 1949   Died 1956

Bred and owned by Mr. and Mrs. Charles E. Wegmann

Ch. Kaffir of Piperscroft (*blk*)
Ch. Puttencove Impetuous (*blk*)
Puttencove Candida (*brn*)
Ch. Carillon Colin of Puttencove (*blk*)
Ch. Carillon Courage, C.D. (*blk*)
Ch. Carillon Colline (*blk*)
Ch. Carillon Celeste (*blk*)

CH. ANNSOWN SIR GAY—*Black*

Ch. Intrepid of Misty Isles (*blk*)
Surrey Snafu (*blk*)
L'Audace Sans Glen (*blk*)
Annsown Sans Souci (*blk*)
Ch. Blakeen Zombie (*blk*)
Blakeen Spooky (*blk*)
Ch. Barbet Baiser (*gr*)

CH. CARILLON DILEMMA, U.D.T.

Whelped January 13, 1956   Died February 7, 1969

Bred and owned by
Blanche Saunders, Carillon Kennels

Ch. Puttencove Impetuous (*blk*)
Ch. Carillon Colin of Puttencove (*blk*)
Ch. Carillon Colline (*blk*)
Ch. Annsown Sir Gay (*blk*)
Surrey Snafu (*blk*)
Annsown San Souci (*blk*)
Blakeen Spooky (*blk*)

CH. CARILLON DILEMMA, U.D.T.—*Black*

Redgio-Labory (*blk*)
Santo-Labory of Carillon (*blk*)
Idyle Labory (*blk*)
Robin Hill of Carillon, U.D.T. (*blk*)
Ch. Carillon Jester, U.D.T. (*blk*)
Petitcote Becky, U.D.T. (*blk*)
Can. Ch. Carillon Jaillir (*blk*)

CH. BEL TOR MORCEAU CHOISI

Whelped: December 18, 1953   Deceased

Bred and owned by Bel Tor Kennels

<pre>
                        Ch. Puttencove Impetuous (blk)
            Ch. Carillon Colin of Puttencove (blk)
                        Ch. Carillon Colline (blk)
        Ch. Annsown Sir Gay (blk)
                        Surrey Snafu (blk)
            Annsown Sans Souci (blk)
                        Blakeen Spooky (blk)
</pre>

CH. BELT TOR MORCEAU CHOISI—*Black*

<pre>
                        Sunstorm's Snuff (brn)
            Ch. Robin Hood (brn)
                        Cartlane Marguerite (brn)
        Ch. Lowmont Lady Cadette (brn)
                        Ch. Puttencove Vim, U.D. (brn)
            Ch. Lowmont Madame d'Aiguillon (brn)
                        Ch. Sunstorm's Harvest (brn)
</pre>

303

CH. ANNSOWN GAY KNIGHT OF ARHILL

Whelped: December 10, 1955   Deceased

Bred by Jane S. Nelson
Owned by Ann Wegmann, Annsown Kennels

Ch. Puttencove Impetuous (*blk*)
Ch. Carillon Colin of Puttencove (*blk*)
Ch. Carillon Colline (*blk*)
Ch. Annsown Sir Gay (*blk*)
Surrey Snafu (*blk*)
Annsown San Souci (*blk*)
Blakeen Spooky (*blk*)

CH. ANNSOWN GAY KNIGHT OF ARHILL—*Black*

Ch. Carillon Courage, CDX (*blk*)
Carillon Conde (*blk*)
Carillon Caprice (*blk*)
Clairedge Cinderella, CD (*blu*)
Sir Anthony (*brn*)
Juliette of Clairedge (*gr*)
Blakeen Vita Nuova (*gr*)

Now to backtrack a bit and start up again with Ch. Annsown Sir Gay. While Sir Gay's four sons in the East—Gigadibs, Morceau Choisi, Ch. Carillon Dilemma and Ch. Annsown Gay Knight of Arhill—were setting their producing records, a bitch from the Pacific Northwest came East to be bred to Gay Knight and as a result the family's influence was spread not only to Canada and the West Coast, but eventually back to England and Europe, where it had all started so many years ago. Gay Knight, a Best in Show winner, was large for his time with a refined head, a long neck, good balance and more angulation behind than his contemporaries. The bitch sent to him was Ch. Wycliffe Jacqueline and she whelped not one, but two famous sons, Ch. Wycliffe Timothy and Ch. Wycliffe Thomas. Thomas and Timothy were both on the large size, sound with good fronts, and well laid back shoulders. Both had lovely expressions with Timothy's a bit finer. Thomas had a bit more rear angulation. Thomas won nine Bests in Show. At Wycliffe Kennels Jean Lyle has put great emphasis on creating a dominant black line, producing only blacks. And indeed, all puppies born at Wycliffe over a twenty year period were all black. However, it is also true that hidden genes lurk unsuspectingly and turn up with the least provocation. This is not necessarily bad; indeed some of the surprises have been spectacular. It also proves that no matter how dedicated a breeder may be, once tight control is no longer exercised by that breeder, the changes in the direction of both type and color may be considerable and occur only a generation or two away from the source. For example, Timothy's son, the Best in Show winner Ch. Wycliffe Virgil (bred to a blue bitch from a silver-apricot cross) produced the beautiful blue Ch. Jocelyene Marjorie, who is the dam of 17 champions, including three of the leading sires in the breed: Ch. Dassin Debauchery, Ch. Dassin's Sum Buddy and Ch. Dassin's Broadway Joe.

Ch. Wycliffe Virgil also sired Eng. Am. Can. Ch. Bibelot's Tall Dark and Handsome, C.D.X., nicknamed "Tramp." Tramp finished in Canada at seven months in five days of showing. He finished in the States at 11 months. He then went through the six months quarantine in England and three days after his release he won the Reserve Challenge Certificate at Crufts, England's most prestigious show. Shown 30 times in England he went Best in Show at 13. He was England's Dog of the Year for 1966. Breed expert Shirley Walne in England credits Tramp as a major influence on the breed there in type, temperament and presentation. Marilyn Willis presented him in the American style, and big coats and bracelets became fashionable. Tramp was a prepotent sire. He sired 53 champions in nine countries. Three were English champions, all Best in Show winners. An untitled son, Sarcell Pacemaker Romulous, sired Eng. Ch. Malibu Beach Boy of Sarcell. Beach Boy sired Eng. Ch. Roushkas Pacific (35 C.C.'s) who in turn sired Eng. Ch. Midshipman at Kertellas Supernova (25 C.C.'s). Pacific and Midshipman are two of the all time top winners in their variety in England and both are champion producers.

Ch. Wycliffe Dudley

Ch. Meuriz of Mayfield

Eng. Ch. Malibu Beach Boy of Sarcell

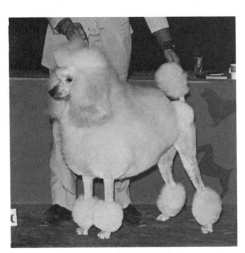

Ch. McDuff of Mayfield

Eng. Ch. Roushkas Pacific

Ch. Moynihan of Mayfield

Ch. Wycliffe Timothy

Standard Chart 3

Ch. Wycliffe Timothy (*blk*) 16
    Ch. Wycliffe Xavier (*blk*) 5
    Ch. Wycliffe Demosthenes (*blk*) 9
        Ch. Tawasentha Anthony of Funtyme (*gr*) 9
    Ch. Wycliffe Dudley (*blk*) 5
        Ch. deRussy Necromancer (*blk*) 10
    Ch. Wycliffe Virgil (*blk*) 50
        Eng. Am. Can. Ch. Bibelot's Tall Dark and Handsome (*blk*) 53
            Eng. Ch. Josato Evorglens Star and Garter (*brn*) 3
            Sarcell Pacemaker Romulus (*blk*)
                Eng. Ch. Malibu Beach Boy of Sarcell (*blk*) 1
                    Eng. Ch. Roushkas Pacific (*blk*) 2
                        Eng. Ch. Midshipman at Kertellas Supernova (*blk*) 2
      Dassin's Daktari (*blk*) 14
        Ch. Meuriz of Mayfield (*blk*) 16
            Ch. McDuff of Mayfield (*apr*) 5
                Ch. Moynihan of Mayfield (*apr*) 6
      Ch. Ker-Mor's Midshipman (*blk*)
      Ch. Jacques Henri XVI (*blk*) 5
        Ch. Fa-Sal's Adonis (*blk*) 5
        Ch. Fa-Sal's James (*blk*)
            Ch. Fa-Sal's Jesse (*blk*) 6

CH. WYCLIFFE VIRGIL

Whelped: April 23, 1960   Died: November 11, 1974

Bred by Jean Lyle, Wycliffe Kennels
Owned by Joan Schilke, Koronet Kennels

Ch. Annsown Sir Gay (*blk*)
Ch. Annsown Gay Knight of Arhill (*blk*)
Clairedge Cinderella, C.D. (*blk*)
Ch. Wycliffe Timothy (*blk*)
Am. Can. Ch. Petitcote Domino, C.D. (*blk*)
Am. Can. Ch. Wycliffe Jacqueline, U.D. (*blk*)
Am. Can. Ch. Carillon Michelle, U.D. (*blk*)

CH. WYCLIFFE VIRGIL—*Black*

Petitcote Baron Chico, C.D. (*crm*)
Am. Can. Ch. Petitcote Domino, C.D. (*blk*)
Carillon Jabotier (*blk*)
Am. Can. Ch. Wycliffe Jacqueline, U.D. (*blk*)
Santo Labory of Carillon (*blk*)
Am. Can. Ch. Carrillon Michelle, U.D.T. (*blk*)
Ch. Carillon Jestina (*blk*)

ENG. AM. CAN. CH. BIBELOT'S TALL DARK AND HANDSOME

Whelped: August 20, 1963   Died: April 1978

Bred and owned by Susan Radley Fraser
Bibelot Poodles, Toronto, Onatrio, Canada

                        Ch. Annsown Gay Knight of Arhill (*blk*)
            Int. Ch. Wycliffe Timothy (*blk*)
                  Int. Ch. Wycliffe Jacqueline, U.D. (*blk*)
Ch. Wycliffe Virgil (*blk*)
                  Int. Ch. Peticote Domino (*blk*)
            Int. Ch. Wycliffe Jacqueline, U.D. (*blk*)
                  Int. Ch. Carillon Michelle, U.D. (*blk*)

ENG. AM. CAN. CH. BIBELOT'S TALL DARK AND HANDSOME, AM. CAN. CDX—*Black*

                        Ch. Annsown Sir Gay (*blk*)
            Ch. Annsown Gay Knight of Arhill (*blk*)
                  Clairedge Cinderella, C.D. (*blk*)
Int. Ch. Lady Joan of Lowmont Int. C.D. (*blk*)
                  Ch. Lowmont Comte de Rochefort (*brn*)
            Lowmont Lady Clarissa (*brn*)
                  Ch. Lowmont Lady Lindy Lou (*blk*)

AM. CAN. CH. WYCLIFFE THOMAS

Whelped April 1, 1959   Died August 13, 1967

Bred and owned by Mrs. Jean M. Lyle

Ch. Carillon Colin of Puttencove (*blk*)
Ch. Annsown Sir Gay (*blk*)
Annsown San Souci (*blk*)
Ch. Annsown Gay Knight of Arhill (*blk*)
Carillon Conde (*blk*)
Clairedge Cinderella, C.D. (*blk*)
Juliette of Clairedge (*gr*)

AM. CAN. CH. WYCLIFFE THOMAS—*Black*

Petitcote Baron Chico (*crm*)
Int. Ch. Petitcote Domino, C.D. (*blk*)
Carillon Jabotiere (*blk*)
Int. Ch. Wycliffe Jacqueline, U.D. (*blk*)
Santo-Labory of Carillon (*blk*)
Int. Ch. Carillon Michelle, U.D.T. (*blk*)
Ch. Carillon Jestina (*blk*)

The saga of Ch. Wycliffe Thomas is a story in itself. Thomas was large, sound and had good shoulders. Mrs. Lyle felt his important contributions as a sire were his size, color and coat plus rear angulation, all coming from his sire Gay Knight. All of these qualities were much needed at that time. His beautiful type she credited to his dam, Ch. Wycliffe Jacqueline.

Thomas was a phenomenal sire with 67 champions to his credit, including 10 Top Producing sons. Thomas had sons and daughters in the East, in the South, in the Midwest, on the West Coast and in Canada.

Thomas' son, Ch. Wycliffe Leroy, a Best in Show winner, sired nine champions including Ch. Christopher Robin of Bushyrun. Christopher Robin sired six champions including the white Ch. Squire's Kelly O'Shayne. Kelly in turn sired one of the world's most titled Poodles, Am. Can. Dutch German Luxembourg (World F.C.I.) Int. Ch. Bibelot's Clean As A Whistle, Am. Can. C.D. Clean As A Whistle, a white, sired 19 champions.

Judging from the perspective of time, Thomas' most influential son would seem to be Ch. Wycliffe Kenneth, who was kept at home to replace his sire. Kenneth was inbred as his dam, Ch. Wycliffe Zara, was also by Thomas. Kenneth closely resembled his sire in type. He also was 26¾ inches tall, an even inkier black, long necked and with more angulation both front and rear. Kenneth had a successful show career winning four Bests in Show owner-handled. As a stud he took second place to his more famous sire until Thomas died, and then just as breeders were beginning to realize his potential, he died of bloat when he was only seven years of age. Time has proven his true value and it can only be left to speculation as to what he might have done with a few years more. As it was, the legacy he left was most impressive.

One of Kenneth's most important litters was out of Can. Ch. Bibelot's Magnificent Maxine (a full sister to Ch. Bibelot's Tall Dark and Handsome), who was sent to England in whelp to him. She went to the Springett Kennels of Marilyn Willis. This famous litter produced seven champions including the noteworthy British sire, Eng. Ch. Springett Darken Democrat, who produced 17 champions all over the world. Democrat's best known son was Eng. Ch. Vicmars Balnoble Royale, who sired 12 champions. Several of these sons are champion producers themselves.

Another of Kenneth's six Top Producing sons was Ch. Wycliffe Thomas Too. Thomas Too was not as spectacular a show dog as his sire and grandsire, Thomas and Kenneth, but he was the next link in the chain to greatness. Thomas Too sired the Best in Show winner, Ch. Wycliffe Xcellente of Shamlot, who was more in the same mold as Thomas and Kenneth. Xcellente was big, bold and beautiful. He sired Top Producers and Best in Show winners. His son, Ch. Clabon Aaron, is a Top Producer. Excellente also sired Wycliffe's next stay at home sire, Ch. Wycliffe Fitzherbert, who is one of the breed's leading stud dogs. Fitzherbert was the sire of five Top Producing sons, including Ch. Fancifaire A OK O'Shea.

Ch. Wycliffe Hadrian

Ch. Wycliffe Varner

Ch. Ascot Julian

Ch. Wycliffe Only Ogden

Ch. Love Story of Torbec

Eng. Ch. Vicmar's Balnoble Royale

Ch. Wycliffe Thomas (*blk*) 67
   Ch. Black Rogue of Belle Glen (*blk*) 19
   Ch. Prince Philip of Belle Glen (*blk*) 19
      Ch. Loribon Gareth (*blk*) 6
      Longleat Tar and Feathers (*blk*)
   Ch. Jacques Le Noir of Belle Glen (*blk*) 7
      Ch. Monfret Bronzini (*brn*) 6
   Ch. Loribon Canadian Caper (*blk*) 8
   Ch. Monfret Music Master (*blk*) 16
      Ch. Janala Y Clef Music Major (*blk*) 5
   Ch. Wycliffe Leroy (*blk*) 13
      Ch. Christopher Robin of Bushyrun (*blk*) 6
         Ch. Squire's Kelly O'Shayne (*wh*)
            Int. Ch. Bibelot's Clean As A Whistle (*wh*) 19
      Ch. Cabal of Bushyrun (*blk*)
         Ch. Meyowne Rudolph (*wh*) 6
   Wycliffe Aeneas (*blk*) 5
   Dassin Doubting Thomas (*blk*) 12
   Bushyrun Dilettante (*blk*)
      Ch. Coqan Baccarat (*blk*) 12
   Ch. Wycliffe Kenneth (*blk*) 66
      Eng. Ch. Springett Darken Democrat (*blk*) 17
         Eng. Ch. Vicmars Balnoble Royale (*blk*) 12
            Australian Ch. Vicmars Right Royal (*blk*) 23
            Eng. Ch. Abendow Captain Cuttle (*blk*) 3
            Eng. Ch. Beguinette Blue Balthazar (*blu*) 4
      Ch. Acadia Quantas (*blk*) 5
      Ch. Wycliffe Varner (*blk*) 16
         Ch. Oakgrove In Command (*blk*) 5
      Ch. Wycliffe Thomas Too (*blk*) 15
         Wycliffe Xanthias (*blk*) 5
         Ch. Wycliffe Xcellente of Shamlot (*blk*) 24
            Ch. Clabon Aaron (*blk*) 15
               Ch. Ascot Julian (*blk*) 6
            Ch. Wycliffe Fitzherbert (*blk*) 81
               Ch. Fancifaire A OK O'Shea (*blk*) 12
               Ch. Fancifaire Acclaim To Fame (*blk*) 7
               Ch. Wycliffe Jaunty Jester (*blk*) 5
               Ch. Wycliffe Only Ogden (*blk*) 24
               Eng. Ch. Wycliffe Ovation For Vulcan (*blk*) 8
      Ch. Wycliffe Lachlan (*blk*)
         Ch. Pannovia's Prankster (*blk*) 5
      Ch. Wycliffe U-Gene C.D.X. (*blk*) 5
      Wycliffe Uranus (*blk*)
         Ch. Wycliffe Hadrian (*blk*) 26
      Ch. Wycliffe Chrichton (*blk*) 11
      Ch. Wycliffe Simeon (*blk*) 5
      Ch. Wycliffe Ulrich (*blk*)
         Ch. Coqan's Bartered Advocate (*blk*)
            Ch. Love Story of Torbec (*blk*) 28
   Ch. Wycliffe Ian (*blk*) 11
   (*See Standard Chart 5*)

313

Ch. Black Rogue of Belle Glen

Ch. Prince Philip of Belle Glen

Am. & Can. Ch. Wycliffe Leroy

Ch. Monfret Music Master

314

AM. CAN. CH. WYCLIFFE KENNETH

Whelped: November 5, 1963   Died: December 3, 1970

Bred and owned by Mrs. Donald Lyle, Wycliffe Kennels

Ch. Annsown Sir Gay (*blk*)
Ch. Annsown Gay Knight of Arhill (*blk*)
Clairedge Cinderella (*blk*)
Int. Ch. Wycliffe Thomas (*blk*)
Int. Ch. Petitcote Domino, C.D. (*blk*)
Int. Ch. Wycliffe Jacqueline, U.D.T. (*blk*)
Int. Ch. Carillon Michelle, U.D.T. (*blk*)

AM. CAN. CH. WYCLIFFE KENNETH—*Black*

Ch. Annsown Gay Knight of Arhill (*blk*)
Int. Ch. Wycliffe Thomas (*blk*)
Int. Ch. Wycliffe Jacqueline, U.D.T. (*blk*)
Int. Ch. Wycliffe Zara (*blk*)
Int. Ch. Carillon Dilemma, U.D. (*blk*)
Can. Ch. Wycliffe Little Lulu, C.D. (*blk*)
Int. Ch. Carillon Michelle, U.D.T. (*blk*)

AM. CAN. CH. WYCLIFFE XCELLENTE OF SHAMLOT

Whelped: October 7, 1971   Died: July 15, 1980

Bred by Jean Lyle, Wycliffe Kennels
Owned by Glenna Carlson, Ascot Kennels

Int. Ch. Wycliffe Thomas (*blk*)
Int. Ch. Wycliffe Kenneth (*blk*)
Int. Ch. Wycliffe Zandra (*blk*)
Int. Ch. Wycliffe Thomas Too (*blk*)
Ch. Wycliffe Martin (*blk*)
Int. Ch. Wycliffe Zandra (*blk*)
Wycliffe Rowena of Highlane (*blk*)

AM. CAN. CH. WYCLIFFE XCELLENTE OF SHAMLOT—*Black*

Int. Ch. Wycliffe Thomas (*blk*)
Int. Ch. Wycliffe Kenneth (*blk*)
Int. Ch. Wycliffe Zara (*blk*)
Int. Ch. Wycliffe Genevieve (*blk*)
Int. Ch. Wycliffe Kenneth (*blk*)
Can. Aus. Ch. Wycliffe Sybil (*blk*)
Can. Ch. Wycliffe Calypso (*blk*)

An untitled son of Kenneth, Wycliffe Uranus, sired the Best in Show winner and Top Producer, Ch. Wycliffe Hadrian. Another Kenneth son, Ch. Wycliffe Ulrich, sired Ch. Coqan's Bartered Advocate. Advocate is the sire of the Canadian Best in Show winner, Ch. Love Story of Torbec, who has 28 champion get and was one of Canada's leading Poodle sires.

Ch. Wycliffe Ian

The story is told that Ch. Wycliffe Ian, a son of Ch. Wycliffe Thomas, was not retained at home because it was suspected he had a white gene. But what one breeder considered unacceptable, other breeders saw as an opportunity. Ian was considered to be more exaggerated and racier in type than his forbears—some felt him too extreme, others loved the type. Ian does not become a revolutionary force in whites, not at this point, but we remind you the white gene was there and it would appear later. A Best in Show winner, Ian was large, refined and typey with a beautiful long lean head. He was short backed with lots of neck and angulation and spirit. Ian had three influential sons: Ch. Wycliffe Martin (21 champions, mostly through Blacknight Kennels), Haus Brau Aladin, and Ch. Wycliffe Murdoch—all blacks. Aladin sired the beautiful headed Best in Show winner, Ch. Winshire Country Gentleman, who, unfortunately like his grandsire Ian, died at an early age, but not before producing a litter out of Ch. Jocelyene Marjorie (a Ch. Wycliffe Virgil daughter) which included Ch. Dassin Debauchery, Ch. Dassin's Sum Buddy and Ch. Dassin's Broadway Joe, three highly influential sires. Ian's son, Ch. Wycliffe Murdoch (bred to an Ian daughter) produced Ch. Haus Brau Clarion, who again was considered an exaggeration of type by many. Clarion sired 33 champions, including Ch. Haus Brau Executive of Acadia.

Ch. Wycliffe Murdoch

Ch. Winshire's County Gentleman

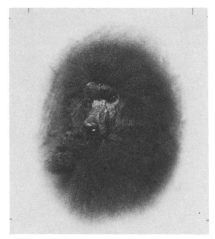
Ch. Alee What Price A Dream

Ch. Eaton Bureaucrat

Eng. Ch. Acadia Detonator of Leander

Ch. Eaton Trustbuster

Eng. Am. Ch. Acadia Stagedoor Johnny
of Leander

Ch. Eaton Affirmed

Ch. Wycliffe Ian (*blk*) 11
    Ch. Wycliffe Martin (*blk*) 21
    Haus Brau Aladin (*blk*)
        Ch. Winshire's Country Gentleman (*blk*) 8
            Ch. Dassin Debauchery (*blk*) 90
                Ch. Jay-En Hurry Sundown (*blk*) 7
                Ch. Langcroft Country Pride (*wh*) 31
                    Ch. Joyfil Jaylee The Avenger (*blk*) 5
            Ch. Dassin's Sum Buddy (*blk*) 25
                Ch. Oak Grove Heaven Forbid (*blk*) 21
                    Ch. Bar J Macho Brand of Kirsch (*blk*) 5
            Ch. Dassin's Broadway Joe (*blk*) 36
                Ch. Dassin Debussy (*blk*) 26
                    Eng. Ch. Dassin Diablo at Tiopepi (*blk*) 6
                    Ch. Shirzon Alex of Cedar Crest (*blk*) 6
    Ch. Wycliffe Murdoch (*blk*) 9
        Ch. Haus Brau Clarion (*blk*) 33
            Ch. Suffolk Casanova of Jo-Val (*blk*) 15
            Can. Ch. Sea Bec Chiron (*blk*)
                Ch. Toujuan's Black Magic (*blk*) 5
            Ch. Haus Brau Executive of Acadia (*blk*) 51
            Ch. Alee What Price A Dream (*blk*) 28
            Ch. Eaton Bureaucrat (*blk*) 5
                Ch. Eaton Trustbuster (*blk*) 7
                    Ch. Calbrecht's Ring of Fire (*blk*) 12
                    Ch. Aliyah Desperado (*blk*) 40
                        Ch. Ravendune Manilow (*blk*) 16
                        Ch. Eaton Affirmed (*blk*) 18
                Ch. Montec's Peter Black (*blk*) 17
                  Ch. Torbec Hey There Peterson (*blk*) 10
                Ch. Ilex Barclay C.D. (*wh*) 5
                Ch. Acadia Command Performance (*wh*) 34
                  Ch. Holyoke Derek (*wh*) 5
                  Ch. Holyoke Henry (*wh*) 5
                  Eng. Am. Ch. Acadia Stagedoor Johnny of Leander (*wh*) 8
                  Ch. Valhalla's In Command (*wh*) 34
                    Ch. Oakgrove Hi Heaven of Lou-Gin (*wh*) 5
                Viscara Vindicator of Mescal (*wh*) 20
                  Ch. Mescal Jeremiah (*blk*) 11
                  Ch. Chalmar Loko Motion (*blk*) 18
            Eng. Ch. Acadia Detonator of Leander (*blk*)
                Eng. Ch. Lentella Son Of A Gun (*blk*)
                    Eng. Ch. Montravia Gay Gunner (*blk*)
                      Eng. Ch. Montravia Tommy Gun (*blk*)

AM. CAN. CH. WYCLIFFE IAN

Whelped May 28, 1963   Died April 24, 1966

Bred by Jean Lyle, Wycliffe Kennels
Owned by Tom and June Hobbs

Ch. Annsown Sir Gay (*blk*)
Ch. Annsown Gay Knight of Arhill (*blk*)
Clairedge Cinderella (*blk*)
Int. Ch. Wycliffe Thomas (*blk*)
Int. Ch. Petitcote Domino, C.D. (*blk*)
Int. Ch. Wycliffe Jacqueline, U.D. (*blk*)
Int. Ch. Carillon Michelle, U.D.T. (*blk*)

AM. CAN. CH. WYCLIFFE IAN—*Black*

Ch. Annsown Gay Knight of Arhill (*blk*)
Int. Ch. Wycliffe Thomas (*blk*)
Int. Ch. Wycliffe Jacqueline, U.D. (*blk*)
Yolande of Wycliffe (*blk*)
Petitcote Top Hat (*blk*)
Sedbergh Mitzi, C.D. (*blk*)
Petitcote Suzy Cue (*crm*)

320

AM. CAN. CH. DASSIN DEBAUCHERY

Whelped October 25, 1971

Bred by F. C. Dickey and Joan Schilke
Owned by Joyce Bachner, Story Tale Kennels

Ch. Wycliffe Ian (*blk*)
Haus Brau Aladin (*blk*)
Ch. Haus Sachse's Rebecca (*blk*)
Ch. Winshire's Country Gentleman (*blk*)
Ch. Wycliffe Murdoch (*blk*)
Haus Brau Cheri Beri Ben (*blk*)
Ch. Haus Brau Angelique (*blk*)

AM. CAN. CH. DASSIN DEBAUCHERY—*Black*

Ch. Wycliffe Timothy (*blk*)
Ch. Wycliffe Virgil (*blk*)
Ch. Wycliffe Jacqueline (*blk*)
Ch. Jocelyene Marjorie (*blu*)
Footprints Go-Boy-Go (*si*)
Mogene's Beauzeaux (*blk*)
Mogene's Amber (*apr*)

AM. CAN. CH. LANGCROFT COUNTRY PRIDE

Whelped July 25, 1975

Bred and owned by
Harold and Marie Langseth, Langcroft Kennels

Haus Brau Aladin (*blk*)
Ch. Winshire's Country Gentleman (*blk*)
Haus Brau Cheri Beri Ben (*blk*)
Ch. Dassin's Debauchery (*blk*)
Ch. Wycliffe Virgil (*blk*)
Ch. Jocelyene Marjorie (*blu*)
Mogene's Beauzeaux (*blk*)

AM. CAN. CH. LANGCROFT COUNTRY PRIDE—*White*

Haus Brau Aladin (*blk*)
Ch. Winshire's Country Gentleman (*blk*)
Haus Brau Cheri Beri Ben (*blk*)
Ch. Langcroft Country Romance (*blk*)
Ch. Haus Brau Clarion (*blk*)
Ch. Haus Brau Intrigue (*blk*)
Ch. Haus Sachse's Rebecca (*blk*)

AM. CAN. CH. HAUS BRAU CLARION

Whelped: May 22, 1967   Died: September 1981

Bred and Owned by Arlene Brown, Haus Brau Kennels

               Ch. Wycliffe Thomas (*blk*)
        Ch. Wycliffe Ian (*blk*)
               Yolanda of Wycliffe (*blk*)
    Ch. Wycliffe Murdoch (*blk*)
               Ch. Annsown Gay Knight of Arhill (*blk*)
        Ch. Wycliffe Jacqueline (*blk*)
               Ch. Wycliffe Theresa (*blk*)

AM. CAN. CH. HAUS BRAU CLARION—*Black*

               Ch. Wycliffe Thomas (*blk*)
        Ch. Wycliffe Ian (*blk*)
               Yolanda of Wycliffe (*blk*)
    Ch. Haus Brau Angelique (*blk*)
               Wycliffe Aristophanes (*blk*)
        Ch. Haus Sachse's Rebecca (*blk*)
               Wycliffe Sophia, C.D. (*blk*)

Ch. Haus Brau Executive of Acadia was acquired by Joy Tongue as a six month old puppy. Even at that tender age his quality was evident. He grew to be 25 inches tall, with a lean pleasing head, a crested neck, short strong back, good legs and feet with lovely hindquarters. He had great showmanship and ability to move and became a top winner with 16 All Breed and Specialty Bests in Show and 37 Group Firsts. He was very loving with people but hated other male dogs. "Zek" was in great demand at stud and was producing exceptionally well when he had an attack of bloat at six years of age. His owner was greatly concerned and retired him from stud although some medical opinion felt it was not hereditary. In his scant five years at stud Zek produced 51 champions including five Top Producing sons.

Zek's most famous offspring was his son, Ch. Acadia Command Performance ("Bart"). Bart resembled his sire in many ways with the same flashy showmanship but he was white and even more spectacular. Shown only 40 times, and for less than a year, he won 36 Group Firsts and 19 Bests in Show—18 of which were All Breed including the 1973 Westminster K.C. Show. Bart died of bloat at just five years of age, but he had already left his mark on the breed as a sire with 34 champions. Ten of these were Best in Show winners. Five of Bart's sons are Top Producers: Ch. Holyoke Derek, Ch. Holyoke Henry, Ch. Valhalla's In Command, Eng. and Am. Ch. Acadia Stagedoor Johnny of Leander and Viscara Vindicator of Mescal.

Vindicator in turn has sired two Top Producers, Ch. Mescal Jeremiah and Ch. Chalmar Loko Motion. Stagedoor Johnny went to England where he became a Specialty Best in Show winner and the most important white sire there in recent years, producing a number of champions before returning to his home on the West Coast. Command Performance's son, Ch. Valhalla's In Command, became a Best in Show winner and in 1983 tied his sire's record with 34 champions to his credit. Command Performance's litter brother, Ch. Ilex Barclay, also a Top Producer was the sire of the highly acclaimed Ch. Lou-Gin's Kiss Me Kate who once held the record of being the top winning dog of all time, all breeds in America.

In the early 1970's, Executive's black son, Eng. Ch. Acadia Detonator of Leander, went to the Leander Kennels of John and Wendy Streatfield where he finished his championship and further spread the Executive influence abroad. Detonator sired Eng. Ch. Leander Son of a Gun. He in turn sired one of England's greatest Standard winners, Eng. Ch. Montravia Gay Gunner, who won an incredible 36 C.C.'s. Gay Gunner's son, Eng. Ch. Montravia Tommy-Gun was Best in Show at the 1985 Crufts Dog Show in London, topping an entry of over 11,000 dogs.

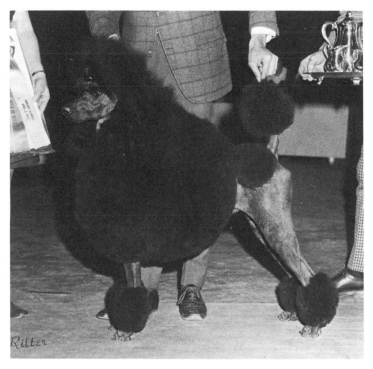

AM. CAN. CH. HAUS BRAU EXECUTIVE OF ACADIA

Whelped: July 30, 1968   Died: July 1, 1982

Bred by Kathleen Kistner and Arlene Brown
Owned by Joy S. Tongue and JoAnna Sering

Ch. Wycliffe Ian (*blk*)
Ch. Wycliffe Murdoch (*blk*)
Ch. Wycliffe Theresa (*blk*)
Ch. Haus Brau Clarion (*blk*)
Ch. Wycliffe Ian (*blk*)
Ch. Haus Brau Angelique (*blk*)
Ch. Haus Sachse Rebecca (*blk*)

AM. CAN. CH. HAUS BRAU EXECUTIVE OF ACADIA—*Black*

Ch. Wycliffe Thomas (*blk*)
Ch. Wycliffe Ian (*blk*)
Yolanda of Wycliffe (*blk*)
Haus Brau Adorable Aegina (*blk*)
Wycliffe Aristophenes (*blk*)
Ch. Haus Sachse Rebecca (*blk*)
Wycliffe Sophia (*blk*)

CH. ACADIA COMMAND PERFORMANCE, C.D.

Whelped: February 3, 1971   Died: February 1976

Bred by Charles & Lois Kletsch
Owned by JoAnna B. Sering

Am. Can. Ch. Wycliffe Murdoch (*blk*)
Ch. Haus Brau Clarion (*blk*)
Ch. Haus Brau Angelique (*blk*)
Am. Can. Ch. Haus Brau Executive of Acadia
Am. Can. Ch. Wycliffe Ian (*blk*)
Haus Brau Adorable Aegina (*blk*)
Am. Can. Ch. Haus Sachse Rebecca (*blk*)

CH. ACADIA COMMAND PERFORMANCE, C.D.—*White*

Am. Can. Ch. Wycliffe Thomas (*blk*)
Am. Can. Ch. Wycliffe Ian (*blk*)
Yolande of Wycliffe (*blk*)
Am. Can. Ch. Chantilly Felice, C.D. (*wh*)
Wycliffe Fabulous Fabian (*wh*)
Chantilly Caprice, C.D. (*wh*)
Jeune Fille D'Orleynes, U.D. (*wh*)

CH. VALHALLA'S IN COMMAND

Whelped April 10, 1975

Bred and owned by
Catherine Kish, Valhalla Kennels

Ch. Haus Brau Clarion (*blk*)
Ch. Haus Brau Executive of Acadia (*blk*)
Haus Brau Adorable Aegina (*blk*)
Ch. Acadia Command Performance, C.D. (*wh*)
Ch. Wycliffe Ian (*blk*)
Ch. Chantilly Felice, C.D. (*wh*)
Chantilly Caprice (*wh*)

CH. VALHALLA'S IN COMMAND—*White*

Ch. Alekai Ahi (*wh*)
Ch. Alekai Luau (*wh*)
Ch. Alekai Pokoi (*wh*)
Ch. Puttencove Perdita (*wh*)
Ch. Alekai Ahi (*wh*)
Puttencove Primrose (*wh*)
Ch. Puttencove Diantha (*wh*)

CH. MONTRAVIA TOMMY-GUN

Whelped February 7, 1981

Bred by Clare Coxall, Tiopepi Kennels, England
Owned by Marita Gibbs, Montravia Kennels, England

                        Eng. Ch. Acadia Detonator of Leander (*blk*)
               Eng. Ch. Lentella Son of a Gun (*blk*)
                    Davlen Chemin de Mar (*blk*)
        Eng. Ch. Montravia Gay Gunner (*blk*)
                    Bibelots Call Me After Dark (*blk*)
               Josato Top Tally (*blk*)
                    Eng. Ch. Josato Vicmars Top That (*brn*)

CH. MONTRAVIA TOMMY-GUN—*Black*

                    Am. Ch. Dassin Debussy (*blk*)
               Eng. Ch. Dassin Diablo at Tiopepi (*blk*)
                    Dassin Broadway Melody (*blk*)
        Tuttlebees Dilemma from Tiopepi (*blk*)
                    Eng. Ch. Man About Town of Torpaz (*blk*)
               Kelrarmo Miss Pink of Tuttlebees (*blk*)
                    Eng. Ch. Josato Pink Gin of Kelrarmo (*blk*)

CH. ALIYAH DESPERADO

Whelped September 23, 1977

Bred by Kurt and Barbara James and Mark Shanoff

                              Ch. Haus'Brau Executive of Acadia (*blk*)
                  Ch. Eaton Bureaucrat (*blk*)
                              Ch. Bel Tor Cause Scandale (*blk*)
            Ch. Eaton Trustbuster (*blk*)
                              Ch. Acadia Command Performance, C.D. (*wh*)
                  Ch. Acadia Commanding of Eaton (*blk*)
                              Eaton Eureka (*blk*)

CH. ALIYAH DESPERADO—*Black*

                              Ch. Haus Brau Executive of Acadia (*blk*)
                  Ch. Alee What Price A Dream (*blk*)
                              Jameslee Beloved Melody (*blk*)
            Ch. Torchlight Mitzvah (*blk*)
                              Ch. Torchlight How Do I Grab You (*blk*)
                  Ch. Torchlight Derling Whervish (*blk*)
                              Ch. Torchlight Truly Truly Fair (*blk*)

Am. Can. Ch. Wycliffe Jacqueline, U.D.T.

In the formative years Bel Tor in the East and Wycliffe in the Pacific Northwest each had their advocates, each stressing the particular virtues of each line. All Standard breeders owe a debt of gratitude to Rebecca Mason at Bel Tor and to Jean Lyle at Wycliffe. These two ladies started with the best they could find at the time—and spent long years selecting and discarding and improving and have made the task much easier for all who followed. In more recent years there has been a blending of the two families with particular success at Acadia, Eaton, Davaroc and Rimskittle, to name only a few of the most successful.

45

Leading Standard Dams

O F THE THREE VARIETIES, the Standard Poodle has by far the largest number of bitches that qualify as Top Producers (dam of three or more champions each). A tabulation of Top Producing dams showed that more than two-thirds were champions themselves.

Standard bitches are noted for the large number of puppies per litter, and litters of ten or more are not uncommon. Breeders can thus select the best from a large number of puppies within each litter.

There has been less mixing of colors than in Miniatures and Toys, and thus less problems with mismarks.

The responsibility that a breeder faces in bringing a big litter of large puppies into the world has itself been an important factor in improving the variety over the last 25 years. Standard puppies grow rapidly, and need lots of room and attention. There has been less demand for Standards than Toys or Miniatures, so they have not been harmed by the commercialism present in the other varieties. As a result, breeders breed only their very best bitches and breed them to the best possible studs.

This insistence on rigid selection, practiced over a few generations, has worked considerably to the betterment of the variety. In the late 1970's and early 1980's the overall quality in Standards is probably the highest among the three varieties of Poodles.

There are 17 Standard bitches who have produced 10 or more champions. Of these 17 bitches, only two are not champions themselves. This speaks well for the old adage that quality produces quality.

The leading Standard dam, with 21 champions, is the black Best in Show winner, Am. Can. Ch. Wycliffe Jacqueline, U.D.T. (Am. Can. Ch. Petitcote Domino, C.D. ex Am. Can. Ch. Carillon Michelle, C.D.X.). Jacqueline was one

Ch. Kah's Kollector's Item (by Ch. Annsown Gay Knight of Arhill ex Ch. Puttencove Black Stella), dam of 14 champions at Monfret Kennels. Owned by Francis P. Fretwell, Monfret Kennels.

Am. & Can. Ch. Lady Joan of Lowmont (by Ch. Annsown Gay Knight of Arhill ex Lowmont Lady Clarissa), last champion from Lowmont Kennel. Dam of 12 champions. Owned by Susan Radley Fraser, Bibelot Kennels.

332

of the foundation bitches of Wycliffe Kennels in the Pacific Northwest. She was the dam of three Top Producing sons and four Top Producing daughters so her influence is widespread.

The blue Best in Show winner, Ch. Jocelyene Marjorie (Ch. Wycliffe Virgil ex Mogene's Beauzeaux) is the dam of 17 champions, including four Top Producers for Dassin Kennels in Ohio.

The brown Molly Brown's Creme de Cacao (Molly Brown's Creme de Moka ex Tory VI) was the foundation bitch and dam of 17 champions for the Jaylee Kennels of Jay and Judy Dazzio in Louisiana.

The black Ch. Kah's Kollector's Item, C.D. (Ch. Annsown Gay Knight of Arill ex Ch. Puttencove Black Stella) went to Monfret Kennels of Francis P. Fretwell in South Carolina, where she produced 14 champions, including two Top Producers.

The black Best in Show winner, Ch. Eaton Busting With Joy (Ch. Eaton Bureaucrat ex Montec's Lady Mizo), is the dam of 12 champions for the Eaton Kennels of Wilmot Eaton Salisbury in Illinois.

The black Am. Can. Ch. Lady Joan of Lowmont, C.D. (Ch. Annsown Gay Knight of Arhill ex Lowmont Lady Clarissa) was the last champion from the Lowmont Kennels. She went to the Bibelot Kennels of Susan Radley Fraser in Canada where she produced 12 champions including the world famous Eng. Am. Can. Ch. Bibelot's Tall Dark and Handsome.

The black Ch. Wycliffe Zandra (Ch. Wycliffe Martin ex Wycliffe Rowena of Highlane) was the dam of 12 champions at Wycliffe Kennels.

The black Can. Ch. Bibelot's Magnificent Maxine (Ch. Wycliffe Virgil ex Ch. Lady Joan of Lowmont) went to England in 1967 to the Springett Kennels of Marilyn Willis in whelp to Ch. Wycliffe Kenneth and produced seven champions including the multiple Best in Show winner and Top Producer Eng. Ch. Springett Darken Democrat. Maxine returned to Bibelot in Canada where she added to her total list of 11 titleholders.

The black Ch. Dassin Six Pac (Ch. DeRussy Necromancer ex Ch. Jocelyene Marjorie) was the dam of 11 champions at the Dassin Kennels in Ohio.

The black Ch. Haus Brau Gayla of Oak Grove (Ch. Wycliffe Varner ex Ch. Haus Sachse's Rebecca) was the dam of 11 champions for the Oakgrove Kennels of Geraldine Routson Seitz in the Pacific Northwest.

The black Am. Can. Ch. Wycliffe Minerva of Tawasentha (Ch. Wycliffe Ian ex Ch. Wycliffe Theresa) after producing five champions at Wycliffe went to the Bushy Run Kennels in Ohio where she produced six more champions.

The white multiple Best in Show winner, Ch. Alekai Pokoi (Ch. Alekai Nohea ex Ch. Ivardon Winter), was the dam of ten champions at Alekai and Mayfair Kennels.

The brown Ch. Bel Tor Brunehilde (Ch. Bel Tor Morceau Choici ex Ch. Bel Tor Beautiful Dreamer) was the dam of ten champions for the Bel Tor Kennels in Connecticut and for Darkin Kennels in Tucson, Arizona.

Ch. Haus Brau Gayla of Oak Grove

The blue multiple Best in Show winner, Ch. Bel Tor Come Hither (Ch. Bel Tor St. Ay Better Mousetrap ex Ch. Bel Tor Head of the Class) was the dam of ten champions for the Darkin Kennels in Arizona.

The white Best in Show winner, Ch. Star Spangled Debutante (Ch. Acadia Command Performance ex Ch. Heather of Blacknight) has produced ten champions for the Terima Kennels of Toni May in California.

The black Am. Can. Ch. Carillon Michelle, C.D.X. (Santo-Labory of Carillon ex Ch. Carillon Jestina) though whelped in the East, went to the Pacific Northwest to produce ten champions for Wycliffe including the leading producing dam in the breed, Ch. Wycliffe Jacqueline.

The black Wycliffe Rowena of Highlane (Ch. Wycliffe Thomas ex Ch. Wycliffe Zara) was the dam of ten champions. Her first litter produced four champions at Wycliffe. She went to the Blacknight (now Dhubhne) Kennels of John and Elizabeth Campbell in California where she produced six more champions in two litters.

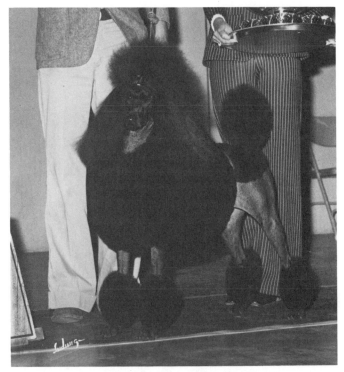

Ch. Eaton Busting With Joy

Ch. Star Spangled Debutante

335

Mrs. George Putnam with a promising young Puttencove.

46

Puttencove Kennels

THE PUTTENCOVE KENNELS of Mrs. George Putnam has established a very recognizable type of Standard and Miniature Poodle, renowned for proud carriage, elegance of head, and sound and delightful Poodle temperament.

Mrs. Putnam has been a key figure in Poodles for so long that many people may not be aware of the significance of her participation and of the depth of her accomplishments. As a young girl she owned her first Poodle in 1903 and showed her for the joy of it. She was a pioneer in a sport that was in its infancy. She struggled along with common sense as her breeding program. Every book which we consider required reading today had not been written by the time she had won a dozen Best in Shows.

The Standards started at Puttencove with a brown bitch puppy, Blakeen Solange, by Ch. Harpendale Monty of Blakeen out of Nunsoe Alter Idem of Blakeen. When the time came, Solange was bred to the great Ch. Blakeen Cyrano, and on May 15, 1936, produced Puttencove Candida—Mrs. Putnam's beloved "Candy". Candida was a lovely-headed, short-bodied, charming bitch and only a slight scar denied her a show career. She was the dam of five champion sons and founded the Puttencove Standards. Candida was bred twice to Ch. Carillon Joyeux producing Ch. Puttencove Peachstone, Ch. Puttencove Blaise and Puttencove Jemima. Candida was also bred to Ch. Carillon Rene to produce the Best in Show winner, Ch. Puttencove Reveille. From Candida's breeding to Ch. Kaffir of Piperscroft came Can. Ch. Puttencove Ivan and Ch. Puttencove Impetuous. Mrs. Putnam won her first all breed Best in Show in 1944 with Ch. Puttencove Impetuous at the Eastern Dog Club. Impetuous was the sire of 11 champions including the famous Ch. Carillon Colin of Puttencove.

Colin, as a handsome black seven weeks old puppy by Impetuous out of Ch. Carillon Colline, was offered to Mrs. Putnam by Blanche Saunders, the famous Obedience expert and owner of Carillon Kennels. Miss Saunders was well aware of the puppy's quality, but she was busy with war work and knew that Mrs. Putnam would give him the opportunity he deserved. This was one puppy that lived up to every expectation and then some. In limited showing, Colin won five Bests in Show, but his lasting importance is based on his great siring ability.

Colin marked a turning point in the black Standard variety. His influence was so great that the majority of black Standards in the ring today are direct descendants. Colin was an impressive dog with great intelligence. He sired a total of 21 champions including Ch. Puttencove Halla's Hugo (sire of six champions), Ch. Puttencove Serenade (dam of six champions) and Ch. Annsown Sir Gay (sire of 22 champions). Halla's Hugo sired Ch. Puttencove Sugar Plum who produced five Prankster champions. An untitled Colin son, Fanfaron Impressario, was the sire of five champions. Sir Gay was a Best in Show winner, and he sired a number of noted producing sons.

The black Ch. Carillon Rene (by Carillon Reveur ex Carillon Francoise), who had been purchased as a six months old puppy, was the head of an important sire line at Puttencove. Rene was the sire of four champions. Bred to Candida he produced Ch. Puttencove Reveille. Rene bred to Puttencove Jemima (ex Candida) gave Ch. Puttencove Grenadier. Grenadier sired four champions including Ch. Puttencove Midshipman (ex Puttencove Miss Impy who was by Ch. Puttencove Impetuous). Midshipman sired 11 champions including Ch. Puttencove Minuteman (ex Puttencove Halla, also by Ch. Puttencove Impetuous). Minuteman was also the sire of 11 champions.

The black bitch Carillon Eve of Puttencove (full sister of Ch. Carillon Courage) was an important producer at Puttencove. Bred to the imported gray Ch. Griseley Labory of Piperscroft, she produced Puttencove Prudence and Puttencove Penelope. Prudence bred to Ch. Carillon Rene gave Ch. Puttencove Samantha (dam of three champions). Samantha bred to the great Colin gave the lovely Ch. Puttencove Serenade, who was the dam of six champions. Serenade's daughter, Ch. Puttencove Spring Song, was the dam of three champions at Monfret Kennels. Puttencove Penelope was bred to Ch. Puttencove Impetuous to produce the outstanding producer Puttencove Halla (dam of five champions). Halla bred to Ch. Puttencove Midshipman produced Ch. Puttencove Minuteman (sire of 11 champions). Halla bred to Colin gave Ch. Puttencove Halla's Hugo (sire of seven champions).

On a judging trip to California in 1952, Mrs. Putnam purchased a white bitch puppy, Astron Lily of Puttencove (by Ch. Pillicoc Barrister ex Ch. Astron Silver Star). Lily was bred to Ch. Loabelo Jonny (grandson of Barrister) to produce the handsome white Ch. Puttencove Promise. Promise had a truly exciting career in the ring and his quality quickly carried him to the top. He was Best of Breed at the Poodle Club of America Specialty in 1957, and Best in

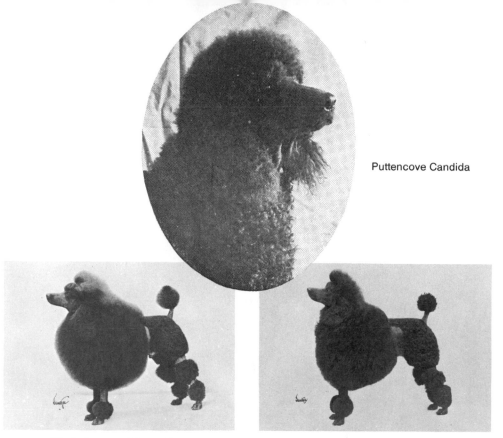

Puttencove Candida

Ch. Puttencove Minute Man

Ch. Puttencove Serenade

Show at Westminster in 1958. Promise was an equally great sire with 29 champions to his credit including Ch. Alekai Nohea, Can. Ch. Calvados de la Fontaine, Ch. Puttencove Kaui and Ch. Tambarine de la Fontaine. Promise's son, Ch. Puttencove Moonshine, was Best of Breed at the parent specialty in 1958 and 1959 and was a multiple champion producer.

In all, Mrs. Putnam bred 54 Standard and 17 Miniature champions. Puttencove won the Poodle Club of America Specialty four times, with three different dogs. Already mentioned was the spectacular Best in Show at Westminster with Ch. Puttencove Promise. In addition, Mrs. Putnam was a past president of the Poodle Club of America, and an honored judge in the show ring.

These accomplishments are even more impressive when viewed in the context of her times. In the days when she was most active, there was no pressure to "finish" your dogs. In fact, Mrs. Putnam believed that bitches belonged in the kennel, and few of them were shown. There were few shows then, often quite far apart, and finishing a champion required perseverance.

Much has been accomplished in the Poodle world since that day in 1931 when Mrs. Putnam gave a Standard Poodle to one of her children and Poodles became a continuing, important part of her life. Her daughter, Helen Sokopp, has become a successful breeder in her own right with her Syrena prefix.

Ch. Bel Tor Morceau Choisi, with
breeder-owner Mrs. J.A. Mason.

Ch. Bel Tor Gigadibs

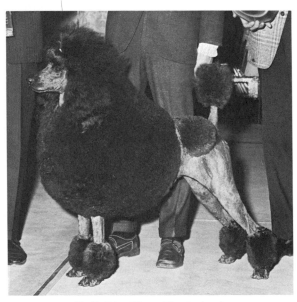

Ch. Bel Tor Where The Action Is

340

47

Bel Tor Kennels

MRS. REBECCA MASON has an incredible ability as a breeder. There have been a total of 158 Poodle champions, in all three varieties but mostly Standards, bearing the Bel Tor prefix—a remarkable record in the annals of dog breeding. In fact, she has bred more A.K.C. Poodle champions than any other breeder.

The name Bel Tor was made up of the first few letters of her name and the names of her daughter and her son: Belinda, Tobias and Rebecca. It was originally Beltore, but was afterwards divided and the last letter dropped and became Bel Tor, and was registered in 1951.

The first litter of Bel Tor Poodles was whelped in March 1942 from Lowmont Lady Juliette, a daughter of Ch. Blakeen Cyrano, and sired by Sunstorm's Merry Messenger (Marechal of Piperscroft ex Eng. Ch. Marlene of Piperscroft). A brown dog, Drambuie, who closely resembled his maternal grandsire, Ch. Blakeen Cyrano, was retained from this litter and later bred to a black bitch, Dubonnette (Ch. Intrepid of Misty Isles ex Antoinette), which Mrs. Mason had bought from Mrs. Olga Rogers. From this litter came Yvette Jeanne and Black Velvet. At that time Mrs. Mason had a prejudice against exhibiting her dogs and, unfortunately, none of these early dogs were shown. In later years, Mrs. Mason changed her mind about showing, and the kennel has vigorously campaigned both light and dark-colored Poodles. The policy of this kennel has been to retire its winners as soon as they have completed their championships, so few have been campaigned as specials.

The impressive records of Bel Tor Kennels are largely based on two litters whelped within a three month period. Mrs. Mason had acquired the brown bitch, Ch. Lowmont Lady Cadette (by Ch. Robin Hood ex Ch. Lowmont Madame d'Aiguillon) as a result of her admiration of the beautiful Madame d'Aiguillon, and the black bitch Ch. Bel Tor Hosanna, as a choice of litter puppy by her Ch. Lowmont Monsieur Hercule Poirot. Both of these bitches were linebred to Ch. Blakeen Cyrano through the Lowmont breeding. After careful thought, Mrs. Mason decided to breed both to the handsome Best in Show winner, Ch. Annsown Sir Gay. Lady Cadette's litter was whelped December 18, 1953 and contained five champions, all with the Bel Tor prefix: Morceau Choici, M'Amie La Belle, Madrigal, Make Believe, and Main Chance. A repeat breeding later produced two more champions—Bel Tor Lothaire and Bel Tor Petite Madelon. Hosanna's litter was whelped on March 6, 1954 and also contained five champions, four with the Bel Tor prefix: Gigadibs, Gasconade, Gentle Julia, Black Sheep, and Ch. Annsown Gay Melodie. The success of these two litters attracted immediate attention to Sir Gay's ability as an outstanding sire.

From these two litters Mrs. Mason retained the two black stud dogs, Ch. Bel Tor Gigadibs and Ch. Bel Tor Morceau Choisi. Gigadibs sired only blacks and whites. Morceau Choisi carried the genes for black, brown and white. By crossing them to each other's daughters and linebreeding in later generations, a continuing succession of Bel Tor champions has been produced.

Ch. Bel Tor Gigadibs, who Mrs. Mason considered almost overdone in every respect, seemed to have that extra something to give to his get and sired 28 champions. A number of his daughters became Top Producers (dam of three or more champions). These include Ch. Bel Tor Oui Oui Mille Fois (five), Ch. Bel Tor Prenez Moi (four), Bel Tor Hussar Chant de Noel (seven), and Ch. Darkin Dubious (three).

Another noted stud at Bel Tor was the refined, stylish black, Bel Tor Salad Days. He was sired by Ch. Torchlight Jackanapes ex Bel Tor Stolen Hour, who was a daughter of Gigadibs and granddaughter of Morceau Choici. Salad Days was the sire of 25 champions.

Bel Tor has been fortunate in having a long list of excellent producing bitches. In addition to those already mentioned there are several mother-daughter combinations which deserve inclusion. Ch. Bel Tor Hosanna (dam of nine champions) was the dam of Ch. Bel Tor Head Of The Class (dam of four champions, three of which are Best in Show winners). Head Of The Class produced the beautiful blue Best in Show winner, Ch. Bel Tor Come Hither, who was the dam of 10 champions. The brown bitch, Ch. Beltore Bright Star (three champions) was the dam in one litter of Ch. Bel Tor McCreery (39 champions) and Ch. Bel Tor Lady Mary (dam of four champions), both named in honor of Lowmont Kennel's owner, Mary McCreery. The black bitch, Ch. Bel Tor Beautiful Dreamer (seven champions), was the dam of Ch. Bel Tor Brunehilde (dam of 10 champions) by Ch. Bel Tor Morceau Choici, and Ch. Bel Tor Destined To Be (dam of three champions) by Bel Tor Gunsmoke.

Ch. Bel Tor Morceau Choisi sired a total of 18 champions including the brown Ch. Bel Tor McCreery and Ch. Bel Tor Vintage Wine (sire of seven). McCreery, who was considered to closely resemble the much admired Ch.

342

AM. CAN. CH. BEL TOR McCREERY

Whelped January 3, 1955   Died July 8, 1966

Bred and owned by Bel Tor Kennels

Ch. Carillon Colin of Puttencove (*blk*)
Ch. Annsown Sir Gay (*blk*)
Annsown San Souci (*blk*)
Ch. Bel Tor Morceau Choisi (*blk*)
Ch. Robin Hood (*brn*)
Ch. Bel Tor Lady Cadette (*brn*)
Ch. Lowmont Madame d'Aiguillon (*brn*)

AM. CAN. CH. BEL TOR McCREERY—*Brown*

Carillon Michel (*blk*)
Lowmont Lord Dion (*blk*)
Ch. Lowmont Lady Joan (*blk*)
Ch. Beltore Bright Star (*brn*)
Drambuie (*brn*)
Yvette Jeanne (*blk*)
Dubonette (*blk*)

Blakeen Cyrano, also had four Top Producing daughters: Ch. Bel Tor Pink Cloud (four), Ch. Bel Tor Lady Mary (four), Ch. Bel Tor Brunehilde (10) and Ch. Bel Tor Philippa (four).

McCreery's 39 champions included Ch. Bel Tor St. Ay Better Mousetrap, a dark red brown, who sired 20 champions. Mousetrap get included Ch. Bel Tor Chance Of A Lifetime (six champions), Ch. Bel Tor Where The Action Is (13 champions and Mrs. Mason's choice as the best she ever bred), Ch. Bel Tor Sandalwood (dam of six champions) and Ch. Bel Tor Away We Go (sire of 10 champions). Away We Go's son, Ch. Bel Tor Darkin Collaboration, sired Ch. Bel Tor All The Trimmings (11 champion get). From Morceau Choisi to All The Trimmings there are six consecutive generations of Top Producing Bel Tor sires.

Ch. Bel Tor McCreery also sired Ch. Rondylo Here's Damon (7 champions) and his litter brother Ch. Bel Tor Andrew of Rondylo. Andrew died young but not before siring the brown Ch. Bel Tor Bringin Home The Bacon. Bacon in turn sired the multiple champion producer Int. Ch. Stormy Lane To Sir With Love and Bel Tor's leading sire Ch. Bel Tor Big Picture. Big Picture ("Pete") had three solid generations of the best Bel Tor behind him. He finished with four majors at 17 months of age. He went on to gain his Canadian, Bermudian, Mexican and CACIB titles. He sired 52 champions including three Top Producing sons: Ch. Rimskittle Right On (22 champions), Ch. Juel Destiny's Show Off (11 champions) and Am. Can. Ch. Torbec A Touch of Class (11 champions) plus two Top Producing daughters, Ch. Bel Tor Blissful (multiple All Breed and Specialty Best in Show winner and dam of six champions at Davaroc) and Ch. Rimskittle Spittin Image (four champions). The Bel Tor and Big Picture influence has continued to spread through its influence on Rimskittle, Davaroc, Juel and Torbec Kennels.

Ch. Bel Tor Noonday Sun

Ch. Bel Tor Blissful

Am. Can. Bda. Mex. Int.
CH. BEL TOR BIG PICTURE

Whelped: September 27, 1969   Died: October 1981

Bred and owned by Bel Tor Kennels

Am. Can. Ch. Bel Tor McCreery (*brn*)
Ch. Bel Tor Andrew of Rondylo (*brn*)
Ch. Bel Tor Here's How (*blk*)
Am. Can. Ch. Bel Tor Bringin Home The Bacon (*brn*)
Int. Ch. Bel Tor Where The Action Is (*blk*)
Bel Tor Something Special (*blk*)
Bel Tor General's Lady (*blk*)

AM. CAN. BDA. MEX. INT. CH. BEL TOR BIG PICTURE—*Black*

Ch. Bel Tor St. Ay Better Mousetrap (*brn*)
Ch. Bel Tor Chance Of A Lifetime (*blu*)
Int. Ch. Bel Tor Head of the Class (*blk*)
Ch. Bel Tor Fortune's Favorite (*blk*)
Ch. Bel Tor Morceau Choisi (*blk*)
Ch. Bel Tor Brunehilde (*brn*)
Ch. Bel Tor Beautiful Dreamer (*blk*)

Am. Can. Ch. Wycliffe Thomas
with his breeder-owner
Mrs. Donald Lyle.

Bel Tor has bred champions in all three varieties including 15 Toy champions. Mrs. Mason's foundation bitch was a black English Toy import, Oldtimbers Royal Romance, who was descended from Montmartre What-A-Boy. Romance bred to Blackabit of Sassafras produced Ch. Bel Tor Touch of Venus and Ch. Bel Tor Thriller. Thriller sired Ch. Bel Tor Elise The Lissome, Ch. Bel Tor Latest Thrill (out of his own daughter) and Bel Tor Nicholas. Nicholas sired four champions—three out of his half sister, Bel Tor Georgiana Luisa Marie (by Thriller). These were Ch. Bel Tor Great New Look, Ch. Bel Tor Impossible Dream and Ch. Bel Tor Impact. Mrs. Mason considered Impact one of her best Toys. His son, Bel Tor Billy B, sired three Bel Tor champions.

In 1985 Mrs. Mason has reduced her kennel to a minimum with only an occasional litter but she still retains a keen interest in the future of her beloved breed.

346

48

Wycliffe Kennels

ONE OF THE MOST IMPORTANT kennels in American
Standard Poodles is the Wycliffe Kennels of Mrs. Donald Lyle in Western
Canada. Starting with the purchase of a black bitch puppy, Carillon Michelle,
from Blanche Saunders in 1952, Jean Lyle has carefully evolved the black
Wycliffe line. Michelle was by the Swiss import Santo-Labory of Carillon ex
Ch. Carillon Jestina. She won her title in the U.S. and Canada, and also held
Am. C.D.X. and Can. U.D.T. degrees. Michelle was the dam of nine champions
including Ch. Wycliffe Hilary of Carillon, Can. Ch. Wycliffe Little Lulu and
Am. Can. Ch. Wycliffe Jacqueline, U.D.T. Hilary, bred to Ch. Carillon
Dilemma, gave Ch. Carillon Gossip and Carillon Glitter (dam of four
champions). Little Lulu was the dam of Ch. Wycliffe Zara (dam of six
champions).

Jacqueline is the leading producing bitch in the breed. She whelped a total of
41 pups in her five litters by four different sires, and from these came 21
champions including seven Top Producers—a record that may stand for some
time to come.

Jacqueline was sent East to be bred to Ch. Annsown Gay Knight of Arhill.
The resulting litter of eight contained six champions, among them Ch. Wycliffe
Thomas (sire of 67 champions), Ch. Wycliffe Timothy (sire of 16 champions),
Can. Ch. Wycliffe Talk Of The Town (dam of 3 champions) and Can. Ch.
Wycliffe Theresa (dam of 10 champions). All four of these were either Best in
Show winners or Best Canadian-bred in Show winners. The fifth and sixth
champion members of this litter were Ch. Wycliffe Twinkling Tiara and Ch.
Wycliffe Theodore.

Jacqueline's previous litter had been sired by Ch. Carillon Dilemma (a son
of Ch. Annsown Sir Gay, thus a half brother of Ch. Annsown Gay Knight of

Arhill). This litter contained five champions including Ch. Wycliffe Nicola, C.D.X. (dam of eight champions). Nicola's daughter, Ch. Wycliffe Victoria of Acadia, was the dam of seven champions. Jacqueline was first bred to Ch. Bel Tor Hugues Capet, (also a Sir Gay son) to produce three champions including Am. Can. Ch. Wycliffe Glamorous Gillian. Gillian's daughter, Ch. Wycliffe Monica, was the dam of four champions.

Jacqueline's last two litters were sired by her son, Ch. Wycliffe Timothy, and from these litters came a total of seven champions including Ch. Wycliffe Virgil (sire of 50 champions) and Ch. Wycliffe Veronica (dam of five champions). Virgil, a Best in Show winner, was the sire of Eng. Am. Can. Ch. Bibelot's Tall Dark and Handsome, who was England's Dog Of The Year for 1966. Tall Dark and Handsome was the sire of 53 champions.

Jacqueline's most famous son was the great black, Am. Can. Ch. Wycliffe Thomas, whelped April 1, 1959. Thomas, a big dog measuring 26½ inches at the withers, was noted for his soundness and superlative disposition. He won from coast to coast. He was Best of Winners at the Poodle Club of America Specialty in 1960 at just 13 months, and completed his championship in just two weeks in the East. He later won many Varieties, Groups and nine Bests in Show. Thomas is one of the leading Standard sires with 67 champions to his credit. His get were important winners and producers from coast to coast. He has 10 Top Producing sons and many Top Producing daughters.

Thomas bred to his daughter Ch. Wycliffe Zara (six champions) produced the Best in Show winner, Am. Can. Ch. Wycliffe Kenneth (66 champions), who

Ch. Wycliffe Thomas Too

Ch. Wycliffe Genevieve

was of the same general type as his sire. Kenneth sired seven Top Producing sons and many Top Producing daughters. Due to siring an excellent English-born litter out of Can. Ch. Bibelot's Magnificent Maxine, which litter was sold to many parts of the world, and to the export of his Best in Show winning daughter Can. Australian Ch. Wycliffe Sybil, C.D., to Australia, Kenneth had more influence world-wide than did his sire Thomas.

Kenneth bred to Ch. Wycliffe Zandra (15 champions) produced Am. Can. Ch. Wycliffe Thomas Too, C.D. (15 champions), who was the next link in the chain. Bred to his half sister Am. Can. Ch. Wycliffe Genevieve (also by Kenneth, and the dam of 11 champions), Thomas Too produced Am. Can. Ch. Wycliffe Xcellente of Shamlot, a Best in Show winner from the classes and sire of 24 champions. Xcellente bred back to his lovely Best in Show winning dam Genevieve gave Wycliffe's next great sire, Am. Can. Ch. Wycliffe Fitzherbert. Mrs. Lyle felt that Fitzherbert had an uncanny resemblance to his double grandsire, Kenneth. Fitzherbert proved to be an exceptional sire in the tradition of Thomas and Kenneth, and his 84 champions total to date has even topped their records as producers of champions.

Mrs. Lyle's most recent choice to continue in the Wycliffe tradition is Am. Can. Ch. Wycliffe Michael, a double grandson of Fitzherbert's, who finished in Canada at just 11 months with a Best Puppy in Show award.

Wycliffe has always been a small suburban "backyard" kennel, with rarely more than three to five adults in residence, and only two or three litters a year. Shortage of space has necessitated keeping only the very best, so brood bitches have also always been show dogs and champions as well. All the top winners retained have always been owner-handled and all of these have lived as family pets.

Mrs. Lyle has concentrated on breeding Poodles with the sturdy well-constructed bodies of the hunter, with the high degree of natural ingenious intelligence and companionability for which the Poodle breed is famous, and Poodles of pure, deep, non-fading black color. She has culled all Poodles which either have a cream littermate, or which ever produced a cream. Consequently no cream puppies have appeared at Wycliffe since 1958.

Because of her strong belief that Poodles are much too smart to live happily and become fully developed in mind and spirit if reared as kennel dogs, Mrs. Lyle has always encouraged purchasers of her show puppies to owner-handle them, so that an unusually high proportion of Wycliffe wins have been achieved by the owners of the Poodles.

Perhaps as a result of this policy, many successful kennels all over the country have been founded on stock from Wycliffe. Some of the best known are Acadia, Annveron, Ascot, Blacknight-Dhubhne, Carylclif, Chalmar, Clabon, Dalwynne, Ledgehill, Loribon, Montec, Pannovia, Rojes and Tawasentha.

Other prominent kennels have made extensive use of Top Producing Wycliffe stud dogs, including Arlea, Belle Glen, Bellepointe, Bibelot, Dassin,

AM. CAN. CH. WYCLIFFE FITZHERBERT

Whelped: July 19, 1974   Died: July 10, 1983

Bred and owned by Mrs. Donald Lyle
Wycliffe Kennels, West Vancouver, Canada

Am. Can. Ch. Wycliffe Kenneth (*blk*)
Am. Can. Ch. Wycliffe Thomas Too, C.D. (*blk*)
Am. Can. Ch. Wycliffe Zandra (*blk*)
Am. Can. Ch. Wycliffe Xcellente of Shamlot (*blk*)
Am. Can. Ch. Wycliffe Kenneth (*blk*)
Am. Can. Ch. Wycliffe Genevieve (*blk*)
Can. Aus. Ch. Wycliffe Sybil, C.D. (*blk*)

AM. CAN. CH. WYCLIFFE FITZHERBERT—*Black*

Am. Can. Ch. Wycliffe Thomas (*blk*)
Am. Can. Ch. Wycliffe Kenneth (*blk*)
Am. Can. Ch. Wycliffe Zara (*blk*)
Am. Can. Ch. Wycliffe Genevieve (*blk*)
Am. Can. Ch. Wycliffe Kenneth (*blk*)
Can. Aus. Ch. Wycliffe Sybil, C.D. (*blk*)
Can. Ch. Wycliffe Calypso, C.D. (*blk*)

deRussy, Fancifaire, Haus Brau, Jaylee, Jay-En, Koronet, Langcroft-Winshire, Nevermore and Oakgrove.

Mrs. Lyle is especially proud of the ability of the Poodles which she raises to reproduce their own quality. No fewer than 14 Wycliffe males have reached the Honor Roll of sires who have produced 10 or more champions, as well as 13 Top Producing bitches with more than five champions each.

A total of 216 Wycliffe Poodles have become champions in nine different countries of the world. One hundred forty-two of these have American championship titles, 114 of these Canadian-born Poodles have Canadian championship titles, and a further 10 have won titles and have been bred from in Great Britain, Holland, Germany, Finland, Bermuda, Mexico and Argentina. In 1982-83, all of the new British champions had Wycliffe blood in their pedigrees. The Wycliffe influence on Standard Poodles is now worldwide, and scarcely a champion in any country of the "western" world does not contain a substantial percentage of Wycliffe blood in its pedigree.

Ch. Jocelyene Marjorie (by Ch. Wycliffe Virgil ex Mogene's Beauzeaux), Standard, shown going Best of Breed at the 1968 Poodle Club of America Specialty under judge Miss Frances Angela (at left). Mrs. Harold Ringrose, club president, is at right. Owned by Joan Schilke and Freeman Dickey, and shown by Mr. Dickey.

49

Dassin Kennels

Although the Dassin Kennels of Freeman C. "Bud" Dickey have bred and finished Miniatures and Toys, they are best known for their beautiful black Standards. Bud Dickey has used his natural instincts as a breeder plus his talents as a top handler to make Dassin one of the breed's leading kennels.

Mr. Dickey showed a German Shepherd in Obedience while he was still in high school. He then acquired and finished a white Standard bitch, Ch. Tour D'Argent Fair Fancy. Fancy produced five champions in her only litter, by Ch. Hallmark Harmony O'Windridge.

In 1964, Mr. Dickey acquired a beautiful black bitch, Ch. Annveron Bacardi Peach (Ch. Carillon Dilemma, U.D., ex Ch. Wycliffe Veronica), known as "Jemima." Jemima was jet black, tall and elegant with a lovely head. She excelled in hindquarters and tailset. When Ch. Annveron Bacardi Peach was bred to Ch. Wycliffe Virgil, she produced the All-Breed Best in Show winner, Ch. Dassin Kissable of Cardon, and Ch. Dassin's Delusion. Jemima bred to Ch. Wycliffe Thomas produced Dassin Doubting Thomas. Although he was never finished, he was an important sire and produced 12 champions. Jemima bred to Ch. Wycliffe Virgil produced another Top Producing son, Dassin Daktari, sire of 14 champions. Jemima was also the dam of Dassin Ruby Begonia (dam of three champions) by Ch. Winshire's Country Gentleman.

In June of 1965, Mr. Dickey saw and fell in love with a beautiful Standard puppy, Jocelyene Marjorie. He talked her owner Joan Schilke into co-owning her with him. Marjorie, Best Puppy in Show at the 1965 Poodle Club of America Specialty, came to live at Dassin when she was 11 months old, and matured into a beautiful blue with a lovely head and great showmanship. She completed her title with several Variety wins and Bests of Breed from the Open

Class, and then as a specials she had Group and Best in Show wins. She was Best of Breed at the 1968 P.C.A. Specialty.

As a producer, Marjorie was even more spectacular. Her first litter, sired by Dassin Doubting Thomas, was whelped October 11, 1969 and all five became champions: Ch. Dassin Blue Tango O'Chal Mar (18 Bests in Show, Best of Breed at 1973 P.C.A. Specialty), Ch. Dassin's Blue Lilac, Ch. Dassin Blue with Envie, Ch. Dassin Butch Cassidy, and Ch. Dassin's Ericka—all Breed and Group winners.

Marjorie's second litter, also by Doubting Thomas, produced four more champions: Ch. Dassin's Black Thorn, Ch. Dassin's Blue Chip, Ch. Dassin's Blue Ingenue and Ch. Dassin Marjorie Morningstar (dam of three champions).

Marjorie's third litter, whelped October 25, 1971, was by a handsome young dog from the Pacific Northwest region, Ch. Winshire's Country Gentleman. This litter contained Ch. Dassin's Sashtie (Group winner), Ch. Dassin's Devastation (Best in Show winner), and three of the leading Standard sires—Ch. Dassin Debauchery (6 Bests in Show, Best of Variety 1974 P.C.A. Specialty), Ch. Dassin's Sum Buddy (3 Bests in Show) and Ch. Dassin's Broadway Joe. Interestingly, type wise Broadway Joe was considered the choice of the litter, but because he was intimidated by Sum Buddy and Debauchery as a puppy, he never really developed the showmanship they did. All three became sires of note. Broadway Joe sired 36 champions including the Best in Show winner and Top Producer, Ch. Dassin Debussy. Debussy was Best of Variety at the 1978 P.C.A. Specialty. Debussy is considered by Mr. Dickey and his partner Joe Vergnetti as the exemplification of the type they are striving to breed.

Marjorie's last litter, whelped April 20, 1973, was by Ch. de Russy Necromancer. This litter produced Ch. Dassin Spartacus, Ch. Dassin Plain Talk and Ch. Dassin Six Pac. Six Pac is the dam of nine champions including Ch. Dassin Rita La Rose, who was Best of Variety at the 1980 P.C.A. Specialty.

Starting with Marjorie's Best of Breed at the 1968 P.C.A. Specialty through the 1983 P.C.A. Specialty when Best of Variety was won by Ch. Dassin De Lux (a Broadway Joe daughter), either Marjorie or one of her descendants has won Best of Variety or higher at either the P.C.A. Parent Club Specialty or the P.C.A. Regional Specialty 12 times.

354

Ch. Dassin Debussy

Ch. Dassin's Sum Buddy

Ch. Dassin Busby Berkley

Ch. Dassin's Broadway Joe

Ch. Blakeen Jung Frau, shown going Best in Show at the 1940 Morris and Essex Kennel Club Show with Geraldine Rockefeller Dodge, presenting trophy; Hayes Blake Hoyt, breeder-owner, handling and George Steadman Thomas, Judge.

50

Standard Kennels
of the Past

BLAKEEN—Hayes Blake Hoyt (*Also Miniatures, Toys*)
CARILLON—Mrs. Whitehouse Walker, Blanche Saunders
CARTLANE—Mildred Hall (*Also Miniatures, Toys*)
DAVDON—Dr. Donald Davidson
ENSARR—Peggy & Bill Githens
LOWMONT—Mary McCreery
MISTY ISLES—Alice Lang Rogers (*Also Miniatures*)
NUNSOE—Jane Lane (Great Britain)
PILLICOC—Alene Erlanger (*Also Miniatures*)
SALMAGUNDI—Mr. & Mrs. Justin Griess (*Also Miniatures*)
TORCHLIGHT—Frances Angela
VULCAN CHAMPAGNE—Nellie Ionides, Shirley Walne (Great Britain)

51

Present Day
Standard Poodle Kennels

THE STANDARD POODLE is enjoying a resurgence in quality and popularity. Raising and placing a litter of 10 or 12 Standard Poodle puppies is not a task to be undertaken lightly. This has resulted in only the best bitches being bred to quality stud dogs. This kind of select breeding practiced for several generations has resulted in a greater uniformity in type among Standards. Today there are many small breeders with just several bitches and only a stud dog or two who breed very selectively. Shipping by air has been a boon making almost any stud dog available. There are very few large kennels with large staffs as in the early days. Concentrating on just a few dogs yields far better results, especially as Poodles flourish best in a family situation.

The following is a list of breeders dedicated to the improvement of the breed:

ACADIA—Joy Tongue Vandervelden
ALEE—Helen Lee James
ALEKAI—Alyce Kaiser, now Wendell J. Sammet
APIELE—Patricia Sendin & Amelia Wewer
ASCOT—Glenna G. Carlson
BEL TOR—Rebecca Mason (*Also Toys*)
BERESFORD—Gladys Renaghan, Maureen Ziko
BIBELOT—Susan R. Fraser (Canada)
BLUE BELL—Ruth Lukens
CALBRECHT—Sharon Calbrecht
CARA VAE—Carl & Sally Brumley

CHALMAR—Marjorie Bauman
DARKIN—Susan North
DASSIN—F. C. Dickey, Joe Vergnetti
DAVAROC—Dr. Sam & Mary Peacock
DE RUSSY—Dr. Jacklyn E. Hungerland
DHUBHNE—John & Elizabeth Campbell
DONNCHADA—Betty Brown, George Brown
EATON—Wilmot Eaton Salisbury
FORZANDO—Lois Nurmi Plawchan
FRENCHES—Rita Price Jones (Great Britain) *Also Miniatures, Toys*
GAYLASNA—Brad & June Noyes
GLORY—Gloria MacKay
GRAPHIC—Florence Graham
HARIANN—Harry & Ann Schneider
HAUS BRAU—Arlene Brown
JAY-EN—Mrs. D. A. & Jack Naegeli
JAY LEE—Jay & Judy Dazzio
JUEL—Judy & Eldon Bishop
KAELEY—Catharine C. Reiley
KAYESETT—Herbert & Muriel Kaye
KORONET—Joan Schilke
LONGLEAT—James & Jenny Lester
LOU-GIN—Lou Dunson
MACGILLIVRAY—Jack & Cindy MacGillivray
MAYFAIR—Anne Seranne & Barbara Wolferman
MAYFIELD—Harriett J. Laws
MARENS—Marcus Ahrens
MONFRET—Francis P. Fretwell
OAKGROVE—Geraldine Seitz
OSEA—Brenda Dennis
PALMARES—Janet Veitch Blannin
PINAFORE—Penny Harney
PUTTENCOVE—Katherine Putnam (*Also Miniatures*)
RIMSKITTLE—James & Anne Rogers Clark
SAFARI—Cynthia & Mary Huff
STORY TALE—Joyce Bachner
SUFFOLK—Jacquelyn Swenson
SYRENA—Helen Sokopp
TERIMA—Toni May
TORBEC—Michelle McIntyre
TORCHLIGHT—Jean Lazarus
VULCAN CHAMPAGNE—now Ann Coppage (Great Britain)

Miss Blanche Saunders with her famous black Standard Poodle, Ch. Carillon Jester, U.D.T., Int. C.D. Jester was the star of two Obedience demonstrations at Yankee Stadium before crowds of 75,000, and was featured on television and in many Obedience films.

52

Poodles In Obedience

by Catharine C. Reiley

THE SPORT OF DOG OBEDIENCE in America celebrated its
50th anniversary in 1983. From the very beginning Poodles figured prominently
in the Obedience story.

In January 1931, Helene Whitehouse Walker imported a brown Standard
Poodle, Nymphaea Jason, from England. She was so delighted with his great
Poodle personality that she imported also his full brother, Nymphaea Jasper,
and his half brother, Ch. Whippendell Poli of Carillon. Mrs. Walker had
decided to become a breeder and it was Poli who gave his name to the
kennel—Carillon.

With the arrival of these three Poodles, Mrs. Walker began to subscribe to
English dog magazines. She became most interested in the Obedience Tests that
were being held in that country. She wondered if something of this type might
not be good for the United States. In the spring of 1931, Mrs. Walker and nine
others joined together to form the Poodle Club of America. Her father, Henry J.
Whitehouse, served as the first President and Mrs. Walker was Secretary-
Treasurer. From 1939 through 1945 she was President of P.C.A. and is now
one of its Honorary Presidents.

Mrs. Walker showed Jason at the Westminster Kennel Club show in 1931,
which turned out to be a fiasco! Mrs. Walker felt that since they had had a long
drive in from the country, Jason should be allowed to relax and even sit while
the other Poodles were being posed and judged. The judge was not impressed,
and Jason did not place. As Mrs. Walker became more adept as a handler, the
three Carillon Poodles, distinctive with orange bows in their topknots, became
regular fixtures at the dog shows. Jason finished his championship in 1933, won

the Group many times, but is best remembered as a great sire with seven champions in a time when difficulties in travel and problems of raising litters made this a remarkable achievement.

Eng. Ch. Whippendell Poli of Carillon earned an even more impressive show record. He made his United States debut in June 1931 and completed his title in April 1932, thus becoming the first Poodle to be a dual bench champion. He won Best of Breed at the first Poodle Club of America Specialty and was the first Poodle to win the Non-Sporting Group at Westminster in February 1933.

At the same time Mrs. Walker was so deeply engrossed in breeding and popularizing the Poodle in the United States, she started another project. Remembering those English magazine articles, she contacted breeders, exhibitors and kennel clubs and proposed that an Obedience Test be held in the fall. The response was small but enthusiastic.

The first All Breed Obedience Test was held in Mount Kisco in October 1933 at Mr. Whitehouse's estate. There were eight entries, three of them Poodles. At this Test the dogs were required to walk at their handler's side off-lead, to come when called, to retrieve a dumbbell on the flat and over an obstacle, to leap a long jump on command, and to remain in the sitting and down positions with their handlers out of sight.

During 1934 two Obedience Tests were held at all-breeds shows and a second private Test was again held in Mount Kisco which included, for the first time, tracking.

In May 1934, Mrs. Walker imported Tango of Piperscroft, C.D.X., an apricot trained for Obedience by Mrs. Grace Boyd. With Tango came instructions on how to deliver voice and hand signals. "I'd go out on the lawn with the letter in one hand and the dog in the other and try to follow directions," Mrs. Walker reminisces, "But I told my father there was only one thing for me to do, and that was to go to the source." It was during that summer that Mrs. Walker spent six weeks in England to gain firsthand knowledge of Obedience and to see what she might better do to establish and promote the sport in the United States.

In the late fall of 1934, Mrs. Walker advertised for kennel help and her ad was answered by Miss Blanche Saunders. She not only obtained help but also the perfect pupil and protege. Mrs. Walker drove to Brewster, New York for the interview and describes her first meeting with Blanche: "She came running to meet me—all energy and enthusiasm. She was in blue jeans, with a red bandana around her head, and had just finished a day's work driving a tractor on the farm. This great energy was to carry her, in fifteen short years, to the top of her profession as a trainer of dogs and their owners. I showed Blanche the routine of the Obedience Tests and the training class knowledge I had brought back from England. Two months later, a lucky accident took place. I lost my voice completely and she offered to pinch hit for me. From then on, *she* conducted all the training classes."

For the next decade, Mrs. Walker and Miss Saunders worked together to

A 1962 photograph of the author with the lady that started it all. From left to right: Miss Blanche Saunders, Mrs. Whitehouse Walker and Miss Catharine Reiley. The dogs, in same order, are: Ch. Carillon Dilemma, U.D.; Kaeley Audacious Coquette, Am. & Berm. U.D.; and Robin Hill of Carillon, Am. & Can. U.D.T.

lay a solid foundation for the new sport. In later years Mrs. Walker said: "Blanche more than carried on where I left off. I am particularly proud that she always had as her goal the first sentence I wrote when asked to explain the purpose of Obedience Tests—to make the dog a better companion to man."

During 1935, six kennel clubs held Obedience Tests at their all-breeds shows. In the summer, Mrs. Grace Boyd visited the United States and brought three of her Obedience trained Poodles and gave demonstrations. In the fall of 1935, Mrs. Walker wrote and published the booklet *Obedience Tests—Procedure for Judge, Handler and Show Giving Club.* Six photos illustrated the various exercises and featured Mrs. Walker and Tango. The sport was mushrooming.

In December 1935, Mrs. Walker wrote the American Kennel Club, enclosing a resume of all the Tests held to date and requesting recognition and approval for the sport. Approval was granted in March 1936. The first licensed Tests conducted under AKC rules were held at North Westchester (12 entries) June 13, 1936 and Orange Kennel Club (16 entries) June 14, 1936. Six dogs received 80% or more of the possible 100 points at both shows and thus became the first C.D.'s in the U.S.A.

With the AKC taking over responsibility for Obedience Tests and with the sport firmly rooted in the East, Mrs. Walker and Miss Saunders were at last free to give their full attention to arousing public interest in the training of dogs in other sections of the country. The famous "trailer trek" took place from September to December 1937. The rear seat of a 1936 Buick was removed and the area remodelled to house three Standard Poodles—Ch. Carillon Joyeux, Carillon Epreuve, U.D. and Carillon Bon Coeur who completed his championship on the trip. The car pulled a 21-foot trailer. They covered 10,000 miles during the ten week trip, giving exhibitions in the Midwest, Southwest and Far West. Talks were given, pamphlets distributed and many new friendships were made. Fortunately the full details of this trip have been recorded by Miss Saunders in *The Story of Dog Obedience* in which she writes: "The ringside was crowded as everyone was anxious to see the two crazy women from New York with their trick Poodles." The cost of the trip was just under five hundred dollars!

Obedience was presented at the Westminster Kennel Club Show in 1939. It was designed by Miss Saunders and staged by Josef Weber. One of the Poodles in that demonstration was Ch. Carillon Courage, C.D.X., who had made history the previous year at the 1938 Tuxedo Kennel Club show by not only winning his Obedience class but also placing first in the Non-Sporting Group.

Carillon Eprevue, U.D.T., first dog of any breed to gain all obedience titles, owned by Carillon Kennels, trained and handled by Blanche Saunders.

The careful attention with which the AKC watched the rapid growth of Obedience was climaxed in early 1939 with the formation of a committee of ten called the AKC Obedience Advisory Committee. Members came from seven states and included Mrs. Walker. It proved most helpful in standardizing Obedience judging throughout the country and set the pattern for similar advisory committees. These have been appointed at periodic intervals and have continued to be a vital force in the development and improvement of the sport over the years.

When war clouds gathered in Europe in 1939 Mrs. Walker reduced her breeding program. In 1943 she closed the kennel and gave Miss Saunders the Carillon name, good will and some brood bitches. During the war years, Miss Saunders worked with Josef Weber in Princeton, New Jersey where dogs were being trained for guard duty at war plants. Upon her return, she resumed breeding and spearheaded many new developments in Obedience.

Demonstrations became even more popular. From 1944 through 1955, Miss Saunders staged exhibitions at Rockefeller Plaza, New York City and at the Yankee Stadium on seven different occasions before crowds of up to 70,000 people. Poodles were always present and were frequently handled by members of the Poodle Obedience Training Club of Greater New York which had been organized in the late 1940's. Miss Saunders served as Head Instructor for their classes. Obedience returned to the Westminster Show in 1947 and 1948 in which two Poodles participated—a Miniature, Ch. Far Away Katy Did, U.D., handled by Laura Niles, and a Standard, Ch. Carillon Jester, U.D.T., Can. C.D., handled by Louise Branch.

Following the War, Obedience took another turn. Emphasis began to be placed on training the family pet to have good manners. The A.S.P.C.A. classes were started in New York City under Miss Saunders' direction and became the model for classes which sprang up in many other cities throughout the country. From 1944 to 1961 it is estimated that over 17,000 dogs and handlers participated in the program, including many of the Poodles who went on to make a name for themselves in Obedience competition. I attended these classes with a Welsh Terrier and was one of the many introduced to the Poodle at that time. Yes, I became hooked and my next dog was a Poodle, and it went even further when I became a breeder and showed my dogs in both breed and Obedience for many years to come.

Both Blanche Saunders' book and film "Training You To Train Your Dog" appeared in 1946. The book was the first "how to do it" in the area of Dog Obedience and was very influential in introducing sound training techniques to Obedience enthusiasts. It is still very much in demand today. The film was narrated by Helen Hayes, Lowell Thomas and Miss Saunders, and Louise Branch was responsible for the photography. *The New Yorker* magazine wrote a profile on Miss Saunders which appeared in the November 24, 1951 issue.

Miss Saunders' travels were extensive. Obedience training "clinics" were established in many parts of the country for people owning and showing dogs and in need of help. Miss Saunders was always willing to give of her time and talents. Such clinics are held today and vary from a weekend to a week's duration. In the late 50's and early 60's, when the clinics were held nearby, Miss Saunders frequently took Ch. Carillon Dilemma, U.D. with her. He is the only Poodle with a Utility title to have taken Best of Variety at Westminster. He accomplished this in 1959 under Mr. Percy Roberts, handled by Miss Christa Skiebe who also handled him to his Obedience titles. There were also times when a demonstration was scheduled and the space was very limited. As a result, my first homebred Miniature, Kaeley Audacious Coquette, Am. Can. Berm. U.D., and I were fortunate enough to join Miss Saunders.

Miss Saunders' death came as she would have wished, quietly and just after doing the thing she loved best, teaching people how to train dogs. It was December 8, 1964 and she had just completed a training session for the Association of Obedience Clubs and Judges. Her last words to the group were typical of her attitude toward training and toward life: "Call me day or night at Bedford, if you need help."

Throughout the years the Poodle has been well represented in the Obedience ring. In 1936 they topped the list of breeds awarded AKC titles with a total of 16. The following year Poodles moved to second position and remained there through 1974. Perhaps one of the reasons that the Poodle remained "up top" in Obedience competition was the interest the early breeders had in the sport. Ch. Cadeau de Noel from the Pillicoc Kennels (owned by the Milton Erlangers) took first place at the first licensed Trial held under AKC rules in June of 1936. Ch. Blakeen Cafe Parfait, a Poodle of Mr. and Mrs. Sherman Hoyt's Blakeen Kennel, not only completed his championship title but also earned his C.D.X. and worked out regularly retrieving game for hunters.

It was in the early 1950's that the Wycliffe Kennels of Mrs. Donald Lyle came into prominence. Her foundation bitch, Carillon Michelle, became Am. Can. Ch. and Am. C.D.X., Can. U.D.T. Michelle did much to popularize the Poodle breed in the Northwest. She was so engagingly wicked and inventive that the resulting laughter was almost worth the wasted entry fees.

In the early 1960's one frequently saw the Standards of Mrs. Joy Tongue's Acadia Kennels attaining breed and Obedience titles. One of the most titled of her breeding was Acadia Cynthia of Wycliffe who went on to become Am. Can. Mex. Bda. Ch., as well as Mex. C.D., Can. C.D.X., T.D., Bda. C.D., T.D. and Am. C.D.X., T.D. In November 1971 this Poodle became the first dog from another country to gain the Bermudian T.D. Another Acadia bred Standard who had a spectacular career was Ch. Acadia Command Performance who took Best in Show at Westminster in 1973 and shortly afterwards earned his C.D. He was well on his way toward his C.D.X. before his untimely death.

The records show that the Standard Poodle dominated in the Obedience ring in the 1940's and 50's, with the Miniatures moving to the forefront in the mid-60's and taking command in the 70's and 80's.

The white Miniatures of the Andechez Kennels of Blanche and Rebecca Tansil have played a prominent role in the emergence of the Miniature as the top working Poodle in Obedience. Many dogs carrying their prefix are listed in various Honor Rolls. One in particular must be mentioned. Their Ch. Andechez Zachary Zee, U.D. was the first breed champion of any variety to gain the coveted OTCh. title, which the American Kennel Club introduced in 1976.

The Obedience Trial Championship differs quite drastically from a breed championship insofar as all striving to attain their OTCh. must compete against those already holding the title. There is no separate class for OTCh.'s as there is for Best of Variety or Best of Breed. Since championship points are only recorded for those dogs who have earned the Utility Dog title, it has become necessary for exhibitors to continue to compete in the Open and Utility classes in order to earn the necessary points for the OTCh.

Requirements for OTCh. are as follows:
1. Shall have won 100 points; and
2. Shall have won a first place in Utility (or Utility B if class is divided) provided there are at least three dogs in competition; and
3. Shall have won a first place in Open B provided there are at least six dogs in competition; and
4. Shall have won a third first place under the conditions of 2 or 3 above; and
5. Shall have won these three first places under three different judges.

The OTCh. championship point schedule awards points for first and second placements in the Utility or Open Classes. The number of points is dependent on the number of dogs competing in the class.

Through the end of 1984, there have been 62 OTCh. champions of record.

An important breeder on the Obedience scene is Mrs. Joe Longo in Miniatures. Her kennel name is Rye Top and all of her Poodles have names starting with T. To date she has gained ten U.D.'s and two OTCh's—a record that stands alone and will not be topped for many years!

Cygnette Des Fabian, Am. Can. Mex. U.D. and Bda. C.D., was Gabrielle E. Fabian's first top competitive Poodle. "Cygnette" made her debut in May 1963 and was in competition for eleven and a half years. She was the Highest Scoring Poodle (*Chips System Ratings*) from 1967 through 1973. "Cygnette" accumulated a lifetime record 834 qualifying scores which included three 200's in the United States and three 200's in Canada. She also was awarded High in Trial 73 times and qualified in both the Open and Utility classes at the same Trial 343 times! Mrs. Fabian's OTCh. Coxinelle Des Fabian was the first Poodle to earn the OTCh. and before she retired at five and a half years of age had accumulated a lifetime total of 664 OTCh. points. This Poodle was one of the canine stars in the AKC Obedience film "200".

Another Andechez Poodle making history in the Obedience ring is OTCh. Andechez There Goes Timothy, owned by Mrs. Barbara Jacoby. This flashy white Miniature placed third in the Super Dog class at the Gaines Eastern

O.T. Ch. Claude De Fabian, the top ranking Poodle according to the AKC listing of the Top 25 by O.T. Ch. Lifetime Points, shown with breeder-owner-trainer Gabrielle Fabian and Judge Mary Happersett. Claude has won 205 First places and 76 High In Trial awards.

O.T. Ch. Andechez There Goes Timothy, shown with his owner-trainer, Barbara Jacoby. Timothy won Highest Score in Trial at the Poodle Club of America Specialty Shows in 1980, 1982 and 1984. He also won the "Super Dog" title at the 1984 Gaines U.S. Dog Obedience Classic—the first Poodle to achieve this award.

Regional in 1981, second in the same class at the 1982 Regional and in 1984 he was the winner of Super Dog at the Gaines United States Classic—the first Poodle ever to achieve this distinction!

The white Miniatures of Mrs. Alice Hartman are equally at home in both the breed and Obedience ring. Her foundation bitch is Ch. and OTCh. White Crest Tracy who has also earned her U.D. in Canada and Bermuda. "Tracy" earned Dog World Awards in both the Novice and Open classes and has over 50 High-in-Trials to her credit. She has also scored several perfect scores of 200. Her daughter, Ch. White Crest Hard Hitting Hannah, U.D., who is also a Can. and Bda. Ch. and Group winner, received *Dog World* Awards in Novice and Open and is only a few points away from her OTCh. It would look as if Mrs. Hartman's white Miniatures might be starting another dynasty. By the time this book is off the press she will have the only mother-daughter Ch. and OTCh.'s in the country.

Throughout the years the Poodle has been and still is a strong contender in the Obedience ring. One can never forget the thrill of watching a well groomed Poodle perform Obedience exercises with head and tail held high, eyes bright and alert, movements fast and precise and that impish—or better still—devilish look which indicates to the handler that innovations in routine may be the order of the day. Poodles love praise from their handlers, applause from an audience and are often far more at home "center stage" than their handlers. Whether scoring 200 or goofing, there is no question that Poodles are in all respect performers—par excellence.

In 1936 the American Kennel Club granted Obedience titles to 36 dogs; in 1983 titles were awarded to 11,689 dogs. In this same time the popularity of the Poodle breed has soared. Such statistics may be impressive but do not tell the whole story. Behind every dog who enters competition there are hundreds of others who never enter the ring. However, their handlers have experienced the joy that comes from owning a well-mannered pet who knows what to do, when to do it and how to do it. The seed that was dropped by Mrs. Walker and Miss Saunders in the 1930's, was nourished in the 40's and 50's, and is flourishing today in the 80's. The sport is still attracting new enthusiasts and still continues to serve as a showcase for the Poodle breed.

Retrieving Poodles of the Greenspring Poodle Club: Stonewood Heidi, bred, owned, and trained by Charles LeBoutillier, Jr.; Wye Town Canis Major, owned and trained by Mrs. Dorman Covington; and Sugar and Spice, owned by Miss Ruth Hyde.

Wye Town Canis Major bringing in his duck.

53

Poodles As Retrievers

SINCE the Poodle is meant to be man's companion, it is only logical that he should also share his pleasure in hunting. Here situations constantly arise to test the Poodle's intelligence and resourcefulness, a natural way to share in his master's activities. Retrieving, an ancient and honorable sport, fits the Poodle temperament perfectly. You will find numerous early paintings, engravings and book illustrations showing Poodles active in the field and retrieving ducks from the water, enjoying this outdoor sport.

But does all this retrieving activity belong to a bygone age? Not at all. In the 1950's a small group of people in Maryland who were members of the Greenspring Poodle Club resurrected in earnest the idea of Poodles as retrievers by field trial and example. Although the Poodle was not recognized as a retriever by the American Kennel Club, those local clubs in the Maryland area holding sanctioned retirever trials permitted Poodles to participate on a non-competitive basis. The results were undeniable. Throughout the tests the Poodle was steady and obedient, picking up all birds assigned to him both on land and in the water. He treated both live and dead birds gently, and delivered them to hand without mouthing. He seemed not to be greatly bothered by gusty weather, cold and choppy water and deep mud. He did not tire noticeably and was as gay and enthusiastic at the day's end as he was at the start.

Nobody had doubted the Poodle's intelligence and ability to learn, but what was questioned was whether Poodles would have the physical stamina to endure the rugged conditions. Also put to rest by these exhibition trials was the ancient theory that Poodles working in the water needed a heavy coat to protect their lungs—which has been responsible for the Poodle's clip for hundreds of years. These dogs were kept in the retriever clip with no more than 1½ inches of hair all over, the face and tail clipped short, and the feet trimmed in the style of the Irish Water Spaniel for added comfort in the heavy going. This short clipped coat did not attract many burrs and the dog could shake it dry quicker than a long one.

Thus began the Greenspring Poodle Club's continuing devotion to the development of their Poodles as first-class hunting dogs. As originally stated by Mr. and Mrs. Gordon Fisher and Mr. and Mrs. Charles Le Boutellier Jr., the prime movers of the club: "The retriever breeding program is aimed toward producing sound and elegant dogs with the distinguishing characteristics of our breed. We are not interested in sacrificing a strong hunting instinct to a soft but glamorous twelve inch coat, nor would we intentionally perpetuate a poor color risk, for instance, simply because of excellence in the field. We consider very carefully the pedigree of each dog working with us."

Ch. Blakeen Cafe Parfait, C.D.X., a son of the famous Int. Ch. Nunsoe Duc de la Terrace of Blakeen, was the foundation of many of the dogs used successfully in the retriever program. Perhaps the star of the Greenspring group was Mr. Le Boutellier's Stonewood Gold Standard, U.D.T., with a truly remarkable personality, who did exceptional work with great style. He was followed by two of his sons—Mrs. Gordon Fisher's Wye Town Canis Minor and Wye Town Canis Major, owned by Mrs. Martha Covington, who was the club's trainer.

Although the largest size Poodle is most often used in hunting, a very high percentage of Poodles, regardless of size, age or varied backgrounds, show great aptitude and joy in retrieving.

Stonewood Gold Standard, "Stevie," presents his bird to his master, Mr. Charles Le Boutellier. Stevie, by Ch. Blakeen Cafe Parfait, C.D.X., was one of the first Poodles in recent times to be trained for retrieving.

54

The Corded Poodle

AT the Poodle Club of America Specialty Show in 1980, Ch. Hasting's Ten, a black Standard bitch, placed second in a large Bred by Exhibitor class under Rebecca Mason and caused a ripple of excitement around ringside. It was the first time a corded Poodle had been shown in America in over fifty years.

The corded Poodle had been tremendously popular at the turn of the century, particularly in England. It is believed to be of German origin and was mentioned by W. R. Furness in 1891 in his book "The American Dog," so it was well established in the United States by that time. The cords which give this Poodle its special look consist of new hair drawn tight near the skin, and the old hair carefully rolled and greased "about the thickness of a crow quill" into long strands to keep it from breaking. These cords "reach far down the shoulders and mingle with those of the neck so as to render the ears almost undistinguishable." The ears of a dog named Lyris, imported into England in the early 1890's, were said to measure 37 inches when held out straight from the head.

There has always been much argument in regard to the texture of coat that will cord successfully. As the years went by it was generally agreed that it was largely a matter of heredity, in which case the coat had a tendency to cord naturally.

The novelty of a corded coat eventually got out of hand, with many of the coats so immensely long that they swept for several feet on the ground, gathering up any debris with which they came in contact. The weight of this hampered the Poodle's natural activity and could even harm him physically. Also the grease developed a bad odor and since the coat could not be combed or properly washed, it was often full of insects. In time the corded Poodle simply went out of fashion.

Early Corded Standard Poodles. Painting by Arthur Wardle.

Ch. Hasting's Ten

The Westminster Kennel Club offered classes for corded Poodles through 1927, although the last corded shown there was probably Jaquerose Fritz in 1912. Only a few corded seem to have finished their American titles between 1900 and 1917. The American Poodle standard adopted by the Poodle Club of America in 1901 stated: "the cords should be thick and strong, hanging in long, ropy cords." By 1959, when the Poodle standard was largely revised, all mention of corded Poodles was dropped. However, in 1978 provision for corded Poodles was reinstated: "hanging in tight even cords of varying length; longer on mane or body coat, head, and ears; shorter on puffs, bracelets, and pompons."

It was at this time, with this renewed opportunity, that Catherine and Michael Pawasarat of Hasting Farm in Maryland decided to recreate the look of corded Poodles of the 1890's. They chose Ch. Hasting's Ten, by their Ch. Rimskittle Roue La Russe out of Ch. Rimskittle Wineglass Sage, and developed an updated version of the historic cording. They did not oil the coat nor allow it to grow to excessive length. The cords were 12 inches long, with corded hip rosettes, and a tall topknot somewhat like the spectacular feathering on a bandmaster's hat. The effect was striking, and Ch. Hasting's Ten became the first multiple Variety and Group winning corded Standard Poodle in recent memory.

Int. Ch. Vichnou de Lamorlaye, winner in Italy, Belgium and France, with small brown Miniature bitch. Breeder-owner, Princesse Amedee de Broglie, Lamorlaye Kennels, Paris, France.

Puppies from the Lamorlaye Kennels in Paris.

55

Poodles in France

by Princesse Amédée de Broglie

It SHOULD BE NOTED that there are differences between French and American methods of breeding and showing.

On the Continent, the kennel clubs of the different European countries follow the rules and regulations of the FCI (Federation Canine Internationale). In France, as elsewhere in Europe (with the exception of Great Britain), Poodles must be bred in the fundamental colors: black, brown and white. In more recent years silver and apricot have also been accepted as regular colors by the Societé Central Canine. But no mixture whatever is allowed when breeding Poodles, not even black to brown.

In France our Poodles are divided into four classifications of height:

Standards, which measure more than 45 centimeters to 58 centimeters with up to 60 centimeters tolerated (that is, over 17.72 inches to 22.83 inches, with up to 23.62 inches tolerated).

Moyens, over 35 centimeters and under 45 centimeters (over 13.78 inches and under 17.72 inches).

Nains, 28 centimeters up to 35 centimeters (11.02 inches and under 13.78 inches).

Toys, under 28 centimeters with no minimum limitation, but the ideal size looked for is 25 centimeters (that is, under 11.02 inches but ideally around 9.84 inches) which is a new classification admitted in 1985.

Confusion often arises when an American inquiry is received for a Standard or a Miniature, because our French definitions of height do not correspond with the American designations.

To be accepted in a French show, Poodles must be in either the "Modern" or "Lion" Clip. This is very much like the English "Saddle" Clip, but the hindquarters are entirely shorn with no pattern left on. There is a pompon left on the end of the tail and ruffles on the hocks. The dog's face is also clipped, but a small moustache is retained and the hair on the forehead and top of the head is shortened and evenly shaped.

In France there is a general rule concerning the registration of dogs, no matter what breed. Each year a letter of the alphabet is taken in sequence; therefore the age of the dog can be known according to the initial letter of his pedigreed name. For example, in 1985 we started at the beginning of the alphabet and the names of all the dogs whelped that year had to begin with "A".

Another rule is that an owner is not permitted, as he is in England, to add his kennel name or prefix to that of any dog he has not bred. The dogs retain their original name, and their new owners have no right to change them in any way, even when they happen to have been privately bred and sold and have no prefix or suffix. Registration in the LOF (Livres des Origines Francais) requires four generations of numbered and registered dogs.

Poodles are a very ancient breed in France, and as we search far back into their origin, we find some very famous strains which have followed through to the present time. We like to find in the pedigrees of our browns, "du Barrois," "de la Gage," and "Maritza"; and in the background of our black Poodles, "de Madjige," "de Puy Valador," and "d'Azay." In our whites, "De Samarobrive" and "Du Briois" are of the utmost value. As the owner of a very large kennel with varied colors and sizes, I have exported as well as imported many Poodles, and I have certainly improved my own stock with the "Von Sadowa," "Sirius" (both German), and "Labory" (Swiss), as well as British and American purchases.

Our French standard of beauty is nearly the same, apart from minor variations, as in all the other countries. Our judges, however, are very exacting in regard to uniformity of color, length of ear leather and number of teeth. Two missing premolars prevent a dog from being registered. Unlike both England and America, our dogs are not judged by points but must obtain one of the mentions, "Excellent," "Very Good," "Good." (There are, by the way, no classes for dogs under ten months old.) Only a first prize in Open Dogs with the mention "Excellent" qualifies a dog for a championship certificate, or CAC (Certificat D' Apitude au Championnat). To become a French champion, a dog must acquire at least three CAC's, one of which must be won at the Annual International Show, held under the auspices of the Societe Centrale Canine de France once a year. Since only one Poodle of each sex and color can obtain the title in any one year, few people realize what an achievement it is to make a French champion.

May these few notes bring a better understanding between the Poodle fanciers of different countries. We would all gain by working together to bring about an even greater perfection of this incomparable breed.

56

Poodle Ailments and Diseases

Poodles as a breed are singularly healthy and normal and subject to few ailments. They are little different from other dogs in their diseases and the remedies for them. To maintain your Poodle in good health, feed him well on nourishing food, see that he gets adequate exercise for his size, give him his routine inoculations and booster shots, and also provide him with the psychological security of knowing you care for him and will protect and help him in times of crisis. This last is not as impossible to do as it might seem. You will quickly develop an incredible rapport with your Poodle, an unspoken language easily understood by both of you.

There are two mistakes owners of Poodles are prone to make. One is to be always running to the veterinarian at the most minute and often imaginary sign of the dog's indisposition; the other is neglect of real and grave illness in the hope or assumption that the Poodle will recover without medical attention. Of the two errors, the former is the most frequent as it is the least harmful. Poodle owners are, as a lot, intelligent and most of them reasonably affluent. They value their dogs, are alert for their indispositions, and are able to afford veterinary services. But it should not be overdone.

The veterinarian is, however, an ace-in-the-hole in time of real Poodle trouble. It is frivolous to bother him with minor illnesses that can as well or better be treated at home; but in the event a Poodle's malady is serious or threatens to become serious, it is best to consult the veterinarian without delay. Do not procrastinate. Having consulted him, accept his counsel and follow his instructions, exactly.

Inoculations

If you bought your Poodle from a breeder, check with him as to when your puppy was inoculated and for what diseases, and ask what future course of inoculations it is best to follow. If your puppy has not been inoculated at all, then this should be done on your first visit with him to the veterinarian.

Poodles may be subject to the usual ailments and problems—ear infections, fleas and ticks, worms, and the once devastating but now fairly easily controlled (by inoculation) diseases—distemper, hepatitis and leptospirosis. Your veterinarian can handle all of these, and the last three should be prevented before they even have the chance to begin, since all can be picked up by your Poodle just by walking down a street.

Distemper was for years the most alarming of all the Poodle diseases and one of the most serious, being a virus that attacked dogs at an early age. Vaccines were discovered and improved and have done a tremendous amount of good in protecting dogs, but there are still bad outbreaks in different parts of the country, new strains of the virus, and every protection should be afforded your Poodle against the disease by having him inoculated just as soon as he is old enough. The same applies to hepatitis, also a virus, and leptospirosis, an infection which attacks either the liver or the kidneys and is carried in the urine of infected dogs. Your Poodle can be immunized against all three of these diseases—distemper, hepatitis and leptospirosis—in a combination vaccination, given to him when he is 6 to 8 weeks old. This is of the utmost importance. It is not 100 percent certain, but an inoculated dog, if unlucky enough to contract any one of these diseases, will not be so severely affected. Your dog should receive a booster shot at anywhere from 10 to 16 weeks, and then be revaccinated annually. If you are overly concerned, or if your Poodle is on the city streets a lot or in contact with other dogs not yours, a more ideal schedule would be to give the second vaccination at 10 to 12 weeks, and a third at 14 to 16 weeks, with an annual follow-up.

The most serious of all diseases is canine parvovirus. It has been of major concern in the dog world since 1978. The effects are lethal and heartbreaking, as puppies can die from it in a matter of hours. The symptoms are vomiting and diarrhea, usually with blood in it, followed by a weight loss, dehydration and death. If your Poodle suffers from any of these, get him to the veterinarian at once. Take no chances. This disease has a high fatality rate. Canine parvovirus has attracted a great deal of attention because of its epidemic possibilities. It has been under study at Cornell University and the Baker Institute's Department of Virology, which has isolated the virus and after lengthy study has developed a vaccine that is safe and effective, with immunity duration as yet unknown, but estimated to last around 18 months. It is a wise idea to ask your veterinarian to give your Poodle a canine parvovirus inoculation at the same time he vaccinates for distemper, hepatitis and leptospirosis.

These are some of the usual diseases that any dog of any breed might encounter. There are also more serious diseases that relate more specifically to Poodles and have been a problem in recent times. However, you may never need to know more than their names.

Hip Dysplasia

The first is canine hip dysplasia. This occurs mainly in Standards and is also found in other large breeds, manifested by lameness in the rear at about four to nine months of age. Dysplasia literally means "bad development." It can be effectively diagnosed by X-raying the pelvis and hips. The problem is that this disease can be inherited and can be passed on indiscriminately, meaning that a dog with seemingly normal hips can produce a dysplastic litter or a litter with both normal and dysplastic puppies. Any of these puppies, in turn, may produce hip dysplasia when they are grown and are bred. If you want a double-check, your veterinarian can send your dog's X-ray to the Orthopedic Foundation for Animals in Columbia, Missouri. The O.F.A. charges a fee for experts to interpret the X-ray and grade your dog's hips. If the X-ray shows normal hips, the O.F.A. issues an O.F.A. number certified at 24 months or older. X-rays at an earlier age will be reviewed but no certified number is given to younger dogs.

Bloat

Many outstanding show dogs as well as pets have been lost in recent years to the dreaded disease known as bloat. This condition may occur in Standard Poodles over two years of age. Bloat is life-threatening and it is essential to act immediately if the dog is restless and tries to vomit with no success. These are usually the first signs. Next, the abdomen becomes severely swollen from gas or fluid, with a drum-like sound on tapping it. Various degrees of shock may also be seen. The stomach may twist 180° or more causing torsion, pinching off the inlet and outlet of the stomach and interfering with the blood supply to the stomach and spleen. Relief is imperative. Get your dog to the veterinarian at once. Surgery may be necessary. There are many theories as to what causes bloat and how to prevent it. One rather extensive study indicates that eating large quantities of dry kibble, drinking large amounts of water, and exercising heavily after eating can at least contribute to the problem.

P.R.A.

Miniature and Toy Poodles may have an inherited eye problem known as progressive retinal atrophy or P.R.A. This ultimately causes blindness. P.R.A. is difficult to diagnose in young puppies. One of the problems is that a dog or bitch may be used for breeding before the disease is discovered and verified. P.R.A. affects the entire retina of the eye. As the Poodle ages, the retina begins to lose cells and becomes thinner. This loss of cells also causes a lack of adequate blood supply. The disease is called progressive because it develops slowly and cannot be stopped. It is called atrophy because the retina is actually wasting away. Eventually, the dog becomes blind. In Poodles it is difficult to diagnose P.R.A. until the dog is three to five years old by means of the ordinary opthalmoscope.

A comparatively new field of veterinary medicine has been created to combat P.R.A. This is in the hands of the Ophthalmologist, a highly trained veterinary eye specialist with new techniques and new machinery, still comparatively rare and not always within easy reach of even the most dedicated Poodle breeders. Your local veterinarian can probably tell you where they are located or can give you the address of the American Veterinary Medical Association, which can supply the information. It will mean traveling to him, as the basic piece of equipment for diagnosis, the electroretinograph, will be housed in his office. It requires a high degree of accuracy in diagnosing P.R.A. The E.R.G., which stands for electroretinography, can give a correct diagnosis of P.R.A. in Poodle puppies nine to ten months of age. This is a very recent advance and could signal a far better understanding of the problem in the years ahead.

An organization called CERF (Canine Eye Registration Foundation), P.O. Box 15095, Station A, San Francisco, CA 94115, has pioneered research in P.R.A., its causes and elimination. At the University of Pennsylvania, Dr. Gustavo Aguirre, VMD, ACVO, is one of the leading specialists in this field.

Most Poodles live long and happy lives, and it would be wishful thinking to imagine there will not be some days of sickness. A good veterinarian will also prove to be a good friend in need. But if possible, it is always best if you can bring your Poodle home for nursing. More than most breeds Poodles welcome attention, and they are sure to get more from you than from a strange person working in a veterinarian's office. When well, the Poodle is self-sufficient and can deal with almost any problem. When ill, his defenses are down and he must rely entirely on you. It should always be remembered that Poodles are extremely sensitive to their owner's thoughts and moods. They need reassurance, to know you think they are not in danger. You should make every effort to be cheerfully affectionate and to encourage them. Never give the dog the idea that you are anxious over his condition. Assume that he needs just a little rest and relaxation. Poodles have fighting hearts and a will to live, especially where their devotion to their owner is involved. Many a really sick Poodle has pulled himself from the very jaws of death by the sheer will to live and not leave the person whom he loves. That is why a Poodle most needs his owner when he is ill, and does better for him than for strangers, no matter how kind and gentle the strangers may be.

INDEX OF ILLUSTRATED PEDIGREES

BIBLIOGRAPHY

ALL OWNERS of pure-bred dogs will benefit themselves and their dogs by enriching their knowledge of breeds and of canine care, training, breeding, psychology and other important aspects of dog management. The following list of books covers further reading recommended by judges, veterinarians, breeders, trainers and other authorities. Books may be obtained at the finer book stores and pet shops, or through Howell Book House Inc., publishers, New York.

BREED BOOKS

AFGHAN HOUND, Complete	Miller & Gilbert
AIREDALE, New Complete	Edwards
AKITA, Complete	Linderman & Funk
ALASKAN MALAMUTE, Complete	Riddle & Seeley
BASSET HOUND, Complete	Braun
BLOODHOUND, Complete	Brey & Reed
BOXER, Complete	Denlinger
BRITTANY SPANIEL, Complete	Riddle
BULLDOG, New Complete	Hanes
BULL TERRIER, New Complete	Eberhard
CAIRN TERRIER, Complete	Marvin
CHESAPEAKE BAY RETRIEVER, Complete	Cherry
CHIHUAHUA, Complete	Noted Authorities
COCKER SPANIEL, New	Kraeuchi
COLLIE, New	Official Publication of the Collie Club of America
DACHSHUND, The New	Meistrell
DALMATIAN, The	Treen
DOBERMAN PINSCHER, New	Walker
ENGLISH SETTER, New Complete	Tuck, Howell & Graef
ENGLISH SPRINGER SPANIEL, New	Goodall & Gasow
FOX TERRIER, New	Nedell
GERMAN SHEPHERD DOG, New Complete	Bennett
GERMAN SHORTHAIRED POINTER, New	Maxwell
GOLDEN RETRIEVER, New Complete	Fischer
GORDON SETTER, Complete	Look
GREAT DANE, New Complete	Noted Authorities
GREAT DANE, The—Dogdom's Apollo	Draper
GREAT PYRENEES, Complete	Strang & Giffin
IRISH SETTER, New Complete	Eldredge & Vanacore
IRISH WOLFHOUND, Complete	Starbuck
JACK RUSSELL TERRIER, Complete	Plummer
KEESHOND, New Complete	Cash
LABRADOR RETRIEVER, Complete	Warwick
LHASA APSO, Complete	Herbel
MASTIFF, History and Management of the	Baxter & Hoffman
MINIATURE SCHNAUZER, Complete	Eskrigge
NEWFOUNDLAND, New Complete	Chern
NORWEGIAN ELKHOUND, New Complete	Wallo
OLD ENGLISH SHEEPDOG, Complete	Mandeville
PEKINGESE, Quigley Book of	Quigley
PEMBROKE WELSH CORGI, Complete	Sargent & Harper
POODLE, New	Irick
POODLE CLIPPING AND GROOMING BOOK, Complete	Kalstone
ROTTWEILER, Complete	Freeman
SAMOYED, New Complete	Ward
SCOTTISH TERRIER, New Complete	Marvin
SHETLAND SHEEPDOG, The New	Riddle
SHIH TZU, Joy of Owning	Seranne
SHIH TZU, The (English)	Dadds
SIBERIAN HUSKY, Complete	Demidoff
TERRIERS, The Book of All	Marvin
WEIMARANER, Guide to the	Burgoin
WEST HIGHLAND WHITE TERRIER, Complete	Marvin
WHIPPET, Complete	Pegram
YORKSHIRE TERRIER, Complete	Gordon & Bennett

BREEDING

ART OF BREEDING BETTER DOGS, New	Onstott
BREEDING YOUR OWN SHOW DOG	Seranne
HOW TO BREED DOGS	Whitney
HOW PUPPIES ARE BORN	Prine
INHERITANCE OF COAT COLOR IN DOGS	Little

CARE AND TRAINING

COUNSELING DOG OWNERS, Evans Guide for	Evans
DOG OBEDIENCE, Complete Book of	Saunders
NOVICE, OPEN AND UTILITY COURSES	Saunders
DOG CARE AND TRAINING FOR BOYS AND GIRLS	Saunders
DOG NUTRITION, Collins Guide to	Collins
DOG TRAINING FOR KIDS	Benjamin
DOG TRAINING, Koehler Method of	Koehler
DOG TRAINING Made Easy	Tucker
GO FIND! Training Your Dog to Track	Davis
GUARD DOG TRAINING, Koehler Method of	Koehler
MOTHER KNOWS BEST—The Natural Way to Train Your Dog	Benjamin
OPEN OBEDIENCE FOR RING, HOME AND FIELD, Koehler Method of	Koehler
STONE GUIDE TO DOG GROOMING FOR ALL BREEDS	Stone
SUCCESSFUL DOG TRAINING, The Pearsall Guide to	Pearsall
TEACHING DOG OBEDIENCE CLASSES—Manual for Instructors	Volhard & Fisher
TOY DOGS, Kalstone Guide to Grooming All	Kalstone
TRAINING THE RETRIEVER	Kersley
TRAINING TRACKING DOGS, Koehler Method of	Koehler
TRAINING YOUR DOG—Step by Step Manual	Volhard & Fisher
TRAINING YOUR DOG TO WIN OBEDIENCE TITLES	Morsell
TRAIN YOUR OWN GUN DOG, How to	Goodall
UTILITY DOG TRAINING, Koehler Method of	Koehler
VETERINARY HANDBOOK, Dog Owner's Home	Carlson & Giffin

GENERAL

AMERICAN KENNEL CLUB 1884-1984—A Source Book	American Kennel Club
CANINE TERMINOLOGY	Spira
COMPLETE DOG BOOK, The	Official Publication of American Kennel Club
DOG IN ACTION, The	Lyon
DOG BEHAVIOR, New Knowledge of	Pfaffenberger
DOG JUDGE'S HANDBOOK	Tietjen
DOG PEOPLE ARE CRAZY	Riddle
DOG PSYCHOLOGY	Whitney
DOGSTEPS, The New	Elliott
DOG TRICKS	Haggerty & Benjamin
EYES THAT LEAD—Story of Guide Dogs for the Blind	Tucker
FRIEND TO FRIEND—Dogs That Help Mankind	Schwartz
FROM RICHES TO BITCHES	Shattuck
HAPPY DOG/HAPPY OWNER	Siegal
IN STITCHES OVER BITCHES	Shattuck
JUNIOR SHOWMANSHIP HANDBOOK	Brown & Mason
OUR PUPPY'S BABY BOOK (blue or pink)	
SUCCESSFUL DOG SHOWING, Forsyth Guide to	Forsyth
TRIM, GROOM & SHOW YOUR DOG, How to	Saunders
WHY DOES YOUR DOG DO THAT?	Bergman
WILD DOGS in Life and Legend	Riddle
WORLD OF SLED DOGS, From Siberia to Sport Racing	Coppinger